Backcountry Skiing Adventures

CLASSIC SKI AND SNOWBOARD TOURS
IN MAINE AND NEW HAMPSHIRE

ALSO AVAILABLE FROM AMC BOOKS

Visit the AMC Bookstore at **www.outdoors.org**

AMC Guide to Winter Camping
The Complete Guide to Trail Building and Maintenance

AMC Guide to Mount Desert and Acadia National Park
AMC Hiking Guide to Mount Washington and the Presidential Range
AMC Maine Mountain Guide
AMC Massachusetts and Rhode Island Trail Guide
AMC White Mountain Guide
North Carolina Hiking Trails
West Virginia Hiking Trails

Nature Walks in Northern Vermont
Nature Hikes in the White Mountains
Nature Walks in the Berkshire Hills
Nature Walks in Southern New Hampshire
Nature Walks in the New Hampshire Lakes Region
Nature Walks in Southern Maine
Nature Walks in Eastern Massachusetts
Nature Walks in Central Massachusetts

At Timberline: A Nature Guide to the Mountains of the Northeast
AMC Field Guide to the New England Alpine Summits
Into the Mountains: Stories of New England's Most Celebrated Peaks
North Woods

Backcountry Skiing Adventures

CLASSIC SKI AND SNOWBOARD TOURS IN MAINE AND NEW HAMPSHIRE

David Goodman

APPALACHIAN MOUNTAIN CLUB BOOKS
BOSTON, MASSACHUSETTS

Cover photograph: Peter Cole
Back cover photograph: Brooks Dodge
All photographs by the author unless otherwise noted
Cover design: Ola Frank
Book design: Carol Bast Tyler

USGS base maps used by permission from Maptech (www.maptech.com).
© Bradford Washburn photograph of Mount Washington
courtesy of Panopticon Gallery, Boston, MA.
Mount Washington and the Presidential Range map courtesy of Bradford Washburn.

Distributed by the Globe Pequot Press, Inc., Old Saybrook, CT.

Library of Congress Cataloging-in-Publication Data
Goodman, David, 1959–
Backcountry skiing adventures: the best backcountry skiing and snowboarding in
Maine and New Hampshire / David Goodman.
p. cm.
Includes bibliographical references (p.).
ISBN 1-878239-64-3 (alk. paper)
1. Cross-country skiing—Maine—Guidebooks. 2. Cross-country skiing—New
Hampshire—Guidebooks. 3. Snowboarding—Maine—Guidebooks. 4. Snow-
boarding—New Hampshire—Guidebook. I. Title.
GV854.5.M2G66   1998
796.93'2'09741—dc21   98-37964
                                                                CIP

10 9 8 7 6 5 4 3 2 1   98 99 00 01 02 03

Contents

To Ariel,
who loves playing
in the snow

Preface

This book is the product of several passions. When I was a college student in the early 1980s, I went on my first cross-country ski outings with friends. We would go to Lincoln Woods around Boston or up to the White Mountains and glide around the forest. I marveled at how my friends, who had been skiing for years, could move so gracefully on snow. I learned by mimicking them, and became proficient through trial and error. My flirtation with skiing quickly became an infatuation.

The high mountains have been another passion. My hikes in the White Mountains led to rock and ice climbing and mountaineering throughout North America and beyond. I have been intoxicated by the high and wild places of the planet. The freedom, the challenge, the special camaraderie shared with friends in the mountains, and the sheer joy of being in a remote setting have been a constant lure. I managed to combine my work and pleasure for a number of years working as a mountaineering instructor for the Hurricane Island Outward Bound School. This kept me in the wild place I love most—my home mountains of New England.

Inevitably skis and high mountains converged. Backcountry skiing has been a way for me to bring together my quest for big mountains and my addiction to the sensual thrill of skiing. In the great tradition of backcountry skiing, I learned my most enduring lessons with my head buried deeply in the eastern snowpack. Slowly and stubbornly, I figured out how to ski the fickle snows of the Northeast.

The Appalachian Mountain Club approached me in 1987 and asked if I would write a book about skiing in New England. The editors left it to my discretion how to approach the subject. I decided to write a book about skiing in the highest mountains of New England. These were the places that everyone except snowshoers and a few die-hard telemarkers assumed were inaccessible in winter. But I knew that skiers had been crisscrossing the high peaks of New England since the 1920s. The only problem was that it had been a half-century since the heyday of such "down-mountain skiing." I had a great deal of fun doing the ski research that winter. And I figured the book would have a loyal audience of about 200 fellow telemark fanatics.

Classic Backcountry Skiing: A Guide to the Best Ski Tours in New England was published by the AMC in December 1988. After it appeared, something happened that I didn't anticipate: a lot of people bought the book. At trailheads around New England, I have come across snow-covered cars with tattered copies of the guidebook lying on the dashboard. The book even garnered two national ski writing awards.

Classic Backcountry Skiing arrived just as telemark skiing was starting to boom. People were looking for alternatives to the increasingly homogenized downhill ski scene. They found it right in their own backyards.

Ten years later, it is time for a fresh look at backcountry skiing in New England. Many things have changed since the original book. Trails have been rerouted, renamed, opened, and closed. Backcountry skiing is now a popular pastime, and telemarkers have become remarkably proficient and creative skiers. People are searching farther afield for ski terrain, and that is a good sign. This guide is merely meant to open the door to the world of backcountry *glisse,* or sliding. The joy of exploration is left to you.

One of the more significant developments since publication of the last book is the explosion in popularity of snowboarding. In my backcountry travels, I periodically come across snowboarders or their telltale tracks. I have snowboarded myself, and have watched in awe the way the best snowboarders float through difficult snow and carve smooth arcs down steep terrain. Riders are now in the position that skiers were in during the 1980s: They are seeking freedom, looking for wilder snow. This guide helps point the way.

Backcountry Skiing Adventures builds on the groundwork laid by *Classic Backcountry Skiing.* Many of the present tour descriptions draw heavily upon information that originally appeared in the earlier edition. But there are many new tours, and considerable new information about old tours. Virtually every tour description has changed.

The sheer quantity of great ski terrain in New England has burgeoned to the point where one guidebook is no longer adequate. *Backcountry Skiing Adventures* is being published in two volumes. This first volume covers backcountry skiing and snowboarding in Maine and New Hampshire. The forthcoming companion guidebook covers backcountry skiing and snowboarding in Vermont, western Massachusetts, and the Adirondacks.

May your mountain journeys be deep.

Acknowledgments

I am grateful to a number of people for their help with the research for this book. Their assistance ranged from joining me on the many miles of trail that I covered, to fact checking certain tours. Thanks to Jack Coughlin, Dave Wichland, Carl Demrow, and Dave Salisbury of the AMC in Pinkham Notch. Thanks also to my ski partners, including Bill Minter, Barry Goodman, Andi Colnes, Jay Lena, Ken Norton, Gary Newfield, Dave Getchell, Annie Getchell, Peter Cole, Betsy Harrison, Andy Chakoumakos, Brendon Bernard, Peter Heddon, Dave Metsky, and Greg Tsoules. To all of you, I say thanks for coming along, and sorry if I stole first tracks.

Among the people who offered valuable comments and advice on this project were Steve Gladstone, Nick Howe, Tom Silocka, Dave Hooke, Chris Mask, Tom Jackman, Rick Boucher, Thom Perkins, Tim Weisser, and Dicky Hall.

Special thanks to Jeff Leich of the New England Ski Museum, Brooks Dodge, and Brooks Dodge III for their patient help with my numerous ski history queries.

Gordon Hardy, Mark Russell, Elisabeth Brady, and Ola Frank—the publisher, editor, production manager, and publicist, respectively, at AMC Books—have been enthusiastic midwives of this book. Thanks also to Austin Sass at Maptech, who gave permission to reproduce USGS base maps from Maptech CD-Rom.

A special tip of my hat to an old friend and mentor, the late Allan Bard. "Bardini" preached that there was "one nation under God and above timberline." He inspired legions of skiers—myself among them—to strike out for the highest ground. We'll miss you, friend.

My deepest thanks go to Sue Minter, my wife, fellow explorer, and skiing inspiration. This book would not have been possible without her inexhaustible help and support.

This book is dedicated to my daughter, Ariel. Whether she chooses to travel on foot, skis, snowboard, or a plastic sled, I hope that she finds the same joy in these mountains over the years that I have found.

Author's Note

This book is about adventures in snow. It is intended for use by both skiers (including freeheel and *randonée*) and snowboarders. The spirit of this book is captured by the French word *glisse*, which is derived from *glisser*—literally, "to slide." Sliding on snow is the essence of our sport. This book is a history, guide, and celebration of New England *glisse* in all its forms.

My tour descriptions rely largely on the language of skiing. That is inevitable: skiing is the oldest of the *glisse* disciplines and skiers constitute the majority of backcountry *glisse* practitioners. New England is also steeped in a rich ski history that I chronicle throughout these chapters.

In the interest of simplicity and consistency, I use "skiing" throughout this book to refer to traveling on snow, whether it be on skis or snowboards. The exceptions to this practice should be apparent, such as when I address issues of specific concern to skiers and snowboarders, particularly in the area of technique and equipment.

Maps of Tour Locations

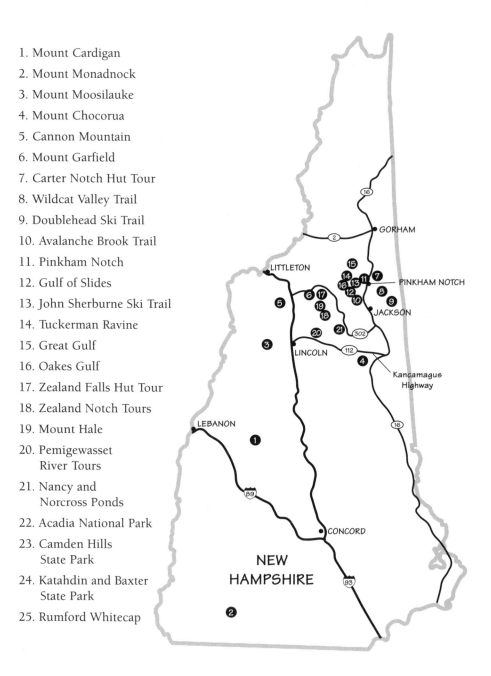

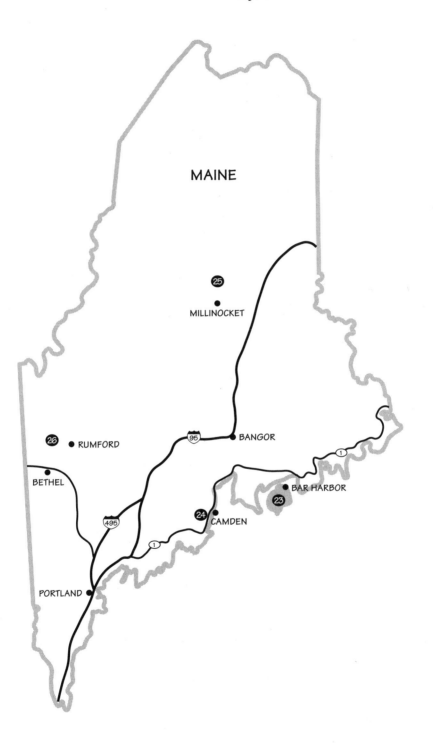

MAINE

㉕
● MILLINOCKET

㉖ ● RUMFORD

95 ● BANGOR

1

● BETHEL

BAR HARBOR ●
㉓

495

㉔ ● CAMDEN

1

PORTLAND ●

SECTION ONE

The Backcountry World

The Backcountry World

WELCOME TO THE WORLD OF BACKCOUNTRY *GLISSE.*

Glisse—derived from the French word that means "to slide"— encompasses all the ways that we enjoy and explore snow. The backcountry is today shared by sliders of every variety, from skiers to snowboarders. Who knows what new inventions will come along in future years that will further expand our enjoyment of the snowy world? I embrace them all in this book. The ethic of all these disciplines is that you earn your turns: When you climb a mountain under your own steam, you have earned the right to descend in whatever manner you find most aesthetic and pleasurable, provided it does not harm the mountain environment.

Skiers and snowboarders have a shared passion: the love of the backcountry world in winter. This world is familiar to many of you. It is the hiking trails you climb in summer, the mountain summits you stop to admire, the trails you wonder about when you look on a map. It includes trailless peaks and well-trodden mountain paths.

To others, this is a new place. You may have been skiing at touring centers at the base of the big peaks. Or you have been snowboarding on the "front side" of many of these mountains, possibly curious about the world that lies on the side of the ridge without chairlifts. This book is about that world.

Backcountry *glisse* is the full spectrum of traveling on snow: going uphill, downhill, across mountain summits, along river valleys. It is skiing and snowboarding off of groomed trails and prepared snow. This style of travel goes by many names. Some call it ski or snowboard mountaineering; others call it *off-piste* (off-trail) skiing or snowboarding, ski touring, mountain skiing, *randonée,* alpine touring, telemarking, Nordic skiing, or cross-country skiing. In some ways it encompasses all of the above, but in other ways it resists categorization. Fifty years ago it was all simply called *skiing.* In spirit—*glisse*—it is all one sport.

Skiers today will find that Nordic ski equipment—so-called telemark gear— is unmatched as an efficient and enjoyable means of travel to reach the best untouched snow in remote places. But the ski techniques, which include telemark and parallel turns, are a hybrid of cross-country and downhill. Backcountry skiing is done in the high mountains, which naturally means that skiing downhill is a major part of the experience. "Down-mountain skiing" was the term that skiers from the 1930s used to describe this style of downhill skiing in the backcountry.

Snowboarders heading into the backcountry are pioneering new ground. Snowboarders follow in tracks blazed by skiers, but they travel with new tools and a fresh eye for adventure. They may come in search of a streamed shaped like a natural half-pipe. They may seek out remote, powdery steep descents. Or perhaps they are content to tour up, down, and wherever the mountain leads them. Riders and skiers are united in their quest for solitude, untracked snow, and a wilder experience.

Backcountry *glisse* is full of surprises. You can glide to quiet places, where the snow is untracked, perhaps changing texture with each mile. Your skis, snowshoes, or snowboards can also take you to exciting places, such as high summits with breathtaking snowfields and expansive views all around.

Backcountry travelers embark on a journey, but there is not necessarily a destination. Be open to whatever comes along. Sometimes the goal of the journey is introspection and solitude; other times, the goal is just to enjoy traveling under your own power through the winter wilderness. Often we go just to have fun. Whatever your motivations, the backcountry journey requires an exploratory mind-set. Bring a spirit of adventure and accept that not everything will turn out quite as planned. Just as the character of a trail changes with each storm, the experience you have each time you fasten on skis or a snowboard and head into the mountains is never the same as it was before.

This is a book about backcountry skiing and snowboarding in the mountains of New England. Since the 1940s, people have been using cross-country skis on the fields and old logging roads of the Northeast, while downhill skiers and snowboarders have been riding chairlifts to get to their ski trails. Most of these skiers have considered wilderness areas to be inaccessible. Throughout the 1930s, however, backcountry skiing in the mountains was a passion pursued by many people in New England. The search for the perfect ski run down a mountain was under way in every corner of the Northeast. The highest peaks of the North Country—Mount Mansfield, Mount Washington, Mount Cardigan, Mount Greylock—all became home to famous ski trails. These trails, with names like Thunderbolt, Nose Dive, Teardrop, and Wildcat, still bring a surge of adrenaline and satisfaction to riders and skiers today.

My intent with this book is to encourage skiers and snowboarders to return once again to the high and wild places of New England. I try to recapture the spirit of adventure that led the skiers of an earlier generation to head to the mountains and explore. The tours in this book are only a sampling.

There are numerous other peaks, open woods, slides, and drainages that offer first-rate skiing and snowboarding to those willing to adventure. Indeed, your own backyard may hold unexplored riches. The world of backcountry *glisse* is, after all, every place in the wilderness where it is white.

The Northeastern Renaissance

Every time skiers or snowboarders push off from a trailhead and vanish into a winter wilderness, they feel like explorers setting off for the New World. Laying first tracks into the snow, we feel as if we are the first visitors to these wild places. But if the snow could speak, it would tell another story. It would simply welcome us back. For we are merely traveling in the tracks of skiers who plied these routes for decades, and then mysteriously vanished.

Backcountry skiing is not a new sport in the Northeast. It is actually a revival of a sport that enjoyed its heyday in the 1930s and has been in a period of dormancy until recently.

The first skiers in New England were Scandinavian loggers and railroad builders in the mid-1800s. They formed the first ski club in the United States in Berlin, New Hampshire, in 1882. It was later named the Fridtjof Nansen Ski Club, after the famous Norwegian Arctic explorer who skied across Greenland in 1888. Skis began appearing in Hanover, New Hampshire, and in North Adams, Massachusetts, by the turn of the century, and the popularity of the sport slowly began to pick up.

Mountain skiing began attracting interest soon after people gained some basic proficiency with the unwieldy new mode of transportation. The first ski ascent and descent of Mount Marcy in the Adirondacks was accomplished in 1911; Mount Washington was skied (via today's auto road) in 1913; and Mount Mansfield in Vermont was first skied in 1914 via the toll road. Ski racing began gaining interest at Dartmouth College in Hanover, New Hampshire, around the same time.

Skiers of this early era would immerse themselves in all aspects of the sport. They were typically proficient at ski jumping, downhill, slalom, and cross-country skiing, sometimes called *langlauf* ("long-run") skiing. Since people would use the same skis for everything, there was little difference between cross-country and downhill skiing except where people chose to ski. In the 1920s, ski bindings consisted of a toe bar with a leather heel strap, much like today's cable bindings. Skis were long, heavy hickory boards without metal edges, and boots were the leather hiking-style variety with a box-shaped toe.

Throughout the 1920s, New England skiers looking for downhill skiing opportunities sought out narrow summer hiking trails, logging roads, and streambeds. This was not the easiest terrain to ski, and skiers soon began searching for more open downhill slopes. Katharine Peckett, the daughter of an affluent inn owner near Franconia, New Hampshire, decided after returning from a vacation in Switzerland to clear a small hill near her father's inn. She opened the first ski school in the United States in 1929. It was around this same time that skiers began to make forays into Tuckerman Ravine. The first official downhill race in the country was held on Mount Moosilauke in 1927. While ski touring through the woods was still an enjoyable pastime, skiers were increasingly drawn to the thrill of a good downhill run, and they would travel long and far to find the mountains with the best downhill skiing.

By the 1930s, skiing had captured the imagination of New Englanders. In 1931, the first "snow trains" for skiers left North Station in Boston headed for New Hampshire, and snow trains to Vermont began rolling out of New York City. Within its first year of operation, the Boston & Maine snow train transported 8,371 passengers to New Hampshire; more than 10,000 skiers boarded the train the following year. Equipment evolved to keep pace with the rising interest in downhill skiing. Skis with metal edges appeared, and steel cable bindings were introduced. These bindings offered the option of latching down the heel cable for skiing downhill on steeper terrain.

A major catalyst for ski activity in the region came about as a direct result of the Depression. The Civilian Conservation Corps (CCC) was created by President Franklin Roosevelt in March 1933 to provide work for unemployed men. It had the dual purpose of addressing national conservation needs and providing jobs. In its nine years of existence, the CCC mobilized 3 million men who worked throughout the United States on reforestation, trail construction, land erosion, fire control, and construction of dams, bridges, and buildings.

The CCC will be remembered best by New England skiers for the numerous ski trails that it built. Vermont was the greatest beneficiary in this regard, since the state's CCC contingent was under the supervision of Perry Merrill, an avid skier. Under Merrill's direction the CCC cut some of the most famous ski runs in the East. Among the trails that still endure are the Nose Dive, Teardrop, Bruce, Ski Meister, Perry Merrill, and (Charlie) Lord Trails on Mount Mansfield. In New Hampshire, the CCC's contributions include the Richard Taft Trail on Cannon Mountain, the Alexandria Trail on Mount Cardigan, the Gulf of Slides Trail near Mount Washington, and the Wildcat Trail on the north side of Wildcat Mountain. Many of its other contributions to skiing in New England are cited elsewhere in this book.

Charlie Lord was the master designer of the CCC trails on Mount Mansfield. Lord, who died in 1997 at the age of 95, once explained to me his formula for creating the high-quality runs for which the CCC became famous: "The only guide we had was we tried to make them interesting for ourselves. We were a selfish bunch, you know. The trails were made for a fairly good skier—not experts, but we tried to pick a route that would challenge us." Very few of the CCC men were actually skiers, since skiing was even then a sport of the middle and upper classes. "But," said Lord, "some of them were quite enthused about skiing" and enjoyed coming out to watch the big ski races that took place on their trails.

The construction of the CCC ski trails initiated a new era of "down-mountain skiing." This was the term used to describe downhill skiing in the backcountry. Down-mountain trails, also called "walk-up" trails because skiers had to hike

Skiing on the Headwall in Tuckerman Ravine, circa 1933. Photo by Winston Pote

up them in order to ski down them, defined the character of skiing in the early 1930s. On some of the longer trails, such as the Bruce Trail on Mount Mansfield, hiking up and skiing down just once took a full day. These outings often proved to be mountaineering adventures as much as they were skiing adventures.

A few select trails were challenging enough to merit classification as Class A race trails. This meant they had approximately 2,000 feet of vertical drop within a specified distance (none of the trail designers seem to recall the exact specifications). The Class A trails of New England included the Nose Dive, Richard Taft Trail, Wildcat Trail, Thunderbolt Trail on Mount Greylock, and the Pine Hill Trail on Wachusett Mountain. These were the only trails where a racer could receive a coveted rating based on his or her time. "A" racers were the fastest, while "B" and "C" racers were close behind.

Ski technique was evolving from telemark and snowplow to styles more suited to racing. Christiania and stem turns, which marked the beginnings of parallel skiing technique, were being advocated by the better coaches, and people quickly abandoned the graceful old telemark in favor of the faster parallel turn.

The popularity of the CCC trails also signaled a subtle change in the direction that skiing was taking. Exploration of the mountains on skis was taking a backseat to skiing on the established down-mountain trails. These wide ski trails were simply a joy to ski. They were a welcome relief from the difficult hiking trails.

Abner Coleman confessed in the Appalachian Mountain Club journal, *Appalachia,* in 1936:

> The direction of the movement in Vermont is following the widespread preference for downhill running. To some extent this delightful obsession is unfortunate, if only because it leaves a lot of ideal terrain to the mercy of snowshoers.
>
> The winter countryside is but little used even by those who live in it. The stampede, rather, both of natives and visitors, has been toward the localities providing down-mountain runs.

The heyday of the down-mountain trails was relatively brief. In 1934, the first rope tow was introduced at a ski hill in Woodstock, VT. Within seven years, J-bars, T-bars, and chairlifts sprang up on almost every major ski mountain in New England. In 1938, an aerial tramway was erected on Cannon Mountain in New Hampshire. The CCC trails often became the nucleus of the new downhill ski areas, as was the case with the Nose Dive on Mount Mansfield in Stowe, the Wildcat Trail in the Wildcat Ski Area, and the Richard Taft Trail in the Cannon Mountain Ski Area. Those trails that were not crowned with a chairlift were often abandoned, to be reclaimed by weeds and shrubs. This was the fate of a number of trails, including the now defunct Chin Clip on Mount Mansfield and the Katzensteig Trail on Wildcat Mountain.

But many of the down-mountain trails survived. Some, like the Snapper Trail on Mount Moosilauke, were preserved as hiking trails, while others, such as the Teardrop and Bruce Trails on Mount Mansfield and the Tucker Brook Trail on Cannon Mountain, were maintained by dedicated local skiers. These people often cleared the trails in defiance of new state and federal regulations that forbade skiing on trails not considered "safe" for the new breed of lift-served skiers. The renegade old-timers, typically alpine skiers from the 1950s and 1960s, were determined to preserve the experience of down-mountain skiing that they grew up with. They were not prepared to part with skiing powder and interesting snow conditions on remote mountain trails, where they could escape the icy mogul fields of the crowded lift-served mountains.

Frazier Noble, one of the down-mountain skiing holdouts who used to maintain the Pine Hill Trail on Wachusett Mountain, eloquently captured the spirit of backcountry skiing, then and now. He explained to me:

> It's hard to convey to people who haven't done any walking for skiing what the experience is about. It's quite different than just buying an impersonal lift ticket and skiing the mountain from the top. You work hard for the run and get far more exercise than you do when just downhill skiing. The scenery is also an important part of it. These trails were not just a slash down a mountain. They had a lot of interesting natural rolls and turns in them. Also, when you walk up you have time

to have long chats with people you're skiing with. That's part of the whole ski experience, too.

The advent of lift-served skiing was the death knell—or at least suspended animation—for backcountry skiing. Those who once flocked to the mountains of the North Country to explore new ski routes were now bombing down the downhill slopes of Vermont and New Hampshire. Skiers of the era recall how the number of people skiing in the backcountry around places like Mount Mansfield dropped from about forty on a typical weekend in the early 1930s to no more than a half-dozen by the mid-1940s.

The evolution in ski equipment epitomized what was happening to the sport of skiing. Rigid downhill boots and bindings that locked the heel down made it impossible to ski uphill or even on flat terrain. The new gear was strictly for going downhill. By the 1950s, the sport of cross-country skiing evolved its own specialized equipment, consisting of lightweight, skinny racing equipment designed for use on prepared, generally flat, ski trails. The schism between "downhill" and "cross-country" skiing was made, and the radically different equipment made it impossible to bridge the divide. This division was to grow even wider until the late 1970s.

People who were cross-country skiing in the mountains in the 1950s and 1960s were a relatively small and hardy bunch. Joe Pete Wilson, a member of the 1960 Olympic biathlon team who skied in the Green Mountains and the Adirondacks, remembers that it was in the mid-1960s, when he was working at a ski resort, that people heard about him and came to ask him about cross-country skiing. He gave a few lessons and answered people's questions. Their curiosity had been piqued when they saw high school and college students out cross-country skiing. There were also many older people who had cross-country skied as kids, or who had parents who skied cross-country. They didn't know what to call the kind of skiing they grew up with; they just thought of it as skiing.

The revival of cross-country skiing was also starting to take place at colleges such as Dartmouth. Dartmouth's downhill ski team and its coach, the late Al Merrill, were nationally renowned. But students noticed that Merrill and a few of his friends "would go out 'touring' after hours," recounted David Hooke in *Reaching That Peak,* a history of the Dartmouth Outing Club (DOC). In 1964, Merrill "was persuaded to give the DOC 'several pointers on ski touring.' By January 1965 ski touring 'was fast becoming the winter's most popular sport.'" In March 1965, a DOC newsletter stated:

> [DOC] managed a surprising number of ski touring trips this winter despite the often filthy snow conditions. Large numbers of men, most of whom traveled on hand-hewn skis garnished with make-shift bindings, glided through weather as diverse as red klister and blue stick. It's a good feeling when your ski sticks on the kick and slides on the glide—an occasional bright eye, raised brow and incredulous mouth numbly muttering "Christ, it works!!!"

A turning point in the revival of cross-country skiing was the sudden availability of inexpensive skis. In the mid-1960s, the first fiberglass downhill skis came on the market. People quickly traded in their old wooden models, which were easily converted into cross-country skis with a little shaving and narrowing to lighten them up. Hooke reports that at Dartmouth, "it is understandable, given the spirit of the times, why touring would have had such appeal: not only was there now a whole lot of obsolete downhill equipment, but converting it and using it would be a great way to get away from 'it all'—meaning lift lines, crowds, and the other trappings of the 'new' Alpine skiing of the day."

In 1970, Joe Pete Wilson and William Lederer coauthored *The Complete Cross-Country Skiing and Ski Touring* (now out of print). It began selling briskly—a sign that change was in the air.

The 1970s saw the growth of cross-country skiing at ski-touring centers. But by the late 1970s another small-scale revival began brewing within the world of cross-country skiing. A small group of mountaineers-turned-skiers, cross-country ski instructors, and alpine skiers who had grown bored with the lift-area scene wanted to add some adventure to their ski experience. They were getting restless, and touring-center skiing was simply not enough to entertain them anymore. In an effort to combine their mountain climbing with their skiing, they began experimenting with using downhill skiing techniques on cross-country skis. Cross-country skiers began parallel skiing, and even revived the defunct telemark turn. Experimentation and brainstorming were at a high pitch among skiers around Stowe and Killington. The audacious and talented Ski-to-Die Club was soon born in the Adirondacks. The publication of Steve Barnett's now classic *Cross-Country Downhill* in 1978 generated further excitement about the potential for Nordic skiing.

With the renewed interest in backcountry skiing came a concurrent evolution in equipment. The lightweight skis and boots of ski tourers and racers were inadequate for the rigors of backcountry skiing. Karhu and Fischer, both with U.S. headquarters in New England, were two of the first companies to respond to the demand from telemarkers and mountain skiers for a heavy-duty ski. The metal-edged Fischer Europa 77 went on sale in the early 1970s, and the skis that have become enduring classics—the Fischer Europa 99 and Karhu XCD-GT—were introduced in 1978. These skis have been steady sellers ever since. Other manufacturers followed suit, and there is now a wide array of choices available to backcountry skiers.

By the early 1990s, so-called "telemark" skiers were a firmly established skiing subculture. Every ski area in the country now has a small cadre of die-hard freeheel skiers. Telemarkers are borrowing technique and equipment from their alpine brethren and have cobbled together a fresh, eclectic, irreverent sport. Freeheelers have honed their technique to a remarkable degree, skiing virtually everywhere that alpine skiers go. And then they go even further, using the benefit of their Nordic heritage to head off into the high mountains. The 1990s witnessed a full-blown revival of backcountry skiing, as skiers fled the increasingly homogenized experience offered at ski areas in search of something wilder, more authentic.

Snowboarders are the latest snow sliders to join in the quest for untamed territory. Jake Burton began making the first snowboards in 1977 from his Londonderry, VT workshop. He soon convinced Stratton Mountain to allow his innovation on its ski slopes. The rest is history: Snowboarding has boomed, its popularity driven by a young new generation of snow sliders. By 1996, the number of snowboarders (3.7 million) for the first time surpassed the total number of people who were cross-country skiing (3.4 million). (In New England, however, there are still twice as many cross-country skiers as snowboarders.)

By the late 1990s, the occasional snowboarder would show up at a New Hampshire trailhead, slap on snowshoes, and disappear. Days later, a skier might come across their distinctive, graceful track— a sign of creative ferment.

There has been enormous cross-fertilization between *glisse* enthusiasts in recent years. Alpine boots have become softer and more flexible, telemark boots are now plastic and stiffer, snowboarders are experimenting with split boards (a.k.a. "skis"), and the skinny Nordic skis of yore have been traded in for fatter alpine-style shaped skis. This process of experimentation has been going on for more than a century: we are simply searching for ever better ways to travel deep into the winter wilderness.

Skiing has come full circle since the 1930s. Skiers and snowboarders are now in the process of rediscovering the techniques and terrain pioneered by an earlier generation. By discovering the uphill part of snow travel, snowboarders have thrown open the door to a vast mountain landscape. And by reclaiming the downhill component of skiing, Nordic skiers have once again opened up the mountains for exploration on skis. The down-mountain trails have had new life breathed into them—or maybe their old spirit restored. This spirit is simply the quest for adventure and a love of the mountains. It has an uncanny way of transcending the barriers of time to bring together everyone who feels its pull.

The Tours

The tours in this book were chosen because they are "classics." Classic tours in New England have a special character. The mountain ranges in this region are unlike any others in the United States. The elevations are small, but the conditions are distinctly alpine.

There are several qualities that are necessary for a tour to be considered a classic.

History. Many of the tours have historic significance. They were trails that formed the hub of down-mountain skiing activity sixty years ago. Many were built by the Civilian Conservation Corps (CCC) in the 1930s. They represent a slice of New England culture as well as some of the best skiing to be found anywhere. The CCC and other trailblazers in New England had their choice of where the best ski runs would go. The enduring quality and popularity of those trails today are a testament to the keen eye they had for choosing the best routes.

Aesthetics. A classic ski or snowboard tour must have scenic value that captures the spirit of New England's mountains and forests. What this area lacks in jagged mountain skylines and vast open bowls it makes up for in picturesque birch forests and accessible mountain summits. A classic tour may travel the full range of New England terrain, or it may showcase one aspect of this special landscape.

Quality of skiing and snowboarding. Classic tours include high-quality skiing and snowboarding terrain. Quality means variety: The best tours hold your interest because they call upon a full range of techniques. A classic ski tour might include skating on flats, diagonal striding on straightaways, skinning up a mountainside, and telemarking or parallel skiing down an exciting powder run. A classic snowboard tour combines the challenge of an ascent with the fun of negotiating natural terrain features, including streambeds, narrow trails, and the dips and rolls of a mountain. This is total skiing and snowboarding—not specialized subdivisions of these sports.

In short, a classic tour has it all.

DIFFICULTY RATINGS FOR SKIERS

The ski tours in this book are intended for experienced cross-country skiers who are comfortable skiing on a variety of terrain. A skier who is proficient on intermediate trails at a ski-touring center should be able to ski most of the routes in this book. None of the tours in this book is intended for novice cross-country skiers except those in the chapter "Easy Day Trips in the White Mountains." These latter trails, though not classics in the sense described here, are nevertheless beautiful and worthwhile tours. They are included in the hope that they will inspire less-experienced cross-country skiers to continue their development and their explorations as backcountry skiers.

Good downhill skiing opportunities are an important part of every classic ski tour described here. No mountain ski tour is complete without them. Indeed, the thrill of a long backcountry downhill run has drawn skiers to the mountains for years. Each tour is rated *moderate, more difficult, most difficult,* or *most difficult/mountaineering.*

Moderate. The terrain includes gentle hills. A good snowplow technique or step turn should suffice for skiing downhill.

More difficult. The terrain includes extended, steeper uphill and downhill sections. Proficiency at turning on steeper terrain—using telemark, parallel, snowplow, kick turns, or other techniques—is necessary.

Most difficult. The terrain includes sustained downhill skiing on trails that are narrow, very steep, or both. The ability to link turns, sometimes quickly, is necessary.

Most difficult/mountaineering. The terrain is steep and exposed, and there may be consequences for falling. These tours require the ability to link turns on steep terrain. They also involve an element of mountaineering judgment as to the safety of the snow and ski conditions.

These difficulty ratings are subjective and extremely variable for any given tour. They describe approximately what the trail would be like to ski in average conditions: moderately heavy powder over a solid base that may be broken up by another skier's tracks. But *conditions are everything.* A tour that is considered "moderate" in powder conditions can be ferocious in breakable crust. An "easy" ski tour can at times challenge the best skiers. You must know your ability to ski in various conditions and know when the conditions of a trail exceed your abilities. There is no shame in deciding to walk down a steep, narrow chute that you are not comfortable skiing; in fact, it takes considerable experience to know your limits.

This is a regional rating system. The rating of each tour is relative to the difficulty of other tours in the Northeast. To compare the difficulty of these tours to routes in other areas of the country, see appendix C, "S System Ratings."

DIFFICULTY RATINGS FOR SNOWBOARDERS

Most of the tours in this book can be snowboarded.

Each tour has been rated for snowboarding. In general, a tour in which there is a sustained downhill on at least half the total distance is considered suitable for snowboarding. Ideally, a good snowboard tour climbs up and rides down, with little need to change equipment on the descent. Where a tour includes rolling terrain—i.e., it follows primarily flat ground, or goes up and down throughout its length—I have noted that it is not suited for snowboarding. In general, snowboarders will want to keep to tours that I have rated *more difficult* or *most difficult*. These routes have the most sustained downhill grade.

Backcountry terrain and snow are quite different than what you will find at a ski area. Wild snow includes crud, crust, powder, ice, and corn—often all in the same run. Practice at a ski area by riding in the trees and along the edges of the trail. Search out soft snow and figure out how to tame its infinite forms. The master class comes when you put it all together in the wilderness.

Riders who are comfortable on intermediate trails at a ski area should be able to negotiate trails that are rated *more difficult*. Trails rated *most difficult* are for advanced riders who are comfortable on all expert (black diamond) ski trails. Tours rated *most difficult/mountaineering* are very steep backcountry gullies and ravines in which you must evaluate the snow conditions and mountaineering hazards to determine whether the routes are safe to ride. These steep runs may have severe consequences if you fall. You should begin with easier tours and work up to harder ones in order to get a feel for this rating system.

The mountains, of course, are not ideal. Even tours that go *mostly* downhill are likely to include some flat or uphill sections. Snowboarders must be equipped, mentally and technically, to negotiate every kind of terrain that a mountain tour will present. *It is crucial that you bring equipment to navigate flat and uphill terrain!* If you don't have snowshoes, you will become more intimate with the snow than you ever hoped to be—usually wallowing up to your waist. The ride down is the reward for those who can reach the summit.

I have skied all these routes, not snowboarded them. My description of how each tour will ride is intended as general guidance. I have directed riders toward routes with a sustained downhill pitch, and away from rolling trails. This is admittedly a rough estimation, and your experience with a trail may differ. At worst, you will do more snowshoeing than expected. This book tries to open the door and point the way; the adventure of discovery is yours.

SLOPE STEEPNESS

The steepness of some routes is often described in terms of the angle of the slope. Most skiers and climbers tend to overestimate slope angles. The most accurate way to determine the steepness of a slope is with an inclinometer. The top-of-the-line compasses made by Suunto and Silva include inclinometers. Life-Link also sells a relatively inexpensive Slope Meter. Becoming proficient in estimating slope angles is especially useful in avalanche hazard assessment, where the difference between a 20-degree slope and 35-degree slope is critical (see "Mountaineering Skills and Avalanches" for more on this subject).

In general, 20-degree slopes are considered advanced-intermediate downhill terrain, such as what is encountered on the Sherburne Trail. Slopes of 30 degrees are advanced downhill terrain. They give pause to the vast majority of Nordic skiers, many of whom resort to traversing and kick-turning to get down a slope of this grade. The middle and lower sections of Hillman's Highway on Mount Washington (see "Tuckerman Ravine" chapter) fits this description. Forty-degree slopes are the realm of expert skiers and riders. It takes considerable experience and skill to be comfortable on slopes of this severity, particularly if the grade is sustained. An example of the latter is the top of the Tuckerman Ravine headwall, just below the Lip.

A WORD ABOUT SNOWMOBILES

Occasionally, these tours intersect or coincide for a short distance with snowmobile trails. There is often considerable antagonism between skiers and snowmobilers, and I am afraid that skiers must bear an equal share of the blame for whatever bad feelings exist. Skiers do not own the mountains. Snowmobilers have as much right to enjoy the outdoors on their designated trails as skiers do on ski routes, however noisy or offensive snowmobiles may be. Furthermore, skiers often depend on the kindness of snowmobilers when an evacuation becomes necessary. I have seen snowmobilers provide help during an emergency, often at great inconvenience to themselves.

Skiers should declare peace. A friendly smile or wave to snowmobilers when you are on one of their trails will go far toward restoring some sense of mutual respect and civility to these encounters in the woods. It will also keep you from getting run over.

Backcountry Snowboarding

Snowboarders have arrived in the backcountry. Riders are heeding the same call of the wild that has lured skiers into the outback for many years. They come with new tools and a fresh outlook. The high and wild places of New England are a great home for these snow sliders.

When snowboarding first became popular in the 1980s, the sport was largely confined to ski areas. After all, riders were "gravity slaves": It seemed impossible that they could go anywhere but downhill. Skiers, especially backcountry enthusiasts, dismissed snowboards as "toys" rather than "tools." All that has changed.

Snowboarders are striking out in search of wilder snow. Western riders have been exploring the outback for years. Eastern riders, like skiers of this region, often have not realized how much great backcountry skiing and riding terrain is here. This guidebook uncovers the limitless backcountry riding possibilities that abound in the New England mountains.

The pioneers of backcountry snowboarding have borrowed freely from all the winter sports to make it possible to travel in the wilderness. They have taken crampons from climbing, poles from skiing, and snowshoes from hikers to get where they want to go. They are even splitting snowboards in two, converting them to temporary skis, in an effort to make one tool do two things. It is a time of great excitement, as snowboarders individually and collectively improvise ways to trample old limitations and expand the boundaries of their sport. Where riders have led, equipment companies are following. Innovative new gear solutions are in the works to allow snowboarders to travel uphill and across the flats.

Knowing how to navigate and take care of yourself in the mountains is essential for backcountry boarding. Regardless of whether you are on skis or snowboards, traveling in the backcountry requires preparation. All of the information in this book about clothing, mountaineering skills, and first aid applies equally to snowboarders as it does to skiers and snowshoers. Refer to those chapters for information on those subjects.

Following is the information that riders need to use this guide and to tour in the New England backcountry.

BACKCOUNTRY SNOWBOARD EQUIPMENT
BASICS: BOOTS, BOARDS, BINDINGS

The basic equipment for snowboarding is evolving and changing so rapidly that any equipment models recommended today will inevitably be gone tomorrow. A few general considerations should guide your choice of basic equipment.

Comfort is king. You will be wearing whatever you bring into the backcountry for most of the day. Your boots, in particular, should be comfortable for walking, climbing, and riding. There are advantages and drawbacks to both soft and hard boots: soft boots are very comfortable for snowshoeing and hiking uphill on moderate terrain, and riding on soft snow, but they are almost useless for kicking steps in hard snow when climbing a steep gully. Hard boots offer exceptional downhill control and can be used with crampons, but they are heavy and clunky going uphill (however, hard boots work well with split boards, since the binding allows the heel to lift). The bottom line is that both styles, provided you have a comfortable fit, will work.

Gear to go everywhere. In a typical mountain tour, you will encounter every kind of snow condition. Powder, crud, crust, and ice are all part of the wilderness scene. Choose a snowboard that does it all. Softer freeride, or all-mountain, boards are best. Boards with a nice balanced flex will respond the most predictably in unpredictable snow.

Simple is better. A basic tenet of backcountry travel is that everything that can break, will break. Bring gear that is easily repairable in the field. Strap-on bindings are more easily jury-rigged if a strap breaks. Step-in bindings have specialized parts on both the boot and board that may be irreparable in the field. For both bindings, carry spare parts, or even a replacement binding that you can slap on in a hurry.

Snowboarding a steep gully in the Great Gulf off Mount Washington.

Touring Gear

On many tours, you will spend most of your day going uphill. Following is the equipment that makes it possible to defy gravity.

Snowshoes. Snowshoes are basic equipment for backcountry snowboarding. What skins are to skiers, snowshoes are to boarders: It's the only way to get up the mountain. Look for lightweight, compact snowshoes with bindings that will fit around your snowboard boots. Snowshoes should have a crampon underfoot to climb on hard snow. Avoid the old wooden snowshoes. They are heavy, difficult to pack, and more prone to break.

Poles. Poles will often enable you to get across a flat area without having to take off your board. They are also useful for snowshoeing. Look for collapsible poles that can fit in your pack. Three-section poles collapse the smallest, and some sectional poles can double as avalanche probes.

Packs. A sturdy day pack is an investment that will last you for many miles and many years. A good winter day pack should have a capacity of 2,000 to 2,500 cubic inches. Look for one of the many models that have an attachment to carry a snowboard and snowshoes.

Wax. The wide surface area of a snowboard makes them prone to drag (i.e., go slowly) in snow. Rub some fluorinated wax on your board. You'll appreciate the glide on long flat runouts.

Split boards. Split boards have become popular among backcountry riders in the West. The snowboard is split down the middle and attaches together with metal clamps. You use your board in two-plank mode (a.k.a. skis) with skins for the climb. Fasten them together into a single snowboard for the descent. This is specialized touring equipment. But if you plan to do a lot of backcountry riding, it's the lightest, easiest way to go.

Repair gear. There is nothing worse than being five miles out on a remote tour and looking down at a broken binding. I know because I've been there. With the mercury plunging, night approaching, and no quick way down, things can get ugly fast. And your gear *will* break. Bring parts to fix your mangled equipment. Anticipate what can break, and be able to fix it. A basic snowboard repair kit should include binding parts (including replacement screws and straps), rope or cord, glue, knife, and a #3 Phillips screwdriver. See the chapter "Clothing and Ski Equipment" for additional suggestions on repair items. And check the chapter "First Aid" for what to bring in a first-aid kit.

Attitude

You earn your turns in the backcountry. Do yourself and other skiers and riders a favor by respecting some time-honored trail etiquette.

Don't posthole the trail! A trail with crotch-deep craters in it is a nasty ride, especially after the holes freeze. Tread softly. Work less. Climb with snowshoes.

Practice powder preservation. Make one snowshoe track instead of packing down the full width of the trail. If possible, snowshoe up the side of the trail so that most of it is left untracked. Take a different trail up than the one you ride down, if you can.

Easy does it. The backcountry is not Disneyland. It's not even a ski area. There is no ski patrol, and help will be a long time coming if you need it. Save the sick air and Mach speed for the resort, where your buddies can see you. Ride conservatively in the backcountry, as if getting hurt were not an option. Because it's not.

Learn the mountains. Outdoor skills are even more important than your half-pipe technique out here. Become mountain savvy: Learn about mountain navigation, winter camping, the environment, and avalanches. Take a course, read a book (see the chapter "Mountaineering Skills and Avalanches"), learn from friends. The more you know, the farther you can go.

Ride friendly. You don't often meet people in the backcountry. When you do, stop and give them room. There's no "right of way" out here—just folks like you who are out to have fun. They'll probably be surprised to see snowboarders. Here's your chance to brag a little and tell them what it's like to ride where they ski or hike.

Keep it clean. Leave no trace of your passage other than your tracks. Carry out all trash, including cigarette butts. (Better yet, leave the butts home and try fresh air instead.)

Help yourself. Bring extra food, water, clothes, a lighter, and a space blanket. Just in case things don't go as planned.

Have fun. It's why we go.

The New England Ski Season

There is usually good snow cover for skiing in the backcountry of northern New England from mid-December through early April. In many years, skiing has begun by Thanksgiving. Likewise, April snowstorms are not uncommon and are sometimes quite substantial. December and February are the months with the heaviest snowfall in the three northern states, with the snow reaching its greatest depth in late February and early March.

Spring skiing in New England begins in early April. Mount Washington is the favorite location. Skiing in Tuckerman Ravine often continues through June. (See the Mount Washington Region route descriptions in this book.) There is also spring skiing at higher elevations and in other ravines of the White Mountains, including Oakes Gulf, the Gulf of Slides, and the Great Gulf.

THE NEW ENGLAND WINTER ENVIRONMENT

Winters in New England are characterized by very cold and wet weather. The cold is intensified in the mountains, where wind exposure is greatest. Data from the weather observatory on Mount Washington illustrates this point.

The summit of Mount Washington (elevation 6,288 feet) is under cloud cover about 55 percent of the time. The average winter temperature is 15 degrees Fahrenheit; the record low temperature is -46 degrees. Average winds in the winter are 44 mph, and winds over 100 mph have been recorded every month of the year. These are admittedly some of the most extreme conditions in New England, but it is better to be prepared for the most severe mountain weather than to be caught off guard in the winter.

Table 1 presents a climatological profile of New England in winter.

TABLE 1
WINTER WEATHER IN NEW ENGLAND

Location	Mean Snow, Sleet Totals (inches)				Mean Temperature (degrees F)			
	Dec.	Jan.	Feb.	Mar.	Apr.	Dec.	Jan.	Feb.	Mar.	Apr.
Pinkham Notch, NH	35.5	31.4	38.2	34.2	16.0	19.9	15.8	17.3	25.6	37.4
Mount Washington, NH	42.5	39.0	40.5	41.8	29.2	9.3	4.8	5.5	12.0	22.5
Woodstock, NH	23.6	21.2	24.2	17.4	3.09	23.5	18.8	21.3	30.4	42.3
Montpelier, VT	23.8	18.2	23.2	17.4	5.0	20.5	15.1	17.5	27.0	40.4
Mount Mansfield, VT*	41.6	36.6	27.8	36.0	24.0	11.1	6.7	11.5	18.0	34.0
Bar Harbor, ME	14.1	16.1	19.5	12.8	2.6	28.2	23.8	24.6	32.5	42.8
Ripogenus Dam, ME (Baxter State Park)	28.2	25.7	26.8	20.9	7.4	17.7	11.9	13.3	23.6	36.6

Source: National Oceanic and Atmospheric Administration, Climatology of the United States, No. 60, 1951–1973. This is most recent available data.
* Source: Mount Mansfield weather station, 1982–1987.

Clothing and Ski Equipment

There is no one right set of clothes or equipment that works for every person. There are, however, some basic guidelines that should be taken into consideration when you are looking for new gear.

DRESSING TO STAY WARM

Clothing for backcountry skiing and riding must keep you warm and relatively dry. Cotton is notoriously unable to do this. When cotton gets wet, it acts like a towel, getting wetter and wetter and drawing out precious body heat and energy.

The best clothes to wear in the winter are those made of synthetics such as polypropylene, polyester, and nylon. These types of clothing are sold under various names, including Capilene, CoolMax, Thermax, and Polarfleece. All these fabrics are similar in that they retain very little moisture and dry from the inside out when they get wet. The body heat of an active skier is usually adequate to dry them.

The most effective way to dress to stay warm in winter is to wear a number of lighter layers rather than one bulky layer. This technique is called *layering*. What keeps you warm is the air trapped next to your body, not clothing. By wearing a number of loose, lighter layers, you can most efficiently trap air, which is warmed by your body.

For layering to be effective, you must peel a layer *before* you begin sweating profusely. Heavy perspiration in the winter can be dangerous. It can lead to dehydration and will saturate your clothes just as if you were standing in the rain.

A typical layering system for an active day of skiing is a polypropylene shirt, a fleece sweater, lightweight fleece pants, and a windbreaker of nylon or Gore-Tex. In your backpack would be a heavier fleece or pile jacket, nylon or Gore-Tex overpants, and a compact down (or equivalent) parka.

Wind protection is especially important in the New England mountains. All the sweaters in your closet won't keep you warm with a 30-mph wind slicing through them. A parka or anorak made of a tightly woven and fast-drying fabric such as Gore-Tex is an essential part of any layering system. As your outer layer, this shell should also be water-resistant. Wet snows are common in New England, and don't be surprised if you encounter rain as well.

A common mistake skiers make when dressing is to throw on a down parka and head up the mountain. In my experience, the temperature would have to be well below zero to be comfortable skiing in a down parka. It is simply too much insulation for an aerobic activity like skiing. A good practice is to start skiing while feeling a bit chilled; you will warm up within a few minutes and save having to undress and repack a few hundred yards down the trail.

THE RIGHT SKIS FOR THE JOB*

Seventy years ago there was only one type of ski. You couldn't really go wrong: You used the same ski for cross-country, ski jumping, and downhill skiing. Today, selecting a ski involves wading through a dizzying forest of specialized gear. There are now different skis for skating, touring on groomed trails, touring off-trail, racing, jumping, lift-area skiing, backcountry telemarking, and alpine touring.

The best skiers can ski most routes on any equipment. That isn't to say it's easy to take skinny cross-country skis down Mount Washington. It's just that high-tech equipment is no substitute for good technique and commitment. Indeed, most of the ski routes in this book—including all of the steepest descents in Tuckerman Ravine—were first skied on seven-foot-long hickory skis with cable bindings. These early skiers simply used what they had. Their passion, boldness, and creativity were far more important catalysts for their mountain explorations than what was under their feet.

Looking for spring skiing in the White Mountains of New Hampshire.

* See "Backcountry Snowboarding" chapter for information on snowboard equipment.

Having said that, your choice of ski equipment *does* matter. Gear has become absurdly specialized, such that it is quite possible to buy equipment that is completely inappropriate for backcountry terrain. The easier backcountry tours can be done in light cross-country gear. But you would find most routes much easier to ski and more enjoyable with equipment that is better suited to a wide range of conditions.

What is the ideal backcountry ski setup? For me, it would be a superlight boot that is fleet on the flats but stiff and solid on the descents, mated with a superlight but indestructible binding, mounted on a superlight ski that is as comfortable flat-tracking as it is busting through crud and descending a steep gully.

Needless to say, this ideal marriage of light weight and uncompromising stability doesn't exist; thus, choosing a ski requires making compromises. No one ski and boot does everything well. Err on the side of what you do most and where you want to go. Lightweight gear is the choice for light touring, while heavier equipment is the choice for more difficult terrain and conditions.

Following are some general suggestions on what to look for in equipment. This discussion is limited to Nordic-style backcountry ski equipment. For recommendations on the latest ski models, and for information on alpine-touring (*randonée*) equipment, see the equipment reviews in magazines such as *Backcountry* and *Couloir*.

BOOTS

Good backcountry boots are the most important investment you will make. The reasons are simple: comfort and control. You will likely be in your ski boots for most of the day. Comfort is king in boot selection: If your feet are comfortable, you will be happy. If your feet hurt, no amount of pretty scenery will arrest your misery. Boots also make a critical difference in your ability to control your skis. If you are upgrading your equipment piecemeal, it makes sense to buy boots first.

Good backcountry ski boots have a more rigid, higher-ankle profile than conventional cross-country boots. Their key attribute is that they are torsionally stiff. This means that when you twist your leg to turn the ski, the twisting motion is transferred directly into turning power on the ski, instead of into just flexing the boot. You are probably familiar with the terrifying sensation of flying downhill on cross-country skis with old boots that flex uselessly in the bindings. A good, stiff boot will add an element of control to your skiing you may never have experienced before.

Leather or plastic boots? Both materials work well, and each has its strengths. Leather boots are very comfortable. Many people have a favorite pair of trusty old leather boots that they have enjoyed touring in for years. The most versatile new leather boots incorporate elements from plastic boots. Having one or two buckles can greatly enhance your control on the downhills, and can do wonders to keep an aging leather boot snug around your foot.

The newest plastic boots are remarkably comfortable. They require little maintenance, stay dry, and have unmatched downhill performance. Take extra care in fitting yourself in plastic boots. One brand may fit your foot, and another may not. You can fine-tune fit problems at an alpine ski shop that is expert at adjusting plastic boots.

You may want to consider buying double boots if you have chronic problems with cold feet. Double boots are heavy but warm. Single boots with insulated supergaiters are another possible solution. (See the section on frostbite in the "First Aid" chapter for more on this.)

Avoid buying too much boot. A clunky, heavy boot will make climbing and touring on the flats feel like a tiresome trudge. If the majority of your skiing is on moderate terrain, opt for a lighter backcountry boot rather than a boot that is oriented to lift-serviced skiing. Skip the ultrastiff telemark racing boots. The stiff collars that reach nearly to your knee will cause you nothing but pain on uphill climbs and long tours. They are strictly for lift-served skiing.

Unless you can find a pair of used boots, be prepared to pay a relatively hefty price for good boots. They are expensive but an investment that should last many years.

Skis

The tours in this book with sections of extended downhill skiing that are rated *more difficult* or *most difficult* are most easily done by the majority of skiers on heavier backcountry skis—commonly called telemark skis. Telemark skis are heavy-duty, metal-edged skis that are designed for maximum control on variable, difficult terrain. They are wider than most touring skis, enabling them to float better in powder and to provide a more stable platform when wearing a pack and skiing on uneven ground. Metal edges are particularly useful in the East, where ice is a fact of life for the backcountry skier.

Metal-edged skis do have a drawback: They are heavy and, consequently, not as enjoyable to ski with on flatter terrain or long tours. Metal-edged skis are not necessary for skiing in powder or on flat terrain where control on downhills is not a primary consideration.

Ski tours rated as *moderate* in this book can generally be skied comfortably on edgeless touring skis, provided you have sturdy boots and reasonably good snow conditions. A good backcountry touring ski should be fairly wide for flotation in deep snow, have ample sidecut to facilitate turning, and be solidly constructed. One way to assess whether a ski fits these criteria is to place it back-to-back with a general-purpose telemark ski; a good edgeless backcountry ski should have a similar profile and similar measurements.

Wide telemark skis—those with measurements of 85 mm or more at the tip—are especially user-friendly in soft snow and on more challenging tours. It is much easier to ski in crud, powder, and heavy snow with the wider, more stable platform.

Camber refers to the arch in the middle of the ski; the space created by this arch is called the wax pocket. A double-cambered ski has a stiff arch, while a single-cambered ski has little or no arch. Double-cambered skis are especially nice for moderate touring, since they hold wax better over the course of a long tour. Single-cambered skis offer more control at high speeds and are especially suited to lift-serviced skiing and more challenging backcountry tours. Single-cambered skis can be waxed (the wax may wear off a little faster than on double-cambered skis) or used with climbing skins. In general, choose a single-cambered ski if you primarily ski at lift areas and on routes rated *more difficult* and *most difficult*. Opt for a single-cambered touring ski if you prefer the more moderate tours.

The debate over which is best, waxless or waxable skis, should really not be so strident. Waxing skis is not that complicated, and it is made even simpler with the two-wax systems that are available (one wax for new snow, another wax for old snow). The tricks of waxing can be learned from other skiers, or simple trial and error. Waxable skis are faster, quieter, and better climbers than waxless skis. Simply put, a fast ski is a fun ski to tour on. However, if you favor moderate tours, only ski occasionally, and just don't want to be bothered with waxing, waxless skis do a fine job.

BINDINGS

Heavy-duty three-pin or cable bindings are the best choice for backcountry skiing. Bindings designed for telemarking are made of strong metal alloys that can take considerable abuse. They are much sturdier and offer greater control than lightweight touring bindings. Getting stranded with a mangled lightweight binding when you are five miles from nowhere should convince you that heavy-duty bindings are worth the extra investment.

The so-called "backcountry" step-in boot-binding systems made by Salomon and Rottefella are fine for moderate touring. For more challenging tours, they do not offer the same level of control and durability as a cable or three-pin binding.

POLES

Adjustable poles are a good choice for backcountry skiing. These poles can collapse or extend, depending on the demands of the terrain; they can be kept long for the uphill climb and shortened for downhill skiing. However, adjustable poles can be exasperating, collapsing when you don't want them to and refusing to adjust. Two-section poles are simpler and less likely to collapse unexpectedly than three-section poles.

If you travel in steep terrain, you should invest in probe poles. These can be joined together to form one long avalanche probe, a useful feature when traveling in slide-prone areas. Note that not all adjustable poles convert to avalanche probes; check to be sure that your poles can screw together.

CLIMBING SKINS

The use of climbing skins on most of these ski tours is strongly recommended. Climbing skins are ski-length strips of fabric with unidirectional hairs. These hairs mat down when skiing forward and grip the snow, preventing the ski from sliding backward. The best skins are made out of nylon or mohair. They mimic the action of early skins, which were actually animal pelts that skiers strapped to the bottoms of their skis in order to ski uphill.

When skiing in the mountains, skiers will often spend at least half a day skiing up steep grades in order to get to a summit or the top of a trail. The ascent on a number of these routes would become so tiring and frustrating without skins that most people would understandably abandon their destination. Skins are actually a safety item in these situations. They permit you to ration your energy efficiently and avoid exhaustion. Being able to gain purchase in any type of snow also enables you to get out quickly if the need arises. Skins can be left on for narrow downhill sections that you find particularly desperate. They will slow you down considerably, but they also make it difficult to turn.

Skins require some care. They should be dried out after each use, folded back together, and stored in a dry place. Adhesive skins require a reapplication of glue every season or two.

Nylon and mohair skins work equally well. Nylon tends to be more durable and dries quicker, while mohair glides better. Look for adhesive skins that are wide enough to cover the bases of your skis; a tail hook is a nice feature, too. Kicker skins—which only cover about half the ski length—also work well on more moderate terrain. Avoid plastic skins. They are cheaper, but they have virtually no forward glide and the attachment straps tend to roll over the edges of the ski when skiing on a sidehill.

Packs

Look for a beefy day pack that is designed to carry skis. Jury-rigged ski attachments can be a constant aggravation. The pack should have a capacity of 2,000 to 2,500 cubic inches. A sternum strap is crucial to stabilize the load when skiing downhill, and a well-padded waist belt makes all the difference in comfort. Cheap packs fall apart. Invest in a good pack, and it will last for years.

Miscellaneous

If you are an avid telemarker, you should invest in **kneepads.** Injuries ranging from bruised to broken kneecaps have been increasingly common among telemarkers, but they can usually be prevented by placing a little foam and plastic between you and the ground. The best protection is the style of kneepads used for skateboarding or in-line skating: They have a molded plastic cup over a layer of closed-cell foam and are available at ski and skate shops. You can also find them in building supply stores (they are used by carpenters).

Eye protection is essential for skiing through trees or on hiking trails. Ski goggles, glacier glasses, sunglasses, or sport shades will all do the job.

Consider carrying a compact **sleeping bag** on more-remote day trips. Having a sleeping bag along is a wise safety precaution, particularly if your party is large or includes some inexperienced skiers.

BACKCOUNTRY REPAIR

Your equipment *will* break. Backcountry skiing is abusive. Skis snap, bindings rip out, poles turn into pretzels, boot pinholes blow out, and packs detonate at the seams. About the only thing that you can count on is that each of these mishaps will occur at the least convenient moment.

Backcountry skiers should be equipped to perform functional field repairs. Below are basic items needed for a repair kit.

Screwdriver. A #3 Phillips screwdriver fits cross-country binding screws. There are several handy palm-size drivers available from ski shops, or you can just buy a stubby screwdriver at a hardware store.

Glue. Quick-drying Super-Glue works well for everything from securing binding screws to reinforcing a broken ski. Pack it securely—it can leak in your pack.

Hose clamps. A small assortment of hose clamps is useful for quickly repairing broken poles and skis. Have some small enough to fit around a pole, and large enough to fit around overlapping broken ski ends.

Aluminum flashing. Aluminum flashing can be used to splint a broken or bent pole or ski. For a pole, wrap a section around the break and hold it in place with hose clamps. Skis can be patched similarly, although it is a more tenuous splint. Curved snow stakes for tents are also very useful for splinting poles.

Screws. Binding screws love to loosen themselves. The best solution is prevention. Put a dab of Shoe-Goo or silicone caulk in the screw holes and under the binding before mounting the binding on the ski. Get into the habit of checking your bindings before each outing to make sure the screws are tight. Always have on hand a small assortment of screws. Extra binding screws can usually be obtained from a ski shop. A few oversized screws are useful in case a binding hole becomes stripped.

Steel wool. Steel wool can be mixed into glue to fill stripped binding screw holes. It hardens like a steel casing around the screw.

Nylon cord. Carry at least ten feet of it. It is invaluable in binding repair. It can be used to replace a lost bail, or rigged like a cable binding.

Knife or multi-tool. Swiss army knives are useful for spreading peanut butter and for doing just about anything else you can imagine. The multi-tools that include pliers, screwdrivers, wire cutters, and a knife are especially useful.

Extra binding. At zero degrees with night approaching, you'll appreciate not having to improvise a binding repair that may not even work. Keep an extra ski binding in the bottom of your pack (ski shops may have an orphaned binding kicking around that they are willing to part with). Use the awl on your Swiss army knife to start a new screw hole if you have to.

Duct tape. When all else fails, so will the duct tape. But have it along anyway. A good way to carry it is to wrap a wad around your poles. And keep a roll in your car to replenish your supply. It's always useful for something.

Mountaineering Skills and Avalanches

Backcountry skiing and snowboarding are just forms of winter mountaineering—hence the term *ski mountaineering,* which aptly describes most of the tours in this book. Skiers and snowboarders need good mountaineering skills to travel safely in the winter wilderness. "Good ski technique," as Steve Barnett writes in *The Best Ski Touring in America,* "rates well behind avalanche knowledge, navigational skills, and camping skills as something you need to know to ski." Some of these skills can be learned from books or classes; others, like good judgment, must be honed by experience.

This book will not attempt to teach mountaineering in any depth, since other books cover the subject thoroughly. A widely respected reference guide is *Mountaineering: The Freedom of the Hills.* However, the skills with which every backcountry skier and snowboarder should be proficient are briefly described below.

MOUNTAINEERING JUDGMENT

Most judgment calls in the mountains ultimately come down to a decision about how big a margin of safety you want to give yourself. In the winter, mountaineers need a larger margin of safety than in the summer. An unplanned night out in the snow without adequate equipment can have serious consequences.

Good judgment in the mountains requires taking into consideration a wide range of variables. Among other things, you must consider the strength of each individual in your party (are they strong skiers? are they in good physical condition?); the condition of each person at the point a decision is being made (is everybody warm? is anybody nearing exhaustion?); the objective hazards your party will encounter (how exposed is the route to the elements? is there significant avalanche danger? what is the weather forecast? what are the snow conditions?); and what you are equipped to accomplish.

Anticipation is critical in the mountains. The more you are prepared for the unlikely, the greater your margin of safety. If you choose to play things close to your limit, you should be prepared for the consequences of the inevitable time when things don't go the way you had planned.

NAVIGATION

Trails can be especially difficult to follow in winter. Blazes on summer hiking trails are often obscured by snow or are difficult to see, particularly during snowstorms. Whiteouts, which are particularly disorienting on exposed mountain ridges, are not uncommon. It is essential, therefore, that skiers be proficient with a map and compass, and carry both of them in the backcountry. A global positioning system (GPS) and altimeter, though both can be helpful for pinpointing your location, are not routinely carried by mountaineers in the East, nor are they necessary.

Maps are the most important items for navigation. Ideally, if you are closely following a map, the compass should rarely have to come out. The two most common types of trail maps are *sketch maps* and *topographic maps*. Sketch maps show the rough outline of trails in an area. They are often not drawn to an accurate scale, may not indicate direction, and do not show changes in elevation. They are useful in combination with topographic maps to determine the approximate location of trails.

A topographic map provides detailed information about the landscape. It is the basic tool of the backcountry traveler. Learning to read topographic maps takes time, but developing a fundamental grasp of how they work is not difficult. Simply put, each contour line represents a change in elevation. The most common contour intervals used on maps published by the U.S. Geological Survey (USGS) are 10, 20, 40, and 100 feet. A few New England maps (notably the Mount Washington quadrangle) have been issued with metric contour intervals. This information is printed at the bottom of each USGS map.

Topographic maps are extremely helpful when planning a ski or snowboard route because you can tailor the tour to the type of terrain you are seeking. Areas with contour lines bunched tightly together indicate steep slopes, while wider spaces between the lines indicate a more moderate grade. You will get a feel for what type of topography to look for on maps by checking a map when you are skiing and seeing how the terrain is depicted.

The best way to stay oriented with a map is to check it frequently, and especially when you arrive at obvious landmarks. This means keeping the map accessible at all times. If you have to dig in your pack to get it, chances are you won't bother until it is too late. Use the map to predict what is around the next bend and what you will encounter in the next half-mile. If the terrain is not what you predicted it would be, you have either miscalculated the distance or are in the wrong place. Either way, you have been alerted to the problem sooner rather than later and can make a quick adjustment.

Maps come in different scales. Most USGS New England maps now come in the 7.5-minute series, which cover an area of about 6 by 9 miles. These maps have a scale of 1:24,000, where about 2.5 inches equals 1 mile.

Map reading in the Northeast can be tricky. Mountaineers accustomed to navigating in big western ranges can easily become confused by the small scale of New England terrain. Distant landmarks are often impossible to sight from the forested trails, and small drainages on the map can be indistinct. The key here is to pay attention to small changes in the terrain and to look around frequently to see how you are oriented to distant landmarks. Navigating here is like skiing here: Our compact landscape makes everything a little more challenging.

A compass is a handheld plastic device with a floating magnetic needle inside that points north—almost. The needle actually points to magnetic north, and the angle of deviation from true north must be corrected depending on where you are on the planet. In New England, magnetic declination ranges from 14 degrees west in Vermont to 20 degrees west in northern Maine. The exact declination for a given area will be printed on your topographic map. This means that if you take a bearing from a map, you should *add* the amount of declination for that area in order to arrive at an accurate bearing to follow. (If you tend to forget whether to add or subtract in the Northeast, think *add*-irondacks.) If you take a bearing from a distant landmark like a mountain summit, you must *subtract* the declination before using the compass bearing on a map. This compensates for the amount that the needle is exaggerating the angle between you and the distant object due to its affinity for magnetic north.

Compasses can be used to establish whether or not you are going in the right direction, to pinpoint your position (by triangulation), or to follow a bearing. The latter is especially useful in dense eastern forests, where following a bearing is sometimes the only way to bushwhack your way out of the deep woods if you've gotten turned around. Remember that compasses are not the only indicators of direction of travel. You can always use the sun: It rises in the east, spends most of its day in the south, and sets in the west. If you've really gotten waylaid, remember that the moon also rises in the east, and the North Star points north.

WINTER CAMPING

Knowing how to comfortably spend a night outdoors in the winter opens up exciting new possibilities for backcountry travelers. Multiday ski tours can be planned to visit the most remote wilderness. It is also important for skiers to know how to spend a night safely in winter in the event you are unexpectedly benighted.

Many of the principles of dressing to stay warm apply to sleeping warm. The key is to preserve and generate as much body heat as possible. This may be done in several ways.

The basic equipment for preserving body heat while sleeping is a sleeping bag and an insulating ground pad. A sleeping bag keeps you warm by trapping air next to your skin. The more loft, or trapped air, a sleeping bag has, the warmer it is. A winter sleeping bag should have roughly six inches of loft, which will keep you warm down to about zero degrees Fahrenheit. Both down and synthetic (such as Polarguard and Quallofil) sleeping bags are appropriate, although down bag users must take care to keep their bags dry. If you do not own a winter sleeping bag, two lighter bags, with one inside the other, should be sufficient.

A good sleeping bag is useless in the snow without insulation beneath it. Air mattresses, such as a Therm-A-Rest, or pads made of closed-cell foam do a good job of insulating you from the snow. The more space between you and the snow, the warmer you will be. In addition to using your sleeping pad, consider sleeping on extra clothes, on an extra sleeping pad, or on your pack. Also, be sure that your sleeping pad is rated to withstand temperatures below zero. Summer pads, although they look the same, will crack at low temperatures.

Winter mountaineers should know how to construct an emergency snow shelter. Snow has remarkable insulating properties; that is one of the reasons hibernating animals can stay alive when they dig into the snow for the winter. If you get benighted without adequate equipment, digging a snow cave may save your life or your extremities. The temperature inside a snow cave can easily be 30 degrees warmer than the outside air. There are many types of snow shelters that work. Find a book that discusses snow shelters (see the "Recommended Reading" list at the back of this book), and spend a day playing with a shovel in your backyard to try your hand at building several different types of shelters.

Even with a good sleeping bag, your body will need enough caloric fuel to generate heat throughout the night. The best fuel is high-carbohydrate foods such as pasta, which should be eaten in quantity before going to bed. In addition, keep a bag of quick-acting, high-energy food such as trail mix next to you as you sleep. If you get cold during the night, eating a few handfuls of gorp (Good Old Raisins and Peanuts) may be all you need to keep your furnace burning.

AVALANCHE AWARENESS

Avalanches pose a serious danger to skiers and snowboarders. The fact that New England does not have a *lot* of avalanches should not be confused with the notion that it does not have *any*. Fortunately, New England has less of the type of terrain and snow conditions that favor avalanches, but it does have its share. And an avalanche in New England is as deadly as an avalanche in Colorado.

White Mountain National Forest Snow Ranger Brad Ray estimates that 20 to 25 potentially deadly avalanches rake the flanks of Mount Washington each winter, although most of them release when no one is around. The notable exception was in 1996, when two skiers died in an avalanche in the Gulf of Slides and a hiker was killed in an avalanche on Lion's Head on Mount Washington.

The danger of avalanches is greatest on slopes of 30 to 45 degrees. This danger is at its peak during a snowstorm and in the first twenty-four hours afterward. In addition, the ravines around Mount Washington are extremely prone to wind loading. Tuckerman Ravine can get a foot or more snow blown into it even without a snowstorm. Wind-loaded slopes and gullies can be very unstable even when there is low avalanche danger elsewhere. A new cornice at the top of a slope is one indication that it has been wind-loaded; avoid these slopes for several days until they settle.

The ski routes described in this book that are most prone to avalanche are Tuckerman Ravine, Katahdin, Gulf of Slides, Great Gulf, and Oakes Gulf. In addition, any ravines, gullies, slides, or steep, open slopes that you might be skiing can avalanche when the necessary combination of conditions exists. If you ski on steep, open terrain, especially around Mount Washington or Katahdin, you should carry standard avalanche safety equipment. This includes a shovel (metal ones are best), avalanche transceiver (you must have a newer, single-frequency model), and probe poles. But carrying rescue gear does not confer immunity: Once you have to resort to locating a buried friend with a beacon, you've already blown it.

The key to traveling in avalanche-prone terrain is prevention. Records show that most avalanche victims trigger the avalanche themselves. *When in doubt, back off.* It simply is not worth it to jump onto a suspect slope. And just because someone else skied a slope does not prove that it is stable. Passing up a tempting powder run takes considerable experience and wisdom.

Assess the snow conditions when you are skiing in avalanche country. First, open your eyes and look around: look for signs of instability on surrounding slopes (cracks, sloughs, settling underfoot). Nearby avalanche activity or debris is a major warning sign of instability. Dig a snow pit as far as you can (to the ground, or at least six feet); look for sliding surfaces within the snowpack—layers of dense

Dig a snow pit to check the avalanche danger.

or icy snow to which recent snow has not bonded. Perform a shovel test to see if the snow shears off at any layer.

The more you develop an interest in backcountry skiing, the more you need to know about avalanches. This is especially true if you plan to venture to mountains in the western United States and elsewhere. Read books, take courses, and ask questions of people with experience in avalanche-hazard assessment. The Appalachian Mountain Club offers a good introductory avalanche course in Pinkham Notch every winter. (See appendix B, "Recommended Reading," for good books on the subject.)

SELF-RELIANCE

Being self-reliant in the mountains has long been a basic ethic of mountaineers. Having the ability to be self-reliant requires proficiency in first aid and mountaineering skills. Just as important as these skills is a mind-set, when heading into the mountains, that you will not count on being bailed out by someone else if an accident occurs. Traveling with this mind-set should factor into your choice of route, equipment, and skiing companions.

Self-reliance is important on a practical level. Rescues take a long time, especially in winter. If an injury is life-threatening, time may be of the essence.

A problem has developed in recent years as people have come to assume that a rescue is just around the corner whenever they head to the hills. Many people have become lazy or careless about preventive safety measures. Being in the mountains without extra clothing, first-aid provisions, and repair equipment is inviting trouble. The odds favoring mishaps always seem to increase in direct proportion to poor preparation.

The increasing presence of cellular phones in the backcountry is perhaps the best example of how people are substituting high-tech gadgets for common sense. Here's a modest proposal for backcountry users: Instead of taking a cell phone, take a first-aid course. Or a mountaineering class. Or an avalanche seminar. Instead of the false security of thinking that you can call 911 from the mountains, take comfort in knowing that you probably don't need to call for help. You can make good decisions, prevent trouble, and take care of yourself. That's the time-tested ethic of mountaineering. And it's your best insurance for being safe and happy in the mountains.

First Aid

Prevention is the key to avoiding winter emergencies. Recognizing signs and being alert to the condition of members of your party are critical. Medical emergencies in winter are a different ballgame than in the summer. The extreme environment increases stress on both the victim and rescuer, and problems can progress from minor to life-threatening in a frighteningly short time.

All backcountry skiers and snowboarders should obtain training in first aid. Accidents can happen easily in the mountains, and your ability to administer the appropriate first aid can be crucial to preempting a harrowing ordeal.

Skiers should always travel with a first-aid kit. The contents of each kit may vary, but at a minimum they should include an assortment of bandages to control bleeding (including a combine dressing or sanitary napkin), materials to treat and care for blisters (Second Skin and Compeed are two of the best treatments), an emergency blanket, and a triangular bandage. I also like to carry two Ace bandages and a lightweight flexible splint called a SAM Splint (made by the Seaberg Company, 800-818-4726, www.samsplint.com). The SAM Splint makes it possible to immobilize an injured extremity quickly and get on your way—an asset when a frigid wind is nipping at you.

Hypothermia and frostbite are the two most common problems in winter. I have been stunned to witness the way that *frostbite and hypothermia can develop and deteriorate extremely fast!* In a sense, these are social diseases: they should not occur if every member of a party is carefully watching out for one another. These conditions are entirely preventable if the early signs are recognized.

HYPOTHERMIA

Hypothermia is a condition in which the temperature of the body core—the area around the vital organs—drops below its normal level of 98.6 degrees. You will need a hypothermia thermometer to definitively measure subnormal temperatures, but the basic signs and symptoms allow you to make a reasonable field diagnosis.

SIGNS

Signs of hypothermia in the early stages include intense shivering, lips and fingernails becoming cyanotic (blue), mental confusion, slurred speech, and clumsiness, especially with the hands. The victim may become apathetic, lag behind, and complain of being cold. This is called *mild hypothermia,* when the body core temperature (taken rectally) is above 90 degrees. Oral temperatures are generally 1 degree lower than rectal temperatures.

Severe hypothermia—when the body core temperature drops below 90 degrees—is life-threatening. A telltale indicator of this stage is that shivering gradually stops. The victim becomes extremely uncoordinated, even unable to walk without help, and speech may be slurred. Severely hypothermic persons often become unusually careless about protecting themselves from the cold: They take off their hats, leave their parkas open, and forget their mittens (this common sign is called "paradoxical undressing"). Victims often deny that there is a problem. Left untreated, this condition can deteriorate until the person is unresponsive or even unconscious.

What is going on here? The body is simply losing heat at a faster rate than it can generate it. The body loses heat in four ways: through evaporation (e.g., breathing), conduction (sitting on the snow or wearing wet clothes), radiation (from exposed skin), and convection (windchill).

The body gains heat from digesting food, engaging in physical activity, being near external heat sources such as a fire or a warm body, and shunting blood from the extremities and the skin to the body core.

TREATMENT

The basic principles of treating mild hypothermia are as follows:

1. *Stop heat loss.* Remove the victim from the cold, wet environment if possible. If you are near a tent or shelter, use them. When far from shelter, one of the most important steps is to *remove wet clothes and replace them with dry clothing.* This includes removing layers of wet polypropylene clothing as well. Hypothermic people are generally unable to generate enough body heat to dry out their clothing, regardless of what "miracle fabrics" they are wearing. Add extra insulation over the dry layers. If you have no dry clothes, at least wrap the person in something windproof, such as a parka or tarp.

These basic remedies are crucial: Just getting dry clothes on a mildly hypothermic partner and feeding him or her can abort the slide. But first you have to notice that your friend is struggling.

2. If possible, *place the victim in a warm environment.* Putting the victim in a sleeping bag with one or two other people all stripped to the waist can be helpful. This is often unnecessary if other measures are taken.

3. If the victim is conscious, *give him or her warm, sweet liquids and high-energy foods, such as trail mix.*

4. *Get moving.* Once your partner is stabilized, exercise will keep him or her warm. It's also the best way to "get out of the woods."

Treatment of severe hypothermia is a much more complicated affair. Most experts agree that a severely hypothermic patient should only be rewarmed in a hospital; even then, the prognosis is not great. If the victim has been hypothermic for a number of hours, metabolic changes have taken place and rewarming too quickly can cause greater harm. The best option is to *evacuate the victim to a hospital with as little jostling as possible.* The victim should not be given warm liquids, since that can cause blood from the body core to rush to the extremities, further depressing the core temperature. The victim should be wrapped in a vapor barrier cocoon consisting of a sleeping bag, a waterproof plastic or coated nylon bag, and a reflective emergency blanket. A severely hypothermic patient may appear dead, but may actually be existing in a "metabolic icebox" with barely detectable vital signs. Administering CPR is generally inadvisable; chest compressions can actually *cause* heart failure in a severely hypothermic patient. A hypothermic patient is not dead until he is warm and dead. Give victims the benefit of the doubt—get them to a hospital.

PREVENTION

Hypothermia is best avoided, not treated. Here are some ways to prevent it:

✳ Eat throughout the day when outdoors in the winter. Your body burns an enormous number of calories to stay warm in the winter. One lunch stop on the trail is inadequate. Have snack foods accessible, and snack often.

✳ Don't wear cotton. If someone in your party is wearing cotton clothing, be especially aware of how that person is faring. In my experience, that person is likely to become mildly hypothermic by late in the day.

✳ Stop evaporative heat loss by shedding layers of clothing *before* you begin sweating.

✳ "If your feet are cold, put on a hat." This old backpacker's axiom is a wise one. Up to 75 percent of the body's total heat production can be lost through the head and neck.

✳ Prevent conductive heat loss by putting on a wind shell *before* arriving at an exposed area such as a summit ridge.

✳ Be extra vigilant on warm, wet days. Skiing when it is 30 to 40 degrees and snowing is classic hypothermia weather. Bring spare dry clothes, and be on the alert.

✳ Check in with your partners. "How're ya doin'?" I annoyingly ask my ski partners throughout the day. Be specific: "Feeling tired? Cold?" Make them think about how they are feeling, and give them a chance to tell you. Then respond: take a rest, add or shed a clothing layer, eat.

✳ Drink lots of fluids.

The last point deserves special mention. Many people assume that dehydration is not a problem in the winter because people don't sweat as much as in summer. This is a serious mistake. The combination of perspiring and exhaling humidified air can dehydrate a skier rapidly. Dehydration is especially problematic for people who are overweight, since they tend to sweat more. A steady loss of body fluids makes a person more prone to frostbite and hypothermia.

Signs of mild dehydration include headaches and brightly colored urine. Prevent this by ensuring that every member of the party has at least a liter of water that is accessible, and make sure people are drinking. Keep your water bottle insulated, or put it inside your parka so that it won't freeze; insulated Camelbak-style hydration systems are useful if it's not too cold. Alcoholic beverages should be avoided; they act as a diuretic, causing further dehydration.

FROSTBITE

Frostbite occurs when body tissue freezes. It can affect any part of the body, but parts that protrude are particularly susceptible. The ears, nose, fingers, and toes must be closely monitored in cold weather.

SIGNS AND TREATMENT

There are two main types of frostbite. *Superficial frostbite* is indicated by patches of gray or yellowish skin that may be hard or waxy to the touch, although underlying tissue is still soft. The affected area feels numb, tingly, or very cold.

The treatment for superficial frostbite is to immediately rewarm the affected body part. This can be done by placing it against warm skin, such as putting a superficially frostbitten foot in a partner's armpit or on his or her stomach, or just placing a warm hand over a numb nose or cheek. Do not rub the affected part, as this can cause deeper tissue damage.

Deep frostbite occurs when a body part—usually hands or feet—is fully frozen, including both skin and underlying tissue. The affected part feels totally numb and wooden, and it is difficult for the victim to move it. Deep frostbite is indicated by pale, waxy skin over solid underlying tissue. The body part feels like a piece of chicken just removed from the freezer.

Field treatment for deep frostbite involves first preventing further injury. Keep the patient warm and make sure no other areas are exposed. Thawing can be done only under sterile conditions, and the affected area cannot be in any danger of refreezing or having to bear weight. Thawing out a frostbitten extremity is extremely painful. It is almost always preferable to ski or walk someone with deep frostbite out to a hospital, where comprehensive medical treatment is available. If you rewarm a foot with deep frostbite in the field, the victim will have to be carried out.

A person with deep frostbite should be evacuated as soon as possible. The victim should be fed plenty of fluids to decrease susceptibility to further injury.

PREVENTION

Don't wait for problems to develop. If someone is complaining of numbness or tingling in the extremities, *stop and deal with it*. Waiting "just until you get to the car" can lead to permanent damage.

Preventing frostbite should be a group effort. When skiing on very cold days, or high on a windy mountain ridge, partners should *check each other continually* for any white splotches on the face, ears, and nose. Other pointers to help prevent frostbite:

✳ Avoid tight boots. They are a prime cause of frostbitten toes. If your boots are snug, it is better to remove one layer of socks than to constrict circulation. Better yet, buy new boots that fit. If you have been frostbitten in the past or have poor circulation in your extremities, consider experimenting with some combination of double boots, insulated supergaiters, and vapor barrier socks.

✳ Mittens are warmer than gloves, especially when used in combination with a glove or mitten liners. Bring spare handgear.

✳ Have adequate wind protection. Snug up your hood on exposed summits. Balaclavas offer additional face protection. Don't venture to the summit on extremely cold, windy days.

✳ Constantly wiggle cold toes and fingers. Run around or do jumping jacks to increase circulation to the extremities. Keep moving.

✳ Avoid direct skin contact with bare metal or cooking fuel.

✳ If someone is frostbitten, they may also be hypothermic. Look for signs of both, and treat accordingly.

RESCUES

If someone is hurt, you must be equipped to stabilize the situation, attempt self-rescue, and as a last resort, go for help. When dealing with an accident, your first responsibility is to yourself and the other uninjured members of your party. You won't be much help if you get hurt falling down the same icy gully that your friend just caromed down. After ensuring that no one else is in danger and the victim's medical condition is stabilized (i.e., they are well packaged and reasonably warm), you must make a decision regarding evacuation. If the victim is able to get him- or herself to a trailhead without suffering further injury, that is always preferable to waiting around in the snow for a rescue party to arrive.

Time is critical in the winter. Do not waste an hour making an improvised litter if you do not think you can drag it out on your own. If you are alone with a helpless partner, you are usually better off seeking the proper equipment and enough people to perform the rescue efficiently and safely than exhausting yourself and becoming a second victim. If you go for help, be sure you know exactly where you left your partner; leave flashing or some type of marker along the way if you are not on a trail. Bring detailed information about the victim's condition and the nature of the injury. This will allow the rescuers to respond in the most appropriate way and know which first-aid equipment to bring. (See appendix D for emergency contact phone numbers.)

A cellular phone is not a substitute for a first-aid kit. Surviving in the mountains depends on good judgment calls, not phone calls. Cell phones frequently do not work in the mountains, especially in winter when their batteries are cold. Do not simply dial 911 and wait for help. It often takes hours to organize a rescue, during which time your condition and that of your partners is deteriorating. If you can possibly get yourself and your party out of the woods on your own power without endangering yourself, you will be much better off.

SECTION TWO

The Tours

NEW HAMPSHIRE

1. Mount Cardigan
2. Mount Monadnock
3. Mount Moosilauke
4. Mount Chocorua
5. Cannon Mountain
6. Mount Garfield
7. Carter Notch Hut Tour
8. Wildcat Valley Trail
9. Doublehead Ski Trail
10. Avalanche Brook Trail
11. Pinkham Notch
12. Gulf of Slides
13. John Sherburne Ski Trail
14. Tuckerman Ravine
15. Great Gulf
16. Oakes Gulf
17. Zealand Falls Hut Tour
18. Zealand Notch Tours
19. Mount Hale
20. Pemigewasset River Tours
21. Nancy and Norcross Ponds

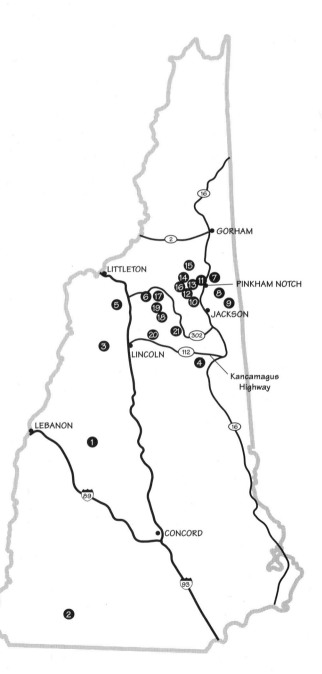

Parking fees: The White Mountain National Forest (WMNF) is charging a fee for all cars parked at a WMNF trailhead at least through the year 2000. This affects the majority of New Hampshire tours in this book. You may purchase a parking permit at any WMNF ranger station. Ranger stations are located in Laconia, Bethlehem, Gorham, Plymouth, and Conway, NH, and in Bethel, ME. In addition, permits are sold at a variety of sporting goods stores and convenience stores in the region. The rangers are vigilant; you will almost certainly be ticketed if you do not have a permit.

A note on maps: All AMC maps that are referenced in these tours refer to the latest (1998) map series. Note that the new map numbers (e.g., Map 5: Carter Range–Evans Notch) do not correspond to older AMC map numbers (where Map 5 was Franconia).

The best map of the Presidential Range of the White Mountains is Bradford Washburn's painstakingly detailed *Mount Washington and the Heart of the Presidential Range* (1988), published by the AMC. It is referred to hereafter as AMC/Washburn *Mount Washington/Presidential Range.*

A good overview map of the entire White Mountain region is the DeLorme *Trail Map & Guide to the White Mountain National Forest* (1995).

Mount Cardigan

THE TOURS
The Alexandria Ski Trail and the Duke's Ski Trail are classic down-mountain runs that descend the east side of the Firescrew–Mount Cardigan summit ridge to the AMC Cardigan Lodge. The Kimball Ski Trail descends through lower-elevation forest. The bald summits of Cardigan and Firescrew offer dramatic views.

DISTANCE
* 3 miles from Cardigan Lodge to summit of Mount Cardigan via Duke's Ski Trail (connecting with Manning and Mowglis Trails)
* Approx. 2.5 miles from Cardigan summit to Cardigan Lodge via the Alexandria and Kimball Ski Trails.

ELEVATION
* *Start* 1,371 feet (Cardigan Lodge)
* *Highest point* 3,121 feet (Mount Cardigan summit)
* *Vertical drop* 1,750 feet

MAPS
AMC Mount Cardigan map, USGS Mount Cardigan (1987). Neither map shows the ski trails clearly. *Mount Cardigan Trails,* available free at Cardigan Lodge, shows all the trails.

DIFFICULTY
* Most difficult (Alexandria Trail)
* Moderate (Duke's Trail & Kimball Trail)

SNOWBOARDING
The Alexandria and Duke's Trails are good snowboard descents. However, hiking and snowshoeing are not allowed on the ski trails. To reach the top of the Alexandria Trail, snowboarders should snowshoe up the Holt/Cathedral Forest/Clark Trails. To ride the Duke's, snowshoe up the Manning Trail to where it intersects with the ski trail.

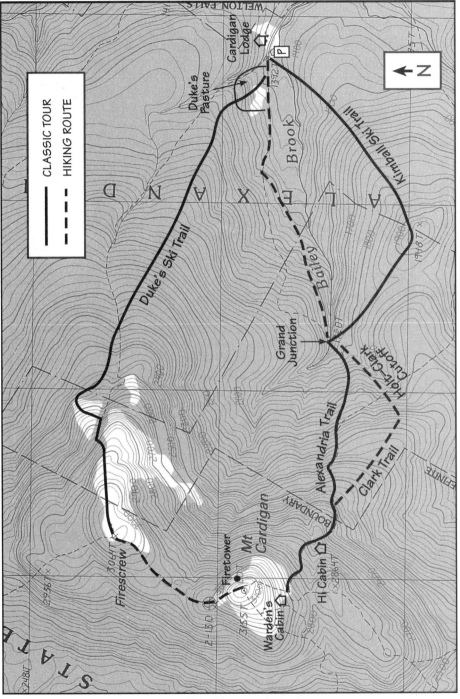

MOUNT CARDIGAN

45

HOW TO GET THERE

From exit 23 on I-93, follow NH 104 west to Bristol, where you turn onto NH 3A west. Follow this to the stone church at the foot of Newfound Lake, continue straight through the crossroad at 1.9 miles, bear right at 3.1 miles, and turn left at 6.3 miles. At 7.4 miles from the church, turn right on a gravel road, then bear right at 7.5 miles at the Red Schoolhouse, and continue to the lodge at 8.9 miles. Brown AMC signs point the way at key intersections. The Shem Valley Road is plowed in winter but is notoriously difficult driving. Drive with care and carry a shovel in case of mishaps.

The ski trails on Mount Cardigan and neighboring Firescrew are among the best and most historic runs in New England. Mount Cardigan, or "Old Baldy" to the locals, was the center of activity for skiers of the Appalachian Mountain Club after the club purchased 600 acres and a barn on the east side of the mountain in 1934. The club's interest was sparked by the fact that Cardigan, at 3,121 feet, is the second highest peak in southern New Hampshire (3,165-foot Mount Monadnock is the highest in the region) and is just over 100 miles from Boston.

The "Appies," as AMC members were called, quickly set about developing the slopes of Cardigan and Firescrew for downhill skiing. The first ski trail to be cut by AMC volunteers was the Duke's Trail on Firescrew. Firescrew got its name from the spiraling plume of fire seen for miles around when the mountain burned in 1855. The trail was named for Duke Dimitri von Leuchtenberg. The duke was a man of Russian nobility who fled his native country during the Russian Revolution. In the 1930s, he was invited by Katharine Peckett to teach skiing at the Peckett's resort in Sugar Hill. He also directed work projects for the Civilian Conservation Corps (CCC) in central New Hampshire. When a group of Appies brought the Duke to Mount Cardigan in 1933, he motioned "with a graceful sweep of his arm" to the pasturelands at the foot of the mountain and claimed it was an ideal place to teach beginning skiers. He then continued walking up the mountain and blazing what became the Duke's Trail, which volunteers dutifully cut in the summer of 1934. True to the duke's prediction, the Duke's Pasture—the slopes just west of the current lodge off the Manning Trail—is still used as a site for AMC ski clinics.

In the winter of 1934, the AMC hired Charles Proctor to teach skiing. A former Dartmouth and Olympic team skier, Proctor was responsible for the design of numerous ski trails in New Hampshire. In 1935, the state of New Hampshire hired Proctor to lay out the Alexandria Ski Trail (named for the nearby town) for expert skiers. The CCC was brought in to provide the labor for the job, and the down-mountain trail was first skied that winter.

The Kimball Ski Trail was another popular run lower on the mountain that was intended for intermediate skiers. It was also cut in the summer of 1934. The trail was named for Helen F. Kimball, a Boston philanthropist who provided funds for the AMC's purchase of the Cardigan Ski Reservation, as the site was known.

Word about Cardigan skiing spread quickly. By 1938, the crowds flocking to Cardigan were straining the capacity of the small AMC lodge. A new lodge was built in 1939 and is still in use today. The hutmaster even ran a rope tow up the Duke's Pasture to accommodate all the people.

Ski traffic on Mount Cardigan dropped off significantly after World War II, a casualty of the lift-served skiing opportunities that blossomed throughout the White Mountains. With the revival of backcountry skiing in the 1980s, skier traffic on Mount Cardigan has once again picked up, and the venerable ski lodge, with bunks for 54 people, is packed nearly every winter weekend. Cardigan Lodge has until recently only been available to groups willing to book the entire facility, but the caretakers may now open the lodge to skiers on a mid-week bed-and-breakfast basis. Lodging information may be obtained by contacting the Cardigan Lodge caretaker at 603-744-8011.

The well-maintained ski trails on Mount Cardigan remain exciting and high-quality ski runs. Skiers can choose one of Cardigan's ski trails and ascend and descend via the same route. Or you can do a 5.5-mile grand tour of Cardigan: ski up either the Duke's or Alexandria Trail, cross the Cardigan-Firescrew ridge on the Mowglis Trail, and descend on the opposite ski trail.

The Duke's Trail is about 1.25 miles long and is easier than the Alexandria Trail. Leaving Cardigan Lodge on the Holt Trail, the slopes of the Duke's Pasture appear shortly on the right. When skiing up the Duke's Trail, you can find the remains of the old rope-tow engine at the top of the pasture; the rusting car chassis from which the engine was taken is on the right.

The Duke's Trail is about 15 feet wide with a moderate 20-degree pitch. It is framed by beautiful old hardwoods. The trail has gentle S-turns near the top that will hold your interest on the descent. The top of the Duke's ends on wide open snowfields—known locally as the "summit slabs"—that lie just beneath the bald cone of Firescrew. Views of the heart of the White Mountains unfold to the north as you weave turns through the widely spaced stunted spruce and fir trees that dot the slabs. Many skiers opt to end their tour here, retracing their tracks down the Duke's Ski Trail. The final ascent to the Firescrew summit on the Manning Trail (climbing due east into the forest from the summit slabs, following yellow blazes) is well worth it for the panoramic views.

To reach the bottom of the Alexandria Ski Trail, follow the Holt Trail 0.8 mile from Cardigan Lodge, cross a bridge over Bailey Brook, and arrive at the three-way trail intersection known as Grand Junction. The Alexandria Ski Trail continues straight ahead. If you want to ski the trail in untracked powder, ascend the mountain from Grand Junction via the Cathedral Forest/Clark Trail, which intersects the top of the Alexandria just below Pajama Ledge (the Alexandria Trail originally continued to the top of South Peak).

The dramatic alpine summit of Mount Cardigan is worth including in your tour. A rime-encrusted firetower crowns the peak. On a clear day, there are com-

Descending the summit slabs on Firescrew, near Mount Cardigan.

manding views of Mount Monadnock to the south; Ascutney, Killington, and Camel's Hump to the west; Mounts Moosilauke and Washington and the Franconia Ridge to the north; and Lake Winnipesaukee to the southeast. In good snow conditions, the summit is flanked by skiable snowfields; in lower-snow periods, the summit cone is not skiable and may require crampons to ascend.

Descending from the summit, the short upper section of the Clark Trail is only about 8 feet wide and can be tricky to negotiate. The reward is the Alexandria Trail. It opens up to about 25 feet in width, and drops 800 vertical feet in 0.75 mile. The trail ranges in steepness from 20 to 25 degrees.

The Alexandria Ski Trail has the characteristics of the best CCC ski trails. It was designed by a skier for skiers. It constantly bends and turns like a restless snake, and often has a sporting double fall line. The trail is wide enough to link turns and have fun on.

The final prize on a descent of Cardigan is to ski the Kimball Trail. This trail is blazed but not signed; consequently, it is often overlooked. After descending the Alexandria, you ski back through Grand Junction. Continue about 100 yards on the Holt Trail, then turn right on an unmarked but obvious trail with blue blazes. After a gradual 15-minute climb, the trail arrives at a clearing on a knoll. The Kimball Trail continues on the left. The mile-long trail is about 15 feet wide and descends gently through a softwood forest. The dark green canopy of the forest gives this trail a warm, deep woods ambience. The trail ends at Cardigan Lodge.

In addition to these down-mountain classics, there are a number of other cross-country ski trails on Cardigan that novice skiers will enjoy. The Back 80, Alleyway, and 93Z trails are fine historic touring trails that meander around the lower flanks of the mountain. The gentle slopes of the Duke's Pasture near the lodge are a good place to practice your telemark technique. A detailed map of the Cardigan ski trails is available in the lodge. Information on ski workshops that take place on Cardigan is available from the AMC (603-466-2727 for workshop information).

The slopes of Mount Cardigan continue to offer high-quality mountain skiing even after more than a half-century. As you swoosh across the Alexandria Trail, picture the person ahead of you in 10-pound hickory skis with cable bindings, bearing down the hill and reveling in the discovery of this "new" sport called skiing. The fine ski trails of Mount Cardigan provide definitive proof that floating through deep snow down the side of a mountain with spectacular views of the New England countryside is a timeless thrill.

OTHER OPTIONS

The West Ridge Trail, which ascends the slopes of Cardigan from Cardigan State Park in Canaan, is popular among skiers approaching the mountain from the west. It is 1.5 miles to the Cardigan summit via this route.

Mount Monadnock

THE TOURS

The Old Ski Path and Red Spot Trail on Mount Monadnock are scenic and historic ski routes. There is also a network of moderate backcountry ski trails around the base of the mountain.

DISTANCE

* 2.9 miles: Old Ski Path Loop round trip from park headquarters

ELEVATION

* *Start* 1,400 feet
* *Highest point* 3,165 feet (summit); 2,500 feet (start of Old Ski Path)
* *Vertical drop* 1,765 feet

MAPS

AMC Grand Monadnock, USGS Monadnock Mountain (1984). For information about the cross-country ski trail network around the base of the mountain, obtain the free sketch map *Monadnock State Park Ski Touring Trails* at the ranger cabin next to the main parking lot at Monadnock State Park.

DIFFICULTY

* More difficult (Old Ski Path Loop)
* Moderate (cross-country trails—see "Other Options" in this chapter)

SNOWBOARDING

Snowboarding is feasible, but not ideal. The Old Ski Path Loop covers rolling terrain, ending on a flat cross-country trail. Snowshoes will be needed for sections of the descent.

PARK FEE

$2.50 per person on weekends/holidays, free on weekdays

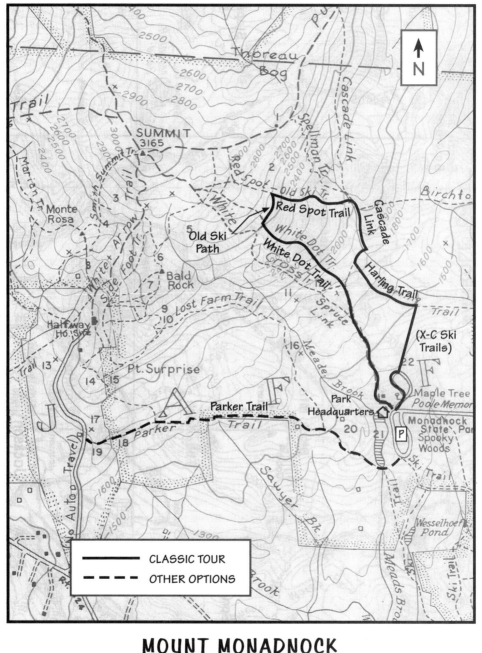

MOUNT MONADNOCK

Base map: AMC Grand Monadnock

HOW TO GET THERE

From Jaffrey, take NH 124 west 2 miles to Dublin Road, and turn right at the sign for Monadnock State Park. Turn left on Poole Memorial Road just beyond the Monadnock Bible Conference. Trails begin from the parking lot at the end of the road.

Mount Monadnock has a special place in the hearts of many New Englanders. Standing alone like a beacon over southern New England, it is the gateway to the mountain ranges to the north. The mountain has been sketched and painted by numerous artists and written about by dozens of writers and poets. Among its best-known fans were Ralph Waldo Emerson and Henry David Thoreau (Thoreau actually lived on the flanks of the mountain in the mid-1800s), who visited the mountain often from their homes in Concord, Massachusetts.

The 3,165-foot summit of Monadnock rises some 2,000 feet higher than the surrounding valleys. From the summit, one can see all six states of New England, the skyscrapers of Boston, and the summit of Mount Washington. This attraction has not been lost on the area's summer hikers, who have made the mountain the second most-climbed peak in the world, after Mount Fuji in Japan (as of 1998, Monadnock averaged 127,000 hikers per year).

Mount Monadnock is an unusual by-product of the glacial era, a rock formation that the ice cap failed to grind down on its impressive journey to the ocean some 20,000 years ago. The mountain is a striking example of a height-of-land that stands alone above an upland plain; the word *monadnock* is now a generic geological term for this phenomenon. The Abenaki Indians, who originally gave the peak its name, were struck by the spiritual aspects of the land. The Abenaki word *monadnock* means "mountain," perhaps a supernatural or holy mountain with an exceptionally good outlook.

As skiing began to increase in popularity in the 1930s, Mount Monadnock was an obvious destination for those seeking snow and challenge. It is the closest big mountain to Boston, where many of the early Appalachian Mountain Club skiers resided. In 1933, the ubiquitous Russian-born nobleman and skier, Duke Dimitri von Leuchtenberg, was retained to lay out a ski trail on Monadnock. The Civilian Conservation Corps cut the trail in February 1935. According to Charles Royce, manager of Monadnock State Park from 1962 to 1972, the original ski trail was the present-day Red Spot Trail, which is still listed on the AMC Grand Monadnock map as "Red Spot-Old Ski Tr." The original ski trail began at the upper junction of the White Dot and White Cross Trails, 0.2 mile below the summit. Royce says that what is presently called the Old Ski Path was originally just a hiking trail that connected the White Dot with the Red Spot Trail. Early skiers on Monadnock would ski the length of the present Red Spot Trail to its junction with the Cascade Link.

Monadnock suffered the curse of many other southern New England ski mountains: the snow was unreliable. Skiers soon drifted off to northerly mountains that offered a more consistent snowpack, such as Cannon Mountain and Mount Washington. By the late 1940s, the Red Spot Trail had grown in and was from then on maintained as a hiking trail.

Cross-country skiing around Monadnock has enjoyed more popularity. From the late 1950s until the mid-1960s, a Swedish guest at the former Ark Hotel (now the Monadnock Bible Conference) cut a network of cross-country ski trails. The former Cedarstrom Ski Trails are still shown on the AMC map in the area south of the park headquarters. In the 1970s, former park manager Ben Haubrich linked together some of Cedarstrom's trails with logging roads and some new trails. This system has endured as Monadnock's present backcountry ski trail network. According to Royce, Haubrich had an ambitious plan to cut an 18-mile ski trail that would circumnavigate Monadnock, but the project was never completed.

Monadnock today is a fine and easily accessible ski destination. There is a wide variety of skiing to be done, and a hike to the summit on a crisp winter day is a scenic feast. An added bonus is the looks and squeals of amazement that you will get from other hikers as you climb the mountain with your skis or snowboard.

The classic ski tour on Monadnock connects with the tracks of the first skiers. From park headquarters, climb the White Dot Trail towards the summit. The White Dot is the main thoroughfare for hikers, and the trail is usually packed down and relatively easy to walk. If you catch it after a snowstorm and before the hikers, the broad White Dot can also be fun to ski right to the bottom. After climbing for 1.1 miles, the trail reaches a broad plateau, where the Old Ski Path leaves to the right.

For the full alpine experience, the treeless Monadnock summit, which lies 0.9 mile farther up the trail, is worth the additional climb. The summit cone is typically windblown and icy and is not skiable. However, in a good snow year it may be possible to ski from the summit. Conditions permitting, the White Cross Trail is the favored descent route. Note that the White Cross Trail does not connect with the Old Ski Path, although the two trails are only about 100 yards apart through the woods. If you have an altimeter, you can cut left off the White Cross Trail at the 2,500-foot elevation and contour briefly through the woods to reach the start of the Old Ski Path. Otherwise, note where the White Cross Trail reaches the third open ledge and widens to about 30 feet, with a 75-foot open slope below you. This is where you contour left to pick up the Old Ski Path. Alternatively, you can ski the White Dot Trail from the summit (you will probably have to remove skis and scramble down the steeper rocky sections), from which the Old Ski Path departs. Nearly all Monadnock hikers stay on the White Dot; the moment you leave it, you will most likely have untracked trails to yourself.

The Old Ski Path begins with nice views to the east over Gilson Pond and surrounding mountains. There are trail signs at both ends, but the trail is not blazed; it is nevertheless easy to follow. The trail is 10 feet wide and twists and

Skiing past a falls on the Parker Trail on Mount Monadnock.

turns for its 0.2-mile jaunt through the woods. It meets the Red Spot Trail with a sharp right-angle turn.

The Red Spot Trail weaves through open forest, where you can make turns through the trees. The trail, which at times constricts to about 5 feet in width, slices through a beautiful, deep green, softwood glade. In low snow some ledges may poke through, but they are easily skirted. Beware of a downhill section with a sharp left turn that has a tree standing in the middle—be prepared to bail out if you don't turn quickly enough!

After a half-mile on the Red Spot Trail, turn right onto the Birchtoft Trail, which descends gently for 0.4 mile until it reaches the Harling Trail. The Harling is a tunnel-like trail that makes for a fun, fast descent. After 0.4 mile, keep your eyes open for a small blue plastic trail sign that reads Junction 14, To State Campground with an arrow pointing right. Turn right here and follow the cross-country trails through the empty campground back to the park headquarters.

A few notes about Monadnock State Park: From November through May, the visitor center is open only on weekends and holidays, during which time there is a $2.50 per person charge. The park campground is open for camping and is free of charge in the winter, and the park will provide water. No pets are allowed in the state park.

OTHER OPTIONS

Mount Monadnock is a great place to get introduced to backcountry skiing. Novice skiers will enjoy the 14-mile network of ungroomed ski trails that crisscross the base of the mountain. A trail map and advice are available from the visitor center on weekends.

A worthwhile day trip that takes in some of the nicest landscape in the area is the loop that can be done from the park headquarters to Gilson Pond. This tour leads through open forest and birch stands. From Gilson Pond, there are views of the Pumpelly Ridge. This is a very enjoyable day of New England woods skiing.

The trails south of the parking lot tend to be the easiest, and the most likely to be skiable with little snow. After an initial drop, these trails travel through marshes and fields. The stretch between Junctions 2 and 4 offers the nicest view of the mountain.

The Parker Trail, just south of park headquarters, is a gentle rolling tour through mixed forest. Old stone walls dart off in different directions, the remnants of previous generations that have inhabited and farmed this historic mountain.

Only 90 minutes from Boston, Mount Monadnock offers a quick escape for urbanites hungry for some New England powder. You may have company—on a nice winter weekend day Monadnock may see 150 people—but you can easily have the mountain to yourself on most of the side trails.

Mount Moosilauke

THE TOURS

The Carriage Road, a historic ski trail, offers a moderate route up and down one of New Hampshire's most scenic mountains. The Gorge Brook Trail is a fun, turn-filled ski route right from the summit. The Snapper Trail offers an easy connector between the two trails. The Moosilauke summit cone is also flanked by large ski-able snowfields.

DISTANCE

* 5.1 miles from Carriage Road to summit
* 5.3 miles on Gorge Brook Trail to summit (from NH 118/ Ravine Lodge Road)

ELEVATION

* *Start* 2,082 feet (NH 118/Ravine Lodge Road); 1,720 feet (bottom of Carriage Road)
* *Highest point* 4,802 feet (Mount Moosilauke summit)
* *Vertical drop* 2,720 feet (summit to NH 118/Ravine Lodge Road)

MAPS

AMC Map 4 (Moosilauke–Kinsman), USGS Mount Moosilauke (1967), and USGS Mount Kineo (1973)

DIFFICULTY

* More difficult

SNOWBOARDING

The Carriage Road, Gorge Brook Trail, and Snapper are all long, sustained descents that are suitable for riding. Each trail has flatter sections that may involve some poling or one-foot pedaling, depending on conditions. Snowshoes will be needed on the 1.6-mile rolling stretch of the Ravine Lodge Road, and to climb the mountain.

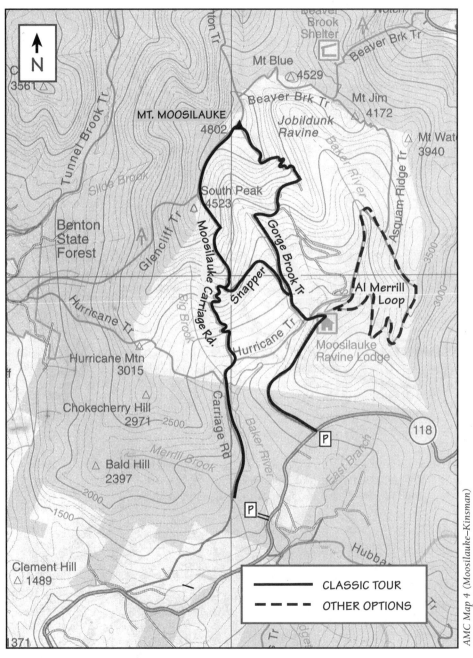

AMC Map 4 (Moosilauke–Kinsman)

MOUNT MOOSILAUKE

HOW TO GET THERE

From I-93, take the North Woodstock exit to NH 112. Go west on NH 112, then west on NH 118. The Ravine Lodge Road is on the north side of NH 118, 7.2 miles west of the junction with NH 112. NOTE: You must have a White Mountain National Forest parking pass to park here, or you will be ticketed. See page 43 for information.

To ski the Carriage Road from the bottom, continue west past the Ravine Lodge Road for 3.2 miles on NH 118. Turn right at a small bridge onto Breezy Point Road (there is a brown sign for Moosilauke Carriage Road here). After 1.6 miles, the road dead-ends at the Carriage Road. Take care not to block the road or driveways when parking.

The history of Moosilauke is intimately tied to the history of the Dartmouth Outing Club (DOC). The DOC began purchasing tracts of land on Moosilauke in 1920 and now owns more than 4,500 acres on the mountain. DOC skiers were a major force in New England ski history, in part because of their activities on Moosilauke. They were greatly assisted by the legendary German ski coach Otto Schniebs, whom they hired in 1930. Schniebs advised the Dartmouth skiers to abandon their stiff, upright skiing style and adopt the technique pioneered by Hannes Schneider at his renowned Arlberg ski school in Austria. This "called for a low crouch, an up-and-down motion, skis apart in the stem position, and use of poles. The graceful telemark went into eclipse," writes Allen Adler in his excellent book *New England & Thereabouts—A Ski Tracing.*

A popular anecdote about Schniebs comes from a talk he gave in Boston. As described in the *American Ski Annual,* Schniebs was posed with a difficult question:

> "Otto," asked a bright-eyed young lady who had the look of one haunted by a deep problem, "what would you do if you were coming down a steep narrow trail a little too fast and there were stumps and trees and ice and things all around?"
>
> "Vell," [Schniebs replied], "either take the damned skis off und valk, or schtem—schtem like Hell!"

Together, the DOC and Mount Moosilauke are responsible for a number of notable skiing firsts. The first organized downhill race in the United States took place on the Mount Moosilauke Carriage Road in April 1927. Called the Moosilauke Down Mountain Race, it had about 15 entrants. The race started at the junction of the Carriage Road and the Glencliff Trail; it was won by Charles Proctor with a time of 21 minutes. Moosilauke also hosted the first invitational club ski races in 1931. In March 1933, the Carriage Road was the site of the first U.S. National Downhill Championship Race. The race was won in 8 minutes by DOC skier Henry ("Bem") Woods, with classmate Harry Hillman (of Hillman's Highway fame in Tuckerman Ravine) coming in a close second.

The late Al Sise raced in that first championship. He recounted to me, "Nobody ever thought of course preparation back then. There were big drifts on the trail, and I flew off one of those and landed on something soft. It turned out to be the guy who started in front of me!" The fallen competitors promptly shared a nip from a brandy flask, and charged off down the mountain.

Sise explained that in other races "the guy who fell the least number of times—say, less than twelve—won on Carriage Road races. As Alex Bright used to say, 'If you didn't fall, it was a sure sign you weren't skiing fast enough!'"

Just before the 1933 national championship on Moosilauke, an inaugural race was held on the Richard Taft Trail on Cannon Mountain. Compared with the narrow Carriage Road with its many switchbacks, the Taft was wide open and steeper. "Those who correctly interpreted this development knew that the future of downhill racing lay on that kind of trail and that the Carriage Road was obsolete," wrote David Hooke in his comprehensive DOC history, *Reaching That Peak*.

Dartmouth skiers were a proud and competitive bunch, and they were determined to have a trail that kept them and their mountain at the forefront of skiing. This led Coach Schniebs to design Hell's Highway, the most famous—and feared—ski trail to grace the side of Mount Moosilauke.

Hell's Highway was cut by Dartmouth students in the summer of 1933. It started from just below South Peak, descending the steep west side of Gorge Brook Ravine to the bottom, where it followed what is now the Gorge Brook Trail to the Ravine Lodge. The result was a trail that was described in a 1939 guidebook to skiing in the East as "the steepest and most difficult trail in New England, requiring expert technique." The upper part of the trail dropped 900 feet in a half-mile, including the famous 38-degree section known as the Rock Garden.

The steepness of Hell's Highway was to be its undoing. The devastating 1938 hurricane that nearly leveled New England caused a landslide on the Rock Garden; the sections of exposed bedrock that remained never again held snow. The trail quickly disappeared into ski lore. The general vicinity of Hell's Highway can be seen today from the Gorge Brook Trail: the prominent treeless slide paths that rake the west walls of the Gorge Brook Ravine lie just right (north) of the fabled ski route.

The loss of Hell's Highway prompted the DOC to search for new ski terrain. The result was the construction of the Dipper and Snapper ski trails in 1939, of which only the latter still exists. "Snapper" was the nickname of Ed Wells, a well-known DOC skier who was involved in designing the trail. It referred to the terse "zingers" that the otherwise reticent Wells would contribute during the nightly bull sessions of the trail crew. The Snapper was primarily a recreational trail, although a few races were held on it.

By the 1980s, the skiing on Mount Moosilauke had become marginal. Both the Snapper and the Carriage Road had grown in to the point where there was barely room enough to make turns. A descent of the Carriage Road typically involved a thigh-burning, 3-mile snowplow down an icy chute. More than one backcountry skier broke equipment or found religion on this run.

A new generation of Dartmouth skiers has restored the luster to Mount Moosilauke. Starting in 1989, the Dartmouth Outing Club took on the ambitious task of rebuilding and redesigning trails on the mountain, in part to make them skiable again. With the aid of a federal transportation grant, scores of chain-saw-wielding volunteers and a bulldozer were let loose on the mountain. The result: the Gorge Brook Trail, Snapper, and Carriage Road are once again first-class ski tours.

Moosilauke is a skiing classic both for its rich ski history and for its dramatic landscape. Skiing up its exposed summit ridge is an exciting alpine experience. Skiers will frequently enjoy a mild climb up, only to battle a raging wind once they break out of the trees in the final push for the summit. Otto Schniebs discovered this the hard way. It is said that Schniebs was lured to the United States by the promise of fine skiing. Upon being brought to Mount Moosilauke, he was appalled when he compared the pathetically small size of the mountain to his native Alps. His attitude changed when he hiked the mountain and was forced to crawl on his hands and knees along the summit ridge because of the ferocious weather. This story is instructive: Use good judgment when determining how to reach the summit in full conditions, or whether to proceed at all. Those climbing to the top may need to skirt the summit cone to one side to avoid catching the full force of the weather.

The summit of Mount Moosilauke is its most dramatic feature. A long, wind-swept, treeless ridge caps the mountain. From the top, there are panoramic views of successive ridges of the White Mountains to the east and the Green Mountains to the west. The view of the massive snowy flanks of Mount Washington is especially impressive from this vantage point. The gentle snowfields that run north of the summit offer the best skiing. As you make turns, you have the sensation of floating over all of New England. Be warned that summit snow conditions can be tricky. You may be skiing on top of windblown crust one minute, bouncing over *sastrugi* (the fragile, rippled snow patterns that grow into the wind) the next, and end up in feathery powder as you traverse through a protected pocket where snow has eddied.

The best skiing on Moosilauke is on the Carriage Road and the Gorge Brook Trail. Thanks to the DOC trail workers, both trails can now be skied in one tour. The Moosilauke grand tour begins on the unplowed Ravine Lodge Road (trailhead directions above). From the NH 118 trailhead, it is a 1.6-mile ski to the Ravine Lodge. Using kick wax on this section will speed your approach. The impressive Ravine Lodge, built in 1937 and owned by the DOC, is closed in the winter due to the prohibitive expense of heating it.

From the lodge, it is roughly equidistant to the summit whether you ascend by the Gorge Brook Trail (3.7 miles), or take the Snapper to the Carriage Rd. to the top (3.4 miles). Do not take the Hurricane Trail to the Carriage Road. The trail is obscure and indirect.

Trail signs at the Ravine Lodge direct you to the hiking trails. Drop down and cross the Baker River, and turn immediately left. You will turn right at the Hurricane Trail junction and quickly hit a short steep rise, which is where you will want to don your climbing skins. After 0.4 mile, you reach the junction with the Snapper, where you must decide which way to ascend.

While both trails are well within the abilities of intermediate skiers—i.e., a reliable snowplow is all you need to get down the mountain—the Carriage Road, being wider and having a more gentle grade, is somewhat easier to descend than the Gorge Brook Trail. So the more ambitious skiers will want to ascend via the Snapper/Carriage Road and descend Gorge Brook, while less advanced skiers should reverse the route. Another factor to consider is that the southeast-facing Carriage Road receives a good deal of sun. On warm spring afternoons, the sun-baked snow on the Carriage Road can be arduous to descend.

The Snapper Trail was completely relocated from its original site in 1991 (the old trail, which crosses the relocated trail near the top, has been abandoned and is rapidly growing in). The new Snapper is 1 mile long, climbing 900 feet from Gorge Brook to the Carriage Road. The trail climbs gradually through a beautiful birch forest, getting steeper as it nears the Carriage Road. Coming down, the Snapper is now a long descending traverse. Watch out for drainage ditches that cross the trail, and beware the final short, steep drop to the Gorge Brook Trail junction.

Carving turns on the summit snowfields of Mount Moosilauke.

The "new, improved" Carriage Road was graded and widened in 1994 by the DOC. The trail is now about 15 feet wide, with an average grade on the upper section of 13 degrees. The Carriage Road has been transformed and is now a delight to ski. Skiers descending the Carriage Road can now swoop several miles of leisurely turns. On the ascent, don't forget to turn around and take in the sweeping views behind you. Note that snowmobilers also use the Carriage Road until just below the junction with the Glencliff Trail (snowmobiles are not allowed on the summit). It is because this is a multi-use recreational trail that the DOC was eligible to receive federal funds to upgrade it.

For those who want to ski the Carriage Road from the bottom, the trail begins at the site of the old Moosilauke Inn (see directions above). The Carriage Road is an obvious, wide path that begins where the plowed road ends, and there will most likely be snowmobile tracks on it. The trail ascends moderately for the first 1.5 miles, then begins climbing more steeply.

The series of switchbacks on the Carriage Road (just below the Snapper Trail junction) were the source of a humorous event that took place during the U.S. National Downhill Championship Race in 1933. Some of the bolder skiers realized that they could save time by cutting through the woods and eliminating the broad turns at the bottom. The brothers Leonard and Hollis Phillips, fresh from training at the Hannes Schneider ski school in Austria, were determined to win the race. They had their father stand at the opening of the cutoff path that they had blazed when they climbed up; he held a long branch in front of the detour so other skiers could not use it. When his sons came by, he swiftly stepped aside, allowing them to fly through the trees and save time. Despite these efforts, however, neither brother won the race.

The Carriage Road is not particularly scenic at lower elevations, where it passes through second-growth hardwood forests. The path intersects with the Snapper 3.1 miles from the start at Breezy Point. From here, it is 2 miles to the summit. Just before the Glencliff Trail junction, the Carriage Road narrows to about 6 feet. This is what much of the road felt like until it was widened. The final mile of the Carriage Road follows a pronounced ridge above treeline, with excellent views in all directions. This section should not be attempted in poor or deteriorating weather conditions, since there is no quick exit from the ridge.

The summit of Moosilauke has a variety of notable historic ruins. In addition to several plaques, there are rock walls that form the outline of a building. These are the remains of the Tip Top House, a summit hotel that burned down in October 1942. Looking down to the southeast, a concrete foundation remains where a summit shelter once stood; it was removed in 1979.

The Gorge Brook Trail was relocated in 1989–90 due to erosion on the old trail. The new trail is a mile longer and detours along the edge of Jobildunk Ravine, a beautiful glacial cirque with large ice flows down the center. Following cairns down from the summit to the southeast, the trail turns briefly to the north and offers spectacular views of Mount Washington from a clearing appropriately dubbed the Balcony. The trail, which is about 8 feet wide in the upper sections, drops into a spruce and fir forest and gradually widens to 15 feet. Gorge Brook offers a fine but forgiving introduction to eastern trail skiing. You turn where the trail turns, relishing surprises around each bend. There is usually ample opportunity to swing through the trees alongside the trail, either for fun or to check your speed.

The DOC skiers who laid out this trail gave it a reasonable grade, so speeds never get too pushy. The middle section just above the Gorge Brook contours gently, allowing you to ride your skis. The final half-mile from the Snapper Trail junction to the Ravine Lodge demands quick turns or a good snowplow through a final chute.

Moosilauke is a big mountain tour. Skiing to the summit and back is a 10-mile day. Plan to spend 8 hours on your skis, leaving the trailhead no later than 10 A.M. To fully appreciate what this grand and historic mountain offers, ski it on a clear day. And don't forget your camera—the hero pictures you can take on the summit snowfields will allow you to enjoy this ski tour year-round.

OTHER OPTIONS

The Al Merrill Loop is a 10-km circuit that leaves from the Ravine Lodge. It follows old roads and is suitable for beginner backcountry skiers. It offers excellent views of Mount Moosilauke. There is a trail map posted on a trailhead kiosk just above the Ravine Lodge.

The Ridge Trail, Beaver Brook Trail, and upper Benton Trail form a longer and more challenging ski route to the summit of Mount Moosilauke (roughly 6 miles from the Ravine Lodge to the summit). Along the way you summit Mount Jim (4,172 feet) and Mount Blue (4,529 feet) and enjoy fine views of Jobildunk Ravine.

Mount Chocorua

THE TOUR
The Champney Falls Trail climbs to the rocky summit of this peak, which dominates views of the White Mountains from the southeast. The trail passes the beautiful Champney Falls and follows an old logging road, which is an enjoyable descent route.

DISTANCE
* 7.6 miles from Kancamagus Highway to summit, round-trip

ELEVATION
* *Start* 1,240 feet (Kancamagus Highway trailhead)
* *Highest point* 3,475 feet (Mount Chocorua summit)
* *Vertical drop* 2,235 feet

MAP
AMC Map 3 (Crawford Notch–Sandwich Range), USGS Mount Chocorua (1987)

DIFFICULTY
* More difficult

SNOWBOARDING
The upper section of the Champney Falls Trail is a continuous descent, with room to carve turns both on and off trail. The final mile between Champney Falls and the trailhead is more moderate, and you may have to pole or snowshoe the bottom section.

HOW TO GET THERE
The Champney Falls trailhead parking lot is marked by a brown USFS sign on the Kancamagus Highway (NH 112), 11.5 miles west of NH 16 in Conway.

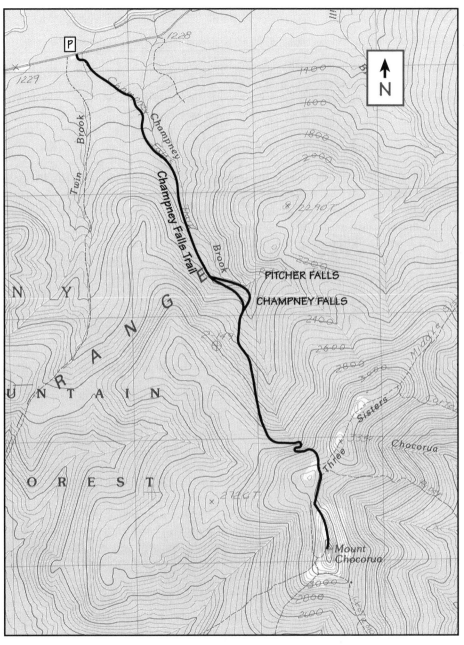

USGS Mount Chocorua (courtesy of Maptech)

MOUNT CHOCORUA

Mount Chocorua is distinctive as a ski tour because of its dramatic alpine qual-ity. Chocorua is a 3,475-foot peak renowned for its craggy summit. It is said to be the most photographed of all the White Mountains, more closely resembling a peak one might find near the Matterhorn than amongst the characteristic glacial domes of the White Mountains.

Chocorua is steeped in colorful history. The legend surrounding the mountain mixes folklore and fact, leaving future generations to discern one from the other. The mountain was named for the Sokosis Indian chief Chocorua, who died on the mountain that now bears his name. That much is not disputed. It is the question of *how* Chocorua died that inflames passion.

One story has it that Chocorua entrusted the care of his son to a local settler named Cornelius Campbell while he traveled to Canada "to consult with his people." Chocorua had enjoyed good relations with the white settlers, and Campbell is said to have been a friend. But Chocorua's son supposedly ingested some fox poison by accident and died. Upon discovering this tragedy, Chocorua slew Campbell's wife and children for revenge. Campbell reputedly pursued Chocorua to the summit of the mountain. Just before being shot by Campbell, the Indian chief declared, "Chocorua goes to the Great Spirit—his curse stays with the white man."

In another popular version of the story, Chocorua's son was not involved at all. White settlers, enraged by an Indian massacre that allegedly occurred in the area, chased Chocorua to the top of the mountain where he leaped to his demise. Several paintings depict Chocorua on a prominent summit boulder on the verge of death. Today's backcountry skiers can retrace the summit climb and ponder the stories as they survey the landscape and imagine the events that have now been immortalized in songs, paintings, and stories.

The Champney Falls Trail is a popular summer hiking route up Chocorua, and it is wide enough to be an enjoyable ski trail. The route ascends a mildly graded logging road that is well marked with yellow blazes. After about a half-mile, the trail climbs up onto the shoulder of Champney Brook via a sharp turn—to be taken note of for the descent. The route soon rejoins the logging road and continues to a trail junction, at 1.4 miles, with a loop trail that drops down slightly to Champney Falls and Pitcher Falls.

The half-mile detour to the falls is well worth it. Champney Falls resembles a small box canyon, appearing incongruously on the northern flanks of the mountain. It looks as if the bedrock simply broke apart, with the water frozen in time as it spilled over the lip of the vertical wall. Watch out for slush and water beneath the falls as you ski around taking in the sights. To rejoin the main path at the other end of the waterfall loop, it will be necessary to remove your skis and scramble up a steep, rocky section of trail.

The trail to the summit continues up the western shoulder of the deepening ravine formed by Champney Brook. The trail has a number of drainage divots, including one where the remains of the telephone wire that led to the now defunct firetower on the Middle Sister can be seen sticking out of the snow. At 2.4 miles,

Stopping to admire frozen Champney Falls on the trail up Mount Chocorua.

the trail begins traversing across the headwall of the ravine via several long, sharp switchbacks. Looking behind you at the first right turn, you will see the deep drainage fall away to provide dramatic views of the Pemigewasset Wilderness to the northwest and the Sandwich Range Wilderness to the west.

After a half-mile of climbing the switchbacks, the route comes to the first of several trail junctions. At the first junction, a trail diverges left to the Middle Sister, one of three "sister" peaks that form the long ridge running northeast from the summit of Mount Chocorua. The Champney Falls Trail continues up a narrow, winding chute toward a treeless knoll. Here you have your first unobstructed view of the rocky summit cone. It is a striking view to the south: when the peak is back-lit by the sun, it has the effect of creating a rainbow shroud around the windy summit rocks. Several trail signs here direct you to the Piper Trail, which brings you the final 0.6 mile to the summit.

The ski tour doesn't just end with a shuffle up the trail. The excitement picks up about a quarter-mile from the summit itself, where trees meet rock and skis must come off. After you take a break to snack and put on wind protection, the mountaineering element of this tour comes into its own. For those planning to continue to the summit, the final leg will require kicking steps into the wind-crusted snow. Climbers must be extremely careful of rime ice, which plasters the rocks. Upon reaching the area right below the summit rock itself, you will have two options to get to the top: easy scrambling around to the right, or if you prefer to reach the summit with a flourish, jamming up a final 10-foot icy crack that tops out right at the USGS benchmark.

The summit views on Chocorua are famous for good reason: a 360-degree panorama greets you. The huge boulder that sits off the northeastern corner of the summit is the one that features prominently in many paintings and drawings of the final moments of Chocorua's life.

From where you left your skis, keep your climbing skins on until you return to the small knoll a half-mile below the summit, since the Piper Trail does some climbing until that point. The next half-mile below this knoll is the most challenging part of the descent. The narrow chute that leads back to the switchbacks is the route down. Unless you have a reliable quick turn, you may opt to keep your skins on until the next trail junction a few minutes away. The descent on the Champney Falls Trail begins with three or four 120-degree switchback corners and then becomes more moderate. The open forest on the left provides abundant tele-marking opportunities, and the trail itself is wide enough to link turns for several miles.

Chocorua is a wonderful introduction to the joys of high mountain skiing and riding in the White Mountains. Its combination of high-quality terrain, spectacular views, and the exciting summit pitch make this a classic ski mountaineering adventure.

OTHER OPTIONS

Mount Chocorua has a number of other hiking trails that make for good skiing. The Bolles Trail, which climbs to the saddle between Mounts Chocorua and Paugus, is an old tote road with a slight grade that makes for easy touring. For those willing to shuttle cars, a recommended continuous route over Chocorua could link up with the Liberty Trail, a moderate route up a wide valley. Numerous other possibilities exist for skiing the trails on the southeast and southwest sides of the peak.

Cannon Mountain

THE TOUR

The Tucker Brook Trail is a legendary 1930s-era down-mountain classic that descends the western side of Cannon Mountain. The trail is accessed from the Cannon Mountain Ski Area (lift ticket required).

DISTANCE

* 3 miles (plus 1 mile from Cannon summit)

ELEVATION

* *Start* 3,520 feet (top of Tucker Brook Trail)
* *Highest point* 4,020 feet (top of Cannon Mountain lifts)
* *Finish* 1,200 feet
* *Vertical drop* 2,820 feet

MAPS

USGS Franconia (1989) shows this trail; AMC Map 2 (Franconia–Pemigewasset) covers this terrain but does not show the trail.

DIFFICULTY

* Most difficult

SNOWBOARDING

The Tucker Brook Trail boasts nearly 3 miles of downhill riding. Save for 200 yards where both skiers and snowboarders must remove gear and hike, this is a great snowboard descent.

HOW TO GET THERE

The top of the Tucker Brook Trail is reached from the Cannon Mountain Ski Area Aerial Tramway or the Cannonball Express (trail directions below). You must shuttle a car to the finish: From the tramway parking lot, get on I-93 north and drive to the next exit (Parkway Exit 3, Route 18 north). Turn left (north) onto NH

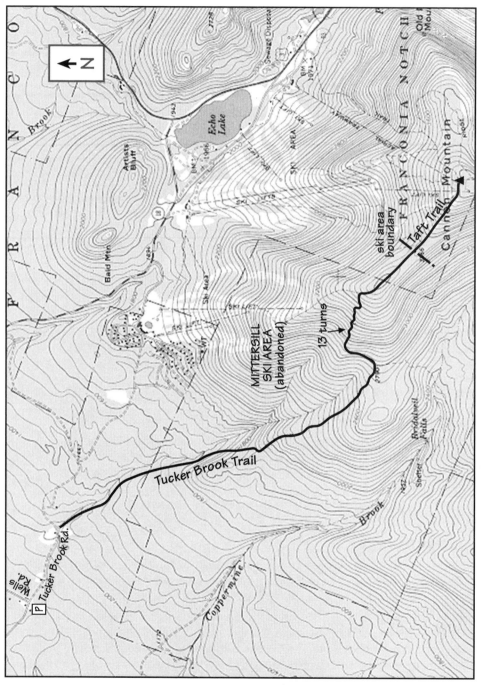

USGS Franconia   (courtesy of Maptech)

CANNON MOUNTAIN

18, pass the Peabody Slopes base area and the Mittersill Alpine Village. At 2.2 miles from I-93, turn left onto Wells Road (dirt road, no sign). Bear left at stop sign, and after 1.4 miles, Tucker Brook Road (no sign) enters from the left and Wells Road turns sharply right. Park on the side of Wells Road, taking care not to block traffic. Tucker Brook Trail comes out where Tucker Brook Road dead-ends, 0.4 mile from Wells Road junction.

In the early 1930s, skiers in the Franconia/Sugar Hill area looked up longingly at the long steep flanks of Cannon Mountain. Their awe was understandable: Cannon is one of the most imposing mountains in the East. Its southeastern face drops off precipitously in a mile-wide cliff that has long challenged rock and ice climbers.

The first Cannon skiers placed their hopes on the western side of the mountain, where they believed the snow fell deepest and held longest. Led by the late Sel Hannah, a former Dartmouth ski team member who went on to become an Olympic skier and a pioneering ski area designer, local skiers banded together in the early 1930s. They cut the Tucker Brook Trail and the Coppermine Trail down the western flanks of Cannon.

The Coppermine and Tucker Brook Trails (Tucker Brook originally branched off from Coppermine at Bridalveil Falls) were audacious propositions in their day. From the summit of Cannon Mountain, these trails descended nearly 3,000 vertical feet in four miles. True to predictions, the trails were reliable stashes of powder, and were loaded with sharp turns to challenge and interest skiers. The most famous part of the descent was the 13 Turns—the fast switchbacks that had to be negotiated right at the start of the run. These trails had everything going for them—except for one detail. They ended up being located on the wrong side of the mountain.

In 1933, the Richard Taft Trail was cut on the north face of Cannon. This fast, steep, wide, Class A race trail set a new standard for down-mountain descents, and it was an instant hit with the Boston-area ski clubs. The Taft was quickly followed by other trails, including Hardscrabble, Cannon, and Ravine. When the state of New Hampshire was deciding in the late 1930s where to site the aerial tramway and the ski area, the obvious choice was to focus on the north face of the mountain, with the Taft and its sister trails as the nucleus of the new ski resort. The tramway from Franconia Notch to the summit of Cannon—the first aerial tramway in the U.S. and a remarkable feat of engineering—opened in June 1938 on the north face. Tucker Brook and Coppermine were swiftly forgotten.

Shortly before his death in 1991, Sel Hannah told me that the location of the tramway and the ski area "seemed ludicrous to me because of the wind in Franconia Notch, and because of what a rough mountain it is." Hannah had lobbied unsuccessfully to locate the ski area on the protected western slopes around the

Tucker Brook Trail and the Coppermine Trail. He was philosophical about losing the debate. "In the end Cannon was good to me," said the man who later founded Sno-Engineering, the international ski-area consulting firm based in Franconia. "I spent my whole life trying to fix the damn mountain."

The Tucker Brook Trail retained a small loyal following of local skiers over the years. People would maintain the trail in the summer, and use the Cannon tramway to access it in winter. The enduring attraction of Tucker Brook, as Hannah noted, was that "it was very fun, it didn't get too much traffic, and it was like old-fashioned skiing: powder snow, no packing, no grooming."

Many things have changed on Cannon since those early days. The Coppermine Trail is now a hiking path that ends at Bridalveil Falls. Mittersill Ski Area, which used to connect with Cannon via the Richard Taft Trail, has been abandoned; its empty trails and rusting lift towers are now an ungroomed powder haunt for Cannon locals. Most of the Richard Taft Trail was lost when Mittersill closed.

But Tucker Brook lives on. It is now an unpatrolled backcountry ski trail that is informally maintained by local skiers. Its upper section incorporates the start of the Richard Taft Trail and the old Coppermine Trail, and its lower section is part of the cross-country ski trail network of the Franconia Inn. The run is frequented by the die-hard community of powder seekers who come in search of the rough-edged ski experience of days gone by.

A word of common-sense caution: Although this trail is accessed via the lifts and trails of the Cannon Mountain Ski Area, *the Tucker Brook Trail is not maintained or patrolled by the ski area.* This is a backcountry ski trail located in the White Mountain National Forest. Ski here with the attitude and preparation appropriate for any backcountry tour. In the event of a mishap, as with any backcountry trail, you are on your own for rescue.

To reach the top of the Tucker Brook Trail, you must take a lift to the summit of Cannon Mountain (the cheap and energetic set can, of course, ski up the Tucker Brook Trail for free). The summit can be reached via the Cannon Mountain Ski Area Aerial Tramway, or by the Peabody and Cannonball Express chairlifts. Since you will have to purchase a full-day ticket to ride these lifts, take a few runs down the trails. Put aside your wilderness ethics for an hour or two and savor the ski history of this mountain. Starting at the tramway base lodge, there are black-and-white photos of early Cannon skiers. For more ski lore, the New England Ski Museum (603-823-7177), located next to the tramway base station, has wonderful exhibits of early New England skiing. The tramway itself was a skiing milestone. The original tramway that was built in 1938 was replaced in 1980 with the current 70-passenger tramway. The cable car is over one mile long and climbs 2,022 feet.

Add to the historic flavor of the day by sampling some of the original ski runs. Start on the Taft Slalom, and drop into Upper and Middle Hardscrabble. The steep serpentine course will give you new respect for your elders.

When you have had enough on the hardpack, it is time to delve into Tucker Brook powder. From the top of the tramway or the Cannonball Express lift, ski down the Taft Slalom. At the bottom of a long straightaway, keep your speed up and go straight, passing a Cannon Mountain Ski Area boundary sign. This was the route of the original Richard Taft Trail. You will soon be climbing uphill a short distance on a wide, well-traveled path; you will likely be joined by other skiers and snowboarders. The trail brings you to the top of a small knoll (this is actually

Navigating the 13 Turns on the Tucker Brook Trail on Cannon Mountain.

3,810-foot Mount Mittersill, according to some maps), from which there are fine views to the south of the wild Kinsman Ridge and the Cannon Balls. Continue down the main trail from this knoll. The trail eventually leads to the top of the abandoned Mittersill Ski Area. This a favorite adventurous detour of Cannon skiers, who cut back to the Peabody Slopes about two-thirds of the way down the mountain. Mittersill has an eerie quality, with its rusting lift towers and a forlorn-looking base village gracing the empty mountain.

To find the start of the Tucker Brook Trail, ski down slowly from the top of the Mount Mittersill knoll, looking for a trail opening on the left. The trail entrance is intentionally discreet. The Tucker Brook Trail begins at 3,520 feet as a 5-foot-wide slot through tight fir trees. This pipeline quickly gives way to a 15-foot-wide ski trail. But the Tucker Brook Trail is no place for cruising: You immediately plunge into the legendary 13 Turns (count them—they're all there). With a pitch of 28 degrees, double fall-line traverses, and rapid direction changes, you will either be on your toes or on your butt. It is a fun, energetic opening act. Don't blow it out too hard at the top, because there are many turns yet to come.

The 13 Turns plunges 600 vertical feet in a half-mile. The trail then contours south at 2,800 feet around the headwaters of Meadow Brook (the misnamed Tucker Brook ski trail actually parallels Meadow Brook. It never comes close to Tucker Brook, which flows next to NH 18). The trail then bends to the right and heads steadily northeast alongside Meadow Brook for the rest of its length. The start of this long straightaway was actually where the original Tucker Brook Trail began; the 13 Turns were part of the Coppermine Trail, from which Tucker Brook departed.

The Tucker Brook Trail changes character dramatically in this lower section. In the next 2.2 miles, the trail widens to about 25 feet, and the grade eases back to 20 to 24 degrees. There is room here for wide, sweeping turns. The woods alongside the trail offer plenty of opportunity to find your own hidden powder areas. By the time you reach the bottom, you should have a good case of turn-cranking thigh burn.

The final mile of the trail is part of the Franconia Inn cross-country ski trail network. Blue trail signs appear and side trails depart on the left. Stay to the right, and you will come out at the end of Tucker Hill Road. Turn left, ski parallel to the road for a half-mile, and you will arrive at the junction of Wells Road where you parked.

The Tucker Brook Trail is surprisingly well traveled. The full spectrum of *glisse* devotees—from telemarkers, to alpine skiers, to snowboarders—pay their respects here. I have skied it several times when the 13 Turns were covered by hardpack moguls. Thanks to its relatively easy access and its great terrain, you would be lucky—or will have risen very early—to claim first tracks. When you reach the bottom, you will have a full appreciation for why this trail has lured so many for so long.

6

Mount Garfield

THE TOUR
A long gradual tour of Mount Garfield, one of the most scenic summits of the White Mountains, via the Garfield Trail. The descent is a moderate sustained downhill.

DISTANCE
❋ 12.4 miles round-trip (from NH 3 trailhead)

ELEVATION
❋ *Start* 1,320 feet (NH 3)
❋ *Highest point* 4,500 feet (Mount Garfield summit)
❋ *Vertical gain* 3,180 feet

MAP
AMC Map 2 (Franconia–Pemigewasset)

DIFFICULTY
❋ Moderate

SNOWBOARDING
This gradual trail will require some walking/snowshoeing on the lower sections of the descent, including a 1.2-mile flat walk in and out on FR 92.

HOW TO GET THERE
From NH 3, park in a plowed parking pullout on the south side of the road at a small sign for Gale River (if you continue 0.3 mile farther east, you will come to Trudeau Road, where there are signs for the Ammonoosuc District Ranger Station). You must have a White Mountain National Forest parking pass for this trailhead, available at the nearby ranger station (this ranger station is scheduled to be moved in the year 2000) or from area convenience stores.

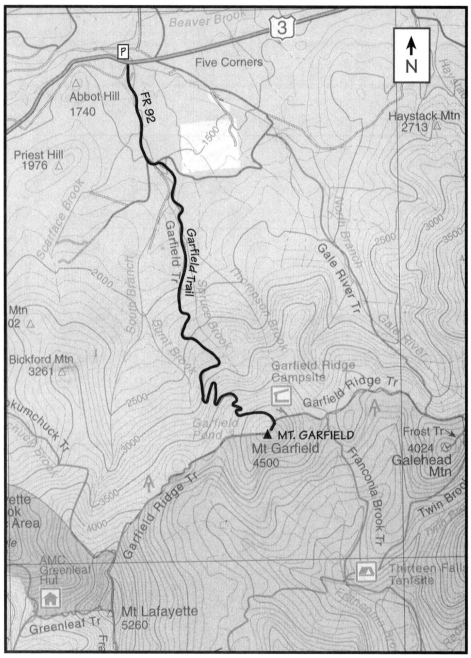

AMC Map 2: Franconia–Pemigewasset

MOUNT GARFIELD

Mount Garfield forms the northern end of one of the most dramatic features of the White Mountains. The spectacular Franconia Ridge, the frosted white knife-edge that can be seen clear across Vermont, comes to an end on the rocky 4,500-foot summit of Garfield. "Garfield rises like a sphinx watching over the valleys of Franconia and Lincoln brooks to the south, providing one of the finest views in the White Mountains, including a spectacular panorama of the higher Franconias to the south," notes the *AMC White Mountain Guide.*

The Garfield Trail is a long ski tour, but its gradual rise allows for a relaxed pace. The trail owes its gentle grade and generous width to the fact that it was once the service road to a firetower that stood atop Mount Garfield, which has long since been dismantled. If you are comfortable with the mileage on this tour, it is an excellent and enjoyable outing for intermediate skiers.

From the parking pullout on NH 3, skiers bear left onto the gated access road (FR 92). This road runs parallel to the South Branch of the Gale River. This is the water supply for the town of Littleton, so take care not to pollute it. Snowmobiles also use this road, so it is likely to have packed snow. Avoid several logging roads that depart on the right. After 1.2 miles, FR 92 turns left across a large bridge. The trailhead kiosk for the Garfield Trail appears on the right.

The trail climbs through a hemlock forest, descending to the banks of Thompson and Spruce Brooks at 0.7 mile. The Garfield Trail crosses Thompson Brook, then intersects a major snowmobile trail at a right angle, which has wooden bridges on either side (the snowmobile trail and bridges do not appear on any hiking maps). Continue skiing straight ahead (due south)—don't cross either snowmobile bridge!

The Garfield Trail continues to climb gradually, its character changing with elevation. The trail is about 10 feet wide. At around 3,000 feet, the trail is transformed into a bright white tunnel of paper birches, with an understory of fir trees. It is a classic New England mountainscape. After a series of switchbacks, the Garfield Trail reaches the forested lower section of the Garfield summit cone, where there is a large area of blowdown. The trail narrows, turns left, and continues up through a conifer forest until the junction with the Garfield Ridge Trail at 4.8 miles. Turning right, the summit of Mount Garfield is 0.2 mile away.

The summit of Mount Garfield is worth the extra hike. A short steep climb delivers you to the rocky summit cone, where you can find the remains of the foundation of the old firetower. Views over the entire Pemigewasset Wilderness unfold below you. To the southeast lies the dramatic ridgeline of the Franconia Range. It is a breathtaking sight. The green rolling interior of the Pemi beckons you to ski onward to explore what lies hidden there. The white gash down the face of Mount Lincoln inspires consideration of a steep wilderness descent. This dreamy vantage point high over a wintry New England is a prize reserved for backcountry skiers.

Take care when descending the narrow, steep stretch of the Garfield Ridge Trail. You soon rejoin the Garfield Trail. The trail begins as a narrow archway through a fir forest, but soon widens. Most of the trail is at a relaxed pitch where you can safely let your skis run, turning when you feel like it. Enjoy the long ride out.

Carter Notch Hut Tour

THE TOUR
Carter Notch is a striking gap with towering rock walls that is home to an AMC winter hut. Skiers can approach on the moderate but scenic Wildcat River Trail from Jackson. Another very challenging option is to ski to the notch via the Nineteen-Mile Brook Trail and ski out over Carter Dome, a high alpine summit.

DISTANCE
❋ 10 miles round-trip to Carter Dome summit (either via Carter Notch or climbing and descending the Carter Dome Trail)
❋ 10 miles round-trip to Carter Notch via Wildcat River Trail

ELEVATION
❋ *Start* 1,487 feet (NH 16 trailhead); 1,400 feet (Carter Notch Road)
❋ *Highest point* 4,832 feet (Carter Dome); 3,388 feet (Carter Notch)
❋ *Vertical drop* 3,345 feet (Carter Dome summit to NH 16); 1,988 feet (Carter Notch to Carter Notch Road in Jackson)

MAPS
AMC Map 5 (Carter Range–Evans Notch), AMC Map 1 (Presidential Range)

DIFFICULTY
❋ Most difficult (Carter Dome Tour)
❋ More difficult (Carter Notch Tour from Jackson)

SNOWBOARDING
There is good riding on the Carter Dome Trail. The top half of the Nineteen-Mile Brook Trail is a steep and exciting downhill ride, while the lower 1.9 miles of this trail will require some walking/snowshoeing. The tour up the Wildcat River Trail is more gradual and is not suitable for snowboards.

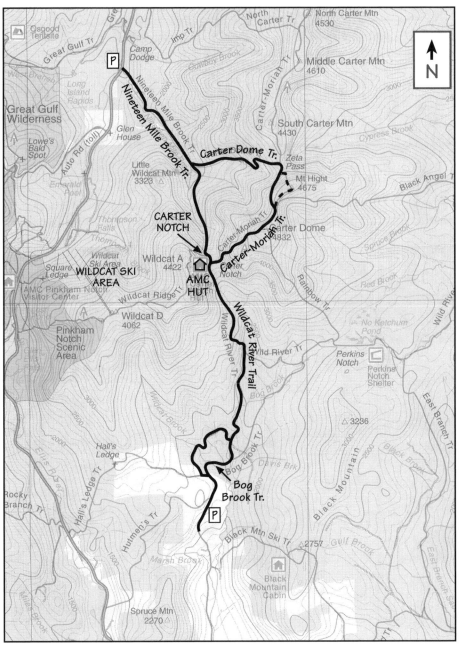

AMC Map 5 (Carter Range–Evans Notch)

CARTER NOTCH HUT TOUR

HOW TO GET THERE

To ski to Carter Notch on the Wildcat River Trail: From Jackson, take NH 16B past the Eagle Mountain House and continue straight on Carter Notch Road for 2 miles. Park at a small plowed Jackson Ski Touring Foundation (JSTF) parking lot on the right (there is no parking beyond this point). See ski trail directions below. It is advisable to check with the JSTF in Jackson (603-383-9355) regarding any trail reroutings at the beginning of this tour.

The trailhead for the Nineteen-Mile Brook Trail is 1 mile north of the Mount Washington Auto Road on the east side of NH 16. A WMNF parking permit is currently required.

Reservations are needed to stay overnight at the AMC Carter Notch Hut. Call the AMC at 603-466-2727.

The Carter Notch area has long been underused by skiers. The ignorance of skiers has been the bliss of snowshoers, as evidenced by the fact that the AMC Carter Notch Hut is packed with the latter every weekend. As a result, there is much ski exploration that has yet to be done in this area. As one of two areas served by an AMC winter hut (Zealand Valley is the other), there are a number of possibilities for overnight hut-based ski tours.

The tours in this area are of a more rugged nature than those accessed from the AMC Zealand Falls Hut. More advanced skiers looking for challenging runs will be well rewarded for the trip into this relatively untamed region.

The 5-mile-long mountain ridge that begins with Shelburne Moriah Mountain in the north and ends with the "E" peak of Wildcat Mountain has always received short shrift from visitors to the area, since it lies in the proverbial shadow of its majestic cousins in the Presidential Range to the west. White Mountain travelers might be surprised, therefore, to learn that six summits on this ridge are over 4,000 feet high, and that some of the most spectacular scenery in the White Mountains is found here.

The most striking feature of this long ridge is Carter Notch. Glaciers scoured out the cleft that separated the Wildcat Ridge from the Carter-Moriah Ridge. Carter Notch was the result: a vertical drop of 1,600 feet from the summit of Carter Dome and 1,200 feet down from Wildcat Mountain. Towering cliffs, two glacial tarns, and numerous giant boulders and blocks strewn haphazardly about the notch floor are the impressive detritus of mountain formation.

There are two ski tours that give access to Carter Notch. Some of the nicest touring is to ski into Carter Notch from Jackson. This is a more moderate tour that lacks the traffic on the Nineteen-Mile Brook Trail. From the JSTF parking lot on the Carter Notch Road (see driving directions above), take the Wildcat Valley Trail to the left (north). Please note: the Wildcat *Valley* Trail goes to the summit of Wildcat Mountain (see "Wildcat Valley Trail" chapter); the Wildcat *River* Trail takes an entirely different route, and ends up in Carter Notch.

Follow the Wildcat Valley Trail (trail 46) for about a mile, then come to a trail junction with the Bog Brook Trail. In 0.7 mile, the Bog Brook Trail crosses three brooks before it intersects the Wildcat River Trail. Follow the Wildcat River Trail as it climbs gradually along the east side of the Wildcat River. A 0.3-mile section of trail just south of Carter Notch is very steep and narrow; you may want to walk this stretch on the descent if you are not comfortable making tight turns. It is about 5 miles from Jackson to Carter Notch. When descending, you can enjoy skiing the glades around the lower section of the Wildcat River Trail.

The tour in on the Nineteen-Mile Brook Trail and over Carter Dome is an exciting high-alpine route with demanding skiing. The negative feature of this route is that it is heavily traveled by snowshoers and hikers. The trails on the west side of Carter Notch develop a hard snowshoe trough, so the skiing can be thankless. The best hope for decent ski conditions on these trails is to hit it mid-week or early after a storm. By contrast, the tour in from Jackson on the Wildcat River Trail is lightly traveled and enjoyable to ski.

The shortest route from NH 16 into Carter Notch is via the Nineteen-Mile Brook Trail; it is a 3.8-mile ski from the highway to the AMC Carter Notch Hut. The lower trail climbs gently alongside the Nineteen-Mile Brook, a beautiful and picturesque drainage that is fed by springs and runoff from Carter Dome and Wildcat. A few sections of the trail become obstructed by ice flows; these sections may be skirted by descending to the brook and skiing carefully around them.

The junction with the Carter Dome Trail is reached after 1.9 miles. The Nineteen-Mile Brook Trail gets progressively steeper from here to the notch. Carter Notch and Wildcat Mountain come into view at a birch glade about a half-mile up from the trail junction. In the final quarter-mile before the notch, the trail pitches up steeply and has several switchbacks. Be warned that descending this top section can be hair-raising and is not recommended!

Built in 1914, the current Carter Notch Hut is the oldest hut still in active use by the AMC. The main hut is made of stone, and there are two separate bunkhouses that sleep a total of forty people. The caretakers are good sources of information about trail conditions and recent precipitation. Check with them if you are in doubt as to your choice of descent routes.

There are a number of skiing options from the hut. One classic tour would include the exciting Carter Dome Trail. The mile-long climb from Carter Notch to the summit of Carter Dome on the Carter-Moriah Trail is extremely steep at the beginning and is best negotiated by carrying your skis and kicking steps up it. If you are skiing this loop from north to south, you would be well advised to descend into the notch in the same fashion.

Throughout the climb you are treated to more and more impressive views down into the notch and across to the cliffs flanking Wildcat. The summit of Carter Dome is covered with low scrub and also offers excellent views. The Carter Dome Trail begins here and coincides with the Carter-Moriah Trail for the next 1.1

miles, except where the two trails diverge briefly around Mount Hight. This section of the trail travels along a wild mountain ridge. It adds an exciting alpine element to the ski tour and is part of what makes this a classic. If you are ascending the Carter Dome Trail, the climb to the Carter Dome summit from Zeta Pass is well worth the extra effort.

The summit of Mount Hight offers some of the best views along the ridge, but it is rocky and usually not skiable. The Carter Dome Trail skirts this rocky peak to the west and is the recommended ski route. The trail follows a tricky sidehill as it slabs down the side of the ridge, making it awkward to ski for about a half-mile.

The descent from Zeta Pass to the Nineteen-Mile Brook Trail offers the best skiing and riding on this tour. The trail follows an abandoned road that used to serve a firetower on the summit of Carter Dome, long since dismantled. The upper section, from Zeta Pass to a tributary that feeds the Nineteen-Mile Brook, is only about 6 to 8 feet wide and drops relatively steeply. Seven sharp switchback turns on this upper section will keep you on your toes. If this trail has been packed by snowshoers, it may be a very hectic ride.

Once the trail crosses to the south side of the tributary, the switchbacks end and the grade becomes much more moderate and considerably wider. This makes for delightful moderate telemarking all the way to the junction with the Nineteen-Mile Brook Trail.

For those wanting a shorter day trip with some enjoyable downhill skiing, a round trip from the NH 16 trailhead to this major brook crossing on the Carter Dome Trail would be a good choice. If you are feeling more ambitious, it is 3.1 miles on the Carter Dome Trail to the Carter Dome summit from the junction with the Nineteen-Mile Brook Trail.

Good judgment must be used in deciding whether to summit Carter Dome during this tour. The Carter-Moriah Ridge, which the trail follows as it drops to Zeta Pass, is exposed to the full force of the elements. If the weather is deteriorating, you should abandon your summit plans. The route down is difficult, and trail conditions on it can vary considerably, depending how heavy the snowshoe traffic has been. Even in good conditions, this tour is for strong skiers and riders.

If you descend from Carter Notch on the Nineteen-Mile Brook Trail, you may opt to walk the steep, narrow top section. The trail becomes more skiable and moderate below the Carter Dome Trail junction. When descending any of these trails, be careful of hikers. You are likely to encounter people here even mid-week.

TRAILS NOT TO SKI

Both the Rainbow Trail and the Black Angel Trail, which leave from the summit of Carter Dome, are narrow, overgrown, and difficult to follow. These trails are for bushwhacking; keep to the other trails for skiing.

Wildcat Valley Trail

THE TOUR
A ski tour from the top of Wildcat Mountain to the town of Jackson, New Hampshire.

DISTANCE
❋ 11 miles

ELEVATION
❋ *Start/highest point* 4,000 feet (Wildcat gondola, upper station)

❋ *Finish* 755 feet (Jackson)

❋ *Vertical drop* 3,245 feet

MAPS
The *Jackson Ski Touring Map,* available at the Jackson Ski Touring Foundation (JSTF) office in Jackson, shows the full length of this trail, as does USGS Jackson (1987). AMC/Washburn *Mount Washington/Presidential Range* map shows the first one-third of this route, and the AMC Map 5 (Carter Range–Evans Notch) and AMC Map 1 (Presidential Range) covers this terrain but does not show the trail.

DIFFICULTY
❋ More difficult

SNOWBOARDING
This trail is not appropriate for snowboarding. It includes frequent stretches of flat and uphill skiing and travels along cross-country ski trails.

FEE
This is a fee trail of the Jackson Ski Touring Foundation (603-383-9355). A reduced-fee ticket for skiing only the Wildcat Valley Trail must be purchased at the Jackson Ski Touring Foundation office in Jackson (located adjacent to the

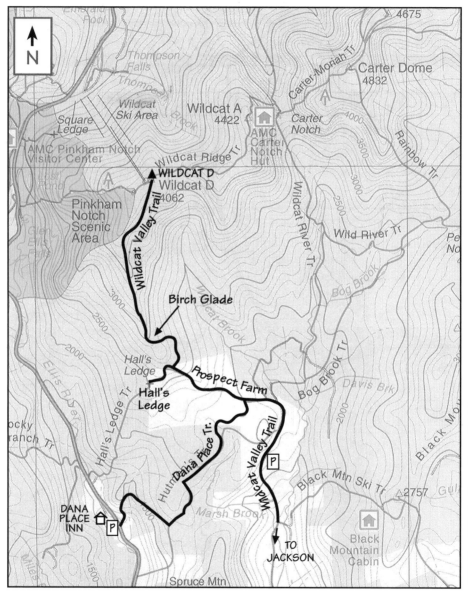

AMC Map 5 (Carter Range–Evans Notch)

WILDCAT VALLEY TRAIL

Jack Frost Ski Shop). Tickets may also be available at the AMC Pinkham Notch Visitor Center and the Wildcat Ski Area; inquire with the JSTF about these locations. Showing your JSTF trail ticket also entitles you to a reduced rate on the Wildcat Ski Area gondola.

HOW TO GET THERE

From Jackson, drive north on NH 16 to the Wildcat Ski Area. Purchase single-ride gondola tickets. The trail begins behind the upper gondola station. If you cannot spot a car in Jackson, contact the JSTF in the morning about arranging a taxi shuttle back to the Wildcat Ski Area in the afternoon.

The Wildcat Valley Trail may be the most popular down-mountain backcountry ski trail in New England today. Cut in 1972 by volunteers for the Jackson Ski Touring Foundation (JSTF), the run was meant to be the adrenaline-pumping jewel in the network of trails that link the town of Jackson with the surrounding White Mountains. Some three decades later, the goal of the original trail crews is still achieved every time an unsuspecting skier drops down off the summit of Wildcat Mountain to begin the 3,245-foot descent into Jackson.

The Wildcat Valley Trail offers a unique New England skiing experience. The ski tour travels the full range of the local mountain environment in its 11 miles. Beginning near treeline between the windswept "D" and "E" peaks of Wildcat Mountain, the trail quickly drops into thick spruce groves that are so familiar in the White Mountains. Over the course of the afternoon that it takes to ski the trail, skiers will pass through old farm pastures, traverse stands of mountain birch, and follow abandoned logging roads. Although it is not a pure wilderness tour, it makes up for what it reveals of human transgressions by providing a glimpse of past decades of New England culture.

This trail has formidable ancestry. One of the most popular of the CCC's down-mountain ski trails from the 1930s was the Wildcat Trail, a Class A race trail on the northwest side of Wildcat Mountain. It boasted a vertical drop of 2,000 feet in a mile and a half, with grades as steep as 33 degrees. The old Wildcat Trail eventually formed the hub of the trail network of the Wildcat Ski Area, and substantially the same route can still be skied today with chairlift access. Since the loss of the Wildcat Trail to the downhill ski area, it took some twenty years for Wildcat Mountain to once again become home to a trail for backcountry skiers looking for challenging down-mountain skiing.

Just because backcountry skiers lost a treasured ski trail to a lift-served ski area doesn't mean they have to reject the convenience that the lift now offers. The easiest and quickest way to the Wildcat Valley Trail is to buy a single-ride gondola ticket to the top of the mountain (discount available to JSTF trail pass holders).

If you are a purist who is racked with guilt about this, you can ski up the mountain, as long as you stay out of the way of oncoming skiers.

The trail begins just behind (south of) the summit cafeteria and upper gondola station. A sign marking the start of the route warns skiers about the difficult nature of the trail. Heed these words if they apply to you: Despite the popularity of this route, it is still a committing undertaking that is not suitable for novice skiers. Rescue is difficult, and the skiing can be fast and treacherous in icy or crusty conditions.

The trail starts inauspiciously: the first 50 feet are typically plastered with windblown ice. The trail then switches back with a few quick blind corners and downhill runs that alternate with flatter terrain. The numerous sitzmarks testify to the technique many people revert to on this section. The trail passes through a beautiful two-acre birch glade that JSTF trail crews improved for skiing. The trail drops steadily, passing the Beth Hendrick Trail, until it reaches Hall's Ledge Trail after 3.2 miles. The short side trail to Hall's Ledge is a traditional lunch stop on the route. It offers dramatic views across the valley into the Gulf of Slides, Tuckerman Ravine, and Huntington Ravine on Mount Washington.

From Hall's Ledge, the trail follows a logging road and takes a mile-long straight, fast drop through the Prospect Farm area. There are several new trails in the Prospect Farm area; keep an eye on the map and take care to follow signs for Trail 46/Wildcat Valley Trail.

At this point, you have skied two-thirds of the vertical drop on this route. Just beyond Prospect Farm, the junction with the Dana Place Trail is reached. From here, the alternatives are to turn right and continue 4.4 miles to the Dana Place Inn via the Dana Place Trail, or to continue straight on the Wildcat Valley Trail another 6.8 miles to Jackson.

The Dana Place Trail follows an old logging road on easy rolling terrain, turning right where it intersects the Marsh Brook Trail after 0.9 mile. After passing through an abandoned apple orchard, the trail then joins the Hutsmen Trail for a short distance. The Dana Place Trail soon turns sharply right, diverging from the Hutsmen, then switches back left and descends to NH 16. The trail comes out halfway between the Dana Place Inn (on the right) and the Blake House.

If you elect to continue on the Wildcat Valley Trail into Jackson, the trail continues straight ahead from the Dana Place Trail junction, eventually crossing open fields and hitting the Carter Notch Road. Skiers must walk on the road for 0.5 mile to Black Mountain Terrace, where they must turn left and pass the town dump before the trail resumes on the right. Be alert for blue plastic blazes as you continue. After 2.2 miles, the trail crosses NH 16B, continues through an old logging area and some fields, and crosses two bridges and the Eagle Mountain Golf Course before again crossing NH 16B 1.7 miles after first crossing it. The trail picks up on the other side of the road and continues for 0.5 mile before ending at the Wentworth Resort in Jackson. At this point you will probably be ready to take advantage of this trail's most pleasant feature: the opportunity to end the route on the doorstep of one of Jackson's several drinking establishments.

Ski conditions on this route can vary considerably. The trail will often have a new dusting of snow up high, even when conditions look dubious in the valley. However, if it has rained recently or there is an icy crust, the skiing is treacherous at best. The JSTF can provide information on current trail conditions.

The Jackson Ski Touring Foundation has instituted a reduced-fee trail ticket for skiing the Wildcat Valley Trail. Skiers should be advised that courtesy patrollers on this and other JSTF trails will charge an extra fee to people who have not purchased a ticket beforehand, and that the reduced-fee ticket is not good for skiing on the other JSTF trails (you may upgrade your ticket in Jackson if you decide to continue skiing on other trails).

9

Doublehead Ski Trail

THE TOUR

The Doublehead Ski Trail was cut by the CCC in the 1930s. It is a wide trail full of interesting twists and turns that leaves from the summit of North Doublehead.

DISTANCE

❋ 1.8 miles to North Doublehead summit

ELEVATION

❋ *Start* 1,480 feet (Dundee Road)

❋ *Highest point* 3,053 feet (North Doublehead summit)

❋ *Vertical gain* 1,573 feet

MAPS

AMC Map 5 (Carter Range–Evans Notch), USGS Jackson (1987), *Jackson Ski Touring Foundation* map (available from JSTF)

DIFFICULTY

❋ More difficult

SNOWBOARDING

The Doublehead Ski Trail is an excellent backcountry snowboard tour. It has a continuous downhill grade and fun banked turns.

HOW TO GET THERE

From the covered bridge in Jackson, take NH 16B, turn right on Dundee Road and bear right over the bridge. After passing the Black Mountain Ski Area, the parking area and brown sign for Doublehead Ski Trail are on the left.

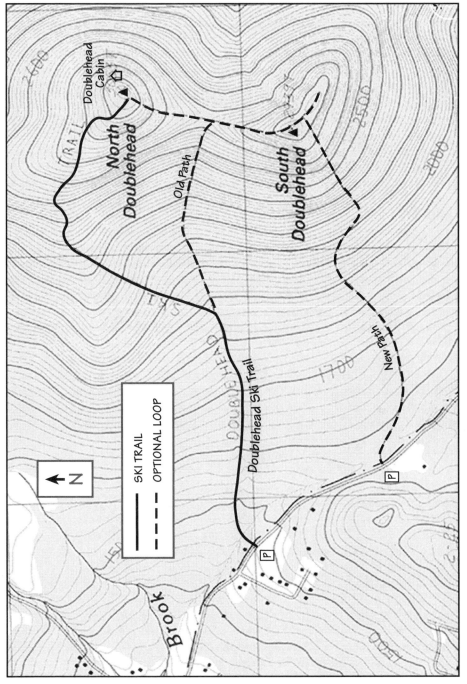

DOUBLEHEAD SKI TRAIL

A tour on the Doublehead Ski Trail is a perfect way to sample the talent and artistry of the master trail builders of the Civilian Conservation Corps (CCC). The Doublehead Ski Trail was built by the CCC in 1934 to meet the growing appetite for skiing in the Mount Washington Valley. Snow trains used to deliver skiers to nearby Glen, and there was a demand for ski terrain in Jackson to accommodate the visitors. Ski trails were duly cut on Black Mountain, Bear Mountain, and North Doublehead. The latter trail retains the classic character of other CCC creations: swooping turns, double fall lines, and a fast descent. It is a well-preserved jewel from an earlier era of skiing.

An early assessment of the CCC's efforts appeared in the December 1934 issue of *Appalachia*. "The lower mile is comparatively moderate in grade, but the upper part is steep enough to be interesting for even the best runners," was the enthusiastic description.

There are several approaches that skiers can take to skiing Doublehead. You can climb and descend the Doublehead Ski Trail; the round trip is 3.6 miles. For more variety—and to preserve the untracked powder on the ski trail—consider making one of two possible loop trips. After climbing the ski trail for 0.6 mile, you can bear right onto the Old Path to reach the North Doublehead summit; this round trip is 3.3 miles, and has the advantage of delivering you back to your car at the trailhead for the Doublehead Ski Trail. The Old Path climbs steeply, arriving at the col between North and South Doublehead, from where it is a steep 0.3-mile climb to the summit of North Doublehead and the start of the ski trail.

Another alternative is to do the Doublehead grand tour: ski up South Doublehead, over to North Doublehead, and down the ski trail. This tour is 3.5 miles round-trip. As with skiing up the Old Path, the climb up South Doublehead is steep near the top, so it is a more strenuous undertaking than simply skiing up North Doublehead.

To ski the South-North Doublehead loop, continue on Dundee Road a half-mile past the trailhead for the Doublehead Ski Trail. The sign for New Path appears on the left. This is the trail up South Doublehead. The trail follows a gradual old logging road for about 0.6 mile, crossing a brook and several ledges. The trail then narrows to 4 to 6 feet in width and climbs up steeply through a beautiful forest of cat spruce and birch trees. If the snow is firm, you may opt to shoulder your skis and hike up this steep pipeline pitch. New Path tops out on the rocky and scenic South Doublehead summit ledges. Turn right and ski briefly to the South Doublehead summit, which has fine views. Turning left (north), the New Path meets the Old Path in the col between North and South Doublehead. The col is dense with birch trees that were heavily damaged in the ice storm of January 1998. The countless snapped tree crowns are the telltale evidence of the devastation wrought by this storm, in which trees were encased in up to six inches of solid ice. Continue climbing, steeply at times, to the summit of North Doublehead.

The North Doublehead summit is home to the Doublehead Cabin. Many CCC trails had a cabin at the top, providing shelter for skiers and winter hikers.

A powder run on Doublehead Ski Trail.

The Doublehead Cabin was built in 1932, and is a fine example of backcountry craftsmanship. The beauty is in the details—from the ship's prows over the gables to the stone chimney that crowns it. The cabin holds eight people and costs $20 per person per day (as of 1998). Overnight reservations must be made two weeks in advance by calling the Saco Ranger Station in Conway at 603-447-5448.

After the narrow confines of the Old and New Paths, the spacious Doublehead Ski Trail that departs from the cabin is a delight. The trail ranges from 15 to 25 feet wide, with a pitch of about 20 degrees. It has a sporting double fall line for most of its descent. The trail avoids the steep ledgy summit slopes of the mountain by detouring around to the northeast from the North Doublehead summit. After this moderate entry, the trail swings back southwest and becomes somewhat steeper. There is plenty of room for turns, and there are lots of them to be had. This trail offers 1.8 miles of steady downhill skiing and riding—make sure you have enough energy left to enjoy it!

The Doublehead Ski Trail can be enjoyed by skiers and snowboarders of many abilities. Experts will revel in the continuous descent. There are enough telemark turns to work up a good thigh burn. The trail is also forgiving enough to be enjoyable to less experienced skiers. It is also wide enough for snowplows and bailouts if needed.

MOUNT WASHINGTON REGION

Mount Washington (elevation 6,288 feet) is the crown of the White Mountains. It is the highest point in the Northeast and the third highest mountain in the East. Standing watch over New England, Mount Washington has long been a magnet for winter explorers. Ice climbers, snowshoers, cross-country skiers, snowboarders, and alpine skiers all share the trails on this mountain as they make their way to their respective meccas. Much of the ski history of this region is presented in the chapter on Tuckerman Ravine.

All of the ski tours described in this section are set in the heart of the White Mountains, offering sweeping views of surrounding peaks and valleys. Some of the routes, such as Tuckerman Ravine and the Gulf of Slides, are unique for New England. They offer wide, open-bowl skiing above timberline, much like skiing in the larger mountain ranges of the western United States. The Mount Washington area is also unusual for its distinctly alpine character. The steep gullies of Oakes Gulf, Great Gulf, and Tuckerman Ravine are classic, elegant high-mountain passageways.

The tours described in this section are only a small sampling of the terrain offered in the White Mountains. There are vast wilderness skiing and snowboarding opportunities in this region. Skiing the classic routes described in this section will, hopefully, inspire winter explorers to strike out in search of other remote but equally rewarding tours.

A note on maps: By far the best map of the Mount Washington region is the AMC's *Mount Washington and the Heart of the Presidential Range* (1988), by Bradford Washburn (denoted hereafter as AMC/Washburn *Mount Washington/Presidential Range*). It is a beautiful and painstakingly precise 1:20,000-scale map by the man who drew the definitive maps of Mount McKinley and Mount Everest. It covers all of the routes described in this section.

Also useful are AMC Map 1 (Presidential Range), available at the AMC Pinkham Notch Trading Post (800-AMC-HILL). The USGS Mount Washington (1982, metric) also covers this terrain.

Avalanche Brook Trail

THE TOUR
A rugged ski trail with good downhill runs from Pinkham Notch to the Dana Place Inn in Jackson.

DISTANCE
❋ 5.5 miles

ELEVATION
❋ *Start* 2,032 feet
❋ *Highest point* 2,650 feet
❋ *Vertical drop* 1,550 feet

MAPS
AMC/Washburn *Mount Washington/Presidential Range* (shows all but the last mile) and the *Jackson Ski Touring Map* (shows all but the first mile; map available from the Jackson Ski Touring Foundation in Jackson) show most of this trail. AMC Map 1 (Presidential Range) covers this terrain, but the trail is not shown.

DIFFICULTY
❋ More difficult

SNOWBOARDING
The Avalanche Brook Trail covers rolling terrain through most of its length. It is not suitable for snowboarding.

HOW TO GET THERE
The trail leaves from the Gulf of Slides Ski Trail, 0.2 mile from the south end of the parking lot at the AMC Pinkham Notch Visitor Center off NH 16. You will have to spot a car where you finish, either at the Dana Place Inn or in the town of Jackson.

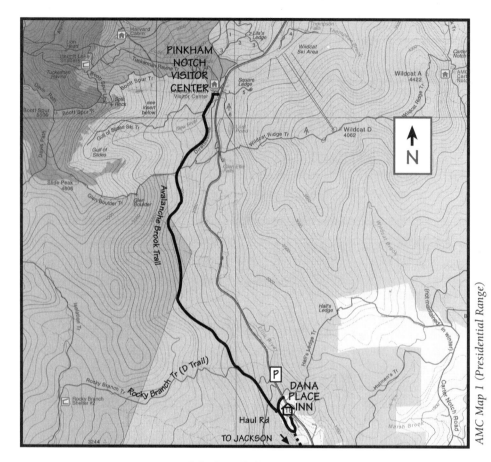

AMC Map 1 (Presidential Range)

AVALANCHE BROOK TRAIL

The Avalanche Brook Trail is an exciting run that passes through mixed forest in the heart of the White Mountains. It goes from Pinkham Notch, the northern center of operations for the Appalachian Mountain Club, to the Dana Place Inn in Jackson.

The Avalanche Brook Trail was cut by volunteers of the Appalachian Mountain Club in 1975. It was designed to link the growing trail network in the town of Jackson with the AMC's ski trail network in and around Pinkham Notch. The original plan was to cut a trail down the east side of NH 16, where the terrain is relatively gentle. When the trail designers could not figure out a way to skirt the precipitous and rocky drop-off around Glen Ellis Falls, they turned their attention to the west side of the valley. The views from the west side were considered superior, but the trail builders had to level out a bothersome sidehill in several places. The final result was the Avalanche Brook Trail.

Once the trail was completed, it became possible to traverse the entire length of Pinkham Notch, beginning on trails from the Glen House (now Great Glen Trails, across from the Mount Washington Auto Road) and skiing all the way to Jackson. The trail now enjoys steady traffic throughout the winter.

This tour, while not a high-alpine experience, travels through interesting mixed forests with a nice variety of terrain. It offers an enjoyable half-day of skiing. When it begins its descent, there is not much time for dallying. It heads fairly fast for the valley floor, dropping more than 1,500 feet in 2.5 miles. The trail runs parallel to NH 16 and is well marked. The route should be skied from north to south, since this maximizes the downhill skiing.

The trail begins at the south end of the parking lot at the Pinkham Notch Camp. A sign at the trailhead informs you that the route follows the Gulf of Slides Ski Trail for the first 0.2 mile. Go straight ahead, cross a wooden bridge over the New River, and watch for a sign pointing left that directs you to the Avalanche Brook Trail.

From Pinkham Notch, there are beautiful views into Huntington Ravine to the northwest, while the craggy summit of Boott Spur lies due west. The Gulf of Slides Ski Trail diverges to the right after 0.2 mile; the Avalanche Brook Trail continues to the left following blue blazes. The trail meanders through hardwood forests for 0.7 mile, then climbs steadily towards the Glen Boulder Trail junction at 1.7 miles. The Avalanche Brook Trail then levels out and contours. The Glen Boulder can be seen above to the west. The trail crosses the lower end of an old avalanche path, the result of a 1967 mudslide from the Glen Boulder ridge above. The trail continues through mixed forest, with beautiful views of the Carter Range across the valley.

Rounding the side of a broad ridge that runs from Slide Peak, the trail descends briefly and then contours at 2,300 feet for another mile. After a gradual climb, the trail crosses a wooden bridge over Avalanche Brook, a deep, ravine-like drainage. From this point, the trail plunges downhill for the next 2 miles. Good trail work has been done on this route by AMC trail crews, with sturdy wooden bridges now spanning most of the deeper drainages.

Once the Avalanche Brook Trail begins its descent, it does not allow much room for graceful swooping turns. This narrow trail is most fun when you are in the mood to ski aggressively and don't mind seeing the birches go by fast. It is, however, a forgiving route: There is ample room to bail out almost anywhere you choose.

After about 5 miles and a fast descent, the trail crosses the Hall Trail (an unplowed road). If you miss this cutoff and come out at the Rocky Branch trailhead, you may continue for a few minutes along the right side of a parking lot (this

Early skiing in Tuckerman Ravine, circa 1932. Photo by Winston Pote

trailhead is also a possible ending point, if you parked a car here). You will join the Hall Trail behind a metal gate on the south end of the lot. Blue blazes continue to mark the way. Within 0.25 mile of the gate, a sign pointing left directs you to the final section of the Avalanche Brook Trail, which intersects with the Highwater Trail behind the Dana Place Inn. From this junction, if you turn left, you will emerge on NH 16 just north of the Dana Place Inn. If you turn right at this junction, the trail soon intersects with the Ellis River Trail, which proceeds another 4.7 miles south on flat ground to the town of Jackson (if you choose to continue to Jackson, you will be on a fee trail of the Jackson Ski Touring Foundation system;

trail tickets may be purchased at the Dana Place Inn). Turning left on the Ellis River Trail brings you to the Dana Place Inn in several minutes.

Finishing up at the Dana Place Inn, you will find clear views to the north across the fields to the snowy summit of Mount Washington and the peaks running south of it.

If you have not spotted a car at the Dana Place Inn or in Jackson, a local taxi service will shuttle skiers back to Pinkham Notch. If possible, make arrangements in the morning for this taxi shuttle by calling the Jackson Ski Touring Foundation at 603-383-9355.

11

Pinkham Notch

THE TOUR

The ski tour travels up the Old Jackson Road, down the Mount Washington Auto Road, and back on Connie's Way Ski Trail. It includes a varied mix of climbing, moderate downhill, and cross-country skiing, all in the shadow of New Hampshire's highest peak.

DISTANCE

❄ 6 miles round-trip

ELEVATION

❄ *Start* 2,032 feet (Pinkham Notch)

❄ *Highest point* 2,600 feet (Mount Washington Auto Road)

❄ *Vertical drop* 568 feet

MAPS

AMC/Washburn *Mount Washington/Presidential Range*, AMC Map 1 (Presidential Range), USGS Mount Washington (1982)

DIFFICULTY

❄ Moderate

SNOWBOARDING

This tour covers rolling terrain and is not suitable for snowboards.

HOW TO GET THERE

Pinkham Notch Visitor Center is located on NH 16, 11 miles south of Gorham, NH, and 20 miles north of Conway. The Old Jackson Road starts from the AMC Pinkham Notch Visitor Center.

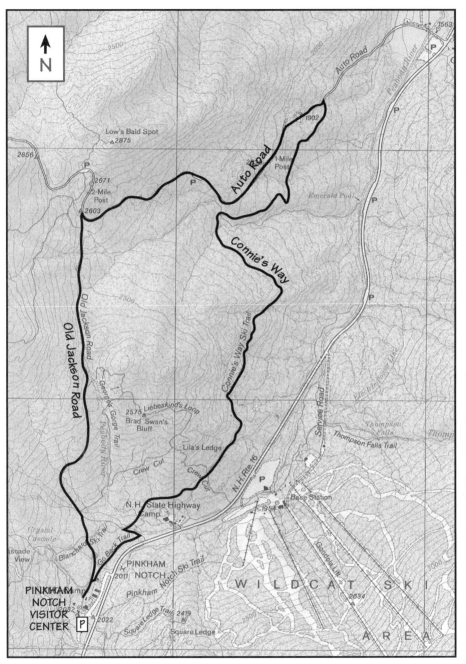

N

Low's Bald Spot
▲2875

2500

2856

P

2671
2-Mile
Post

2603

Auto Road

1902

1-Mile
Post

Auto Road

2000

Peabody River

1563

P

P

P

Emerald Pool

P

Old Jackson Road

Old Jackson Road

Connie's Way

Connie's Way Ski Trail

P

Georges Gorge Trail

Peabody River

2500

2575
Brad Swan's
Bluff

Liebeskind's Loop

Lila's Ledge

Crew Cut

Crew Cut

Service Road

Electric Power Line

Thompson
Falls

Thompson Falls Trail

Thomp

N.H. Rte. 16

P

Base Station

1954

Blanchard Ski Trail

Crystal
Cascade

Cascade
View

Go Back Trail

N.H. State Highway
Camp

PINKHAM
NOTCH

2011

Pinkham Notch Ski Trail

Pinkham Notch Ski Trail

Gondola Lift

W I L D C A T   S K I

PINKHAM
NOTCH
VISITOR
CENTER P

2022

Square Ledge Trail

Square Ledge

2419

2634

A R E A

2500

3000

PINKHAM NOTCH

Mount Washington and the Presidential Range, © *Bradford Washburn*

Pinkham Notch is a hub of activity for backcountry travelers in the White Mountains. The AMC Pinkham Notch Visitor Center offers meals and a wealth of information, both published and anecdotal. The AMC Joe Dodge Lodge accommodates more than 100 guests. Pinkham Notch is also the busiest trailhead in the northern mountains.

The original Pinkham Notch Camp was first constructed in 1920. It was used as a three-season base of operations for the Appalachian Mountain Club. It opened in the winter for the first time in 1929–30. When the Pinkham Notch Highway (now NH 16) was plowed from Jackson that winter, skiers welcomed the opportunity. It marked "the beginning of a new era in winter travel," wrote Winston Pote, who skied and photographed the White Mountains in those years. Nevertheless, the plowing was a source of contention at the Jackson town meeting that year. "Who would want to go up there in the winter anyway?" demanded some of the residents, reported Pote in his excellent chronicle *Mount Washington in Winter.*

The advent of a plowed road to Pinkham Notch eliminated an arduous 12-mile snowshoe from Jackson. But driving a car didn't necessarily make the going easier. Pote describes what it took to drive in the mountains in those days:

> Winter road conditions, despite the improved snowplowing, remained troublesome. High winds formed deep drifts in the mountain passes. Snow alternately thawed and refroze, and by March there were deep ruts of ice, sometimes filled with water. One always carried shovels, and an axe came in handy if one met another car in the same rut and had to chop out a path around it.

Pinkham Notch is a natural attraction to skiers. It is the starting point for trips into Tuckerman Ravine and Gulf of Slides. There are also a variety of shorter ski tours that start right from the AMC Visitor Center.

The ski tour that begins on the Old Jackson Road (OJR) is a traditional favorite of Pinkham Notch visitors. It is part of a fun, energetic half-day loop. The OJR is part of the Appalachian Trail.

The Old Jackson Road was once, as its name suggests, the main road through Pinkham Notch. Nineteenth-century travelers would come down from Gorham, travel two miles up the Mount Washington Carriage Road (now the Auto Road), and descend to Jackson on the OJR. It was a circuitous route, and inevitably a direct road was cut along the valley floor in the present location of NH 16.

The OJR leaves from the Tuckerman Ravine Trail about 50 yards from the trailhead, which is located behind the AMC Visitor Center. In 0.3 mile, the trail crosses the Blanchard Loop, which connects with the Go Back Trail and Connie's Way, the preferred return route. The OJR crosses several brooks and begins climbing at a steady, steeper grade, ascending 500 feet in 0.8 mile. The OJR is less than 10 feet wide for most of its length. If you choose to descend this way, you will need a solid snowplow or a quick turn—there isn't much room to maneuver.

Ascending the Old Jackson Road on Mount Washington.

As the OJR climbs, there are views to the south and west of Huntington Ravine, Tuckerman Ravine, and the southern slopes of the Gulf of Slides. These views reinforce the feeling of being in a big mountain environment. The trail traverses through beautiful mature hardwood stands along its journey. After 1 mile, the trail enters a sunny plateau. This is a natural choice for a trailside picnic spot.

At about 1.5 miles, the OJR comes to a large brook crossing. The summer hiking trail makes a hard left here, but skiers should continue straight, crossing the brook and climbing briefly. The Mount Washington Auto Road lies just ahead. (Note: The hiking maps do not show this winter shortcut to the Auto Road.) The OJR ends after 1.6 miles when it emerges just below the 2-mile mark on the Mount Washington Auto Road. For skiers, the obvious choice at the Auto Road is to take full advantage of the wide open spaces and make some turns. The road is gentle enough that you can negotiate it with a good snowplow, or you can carve turns to your heart's content.

The Mount Washington Auto Road was built between 1855 and 1861. It is 8 miles long and climbs at a gentle grade to the summit of Mount Washington. From mid-May to mid-October, this is a commercial toll road for cars. It is also the site of an annual car race, a running race, and a bicycle race.

The road is snow covered and closed to public vehicle traffic for the other half of the year. Until the mid-1990s, the Auto Road was not usually very good for skiing, since it is churned up daily by snowcats bringing supplies and staff up to the Mount Washington Observatory on the summit. In 1994, the Great Glen Trails cross-country ski center opened and began grooming the lower 4 miles of the Auto Road for skiing, vastly improving the ski experience. (Great Glen Trails is owned by the Mount Washington Auto Road Company.) Great Glen also offers a snowcat skier shuttle that brings skiers halfway up the mountain. The Auto Road is now officially part of the Great Glen ski trail network, and a trail pass must be purchased to ski the road. An exception is made for skiers who are skiing the 1.3 miles from OJR to Connie's Way; no trail pass is required for skiing this section of the road. However, if you decide to continue farther up or down the Auto Road, you will need to purchase a trail pass. For more information about skiing the Auto Road, the shuttle, or the 20-km backcountry trail network maintained by Great Glen Trails, contact 603-466-2333.

After relishing the open space and views on the Auto Road, it is time to return to the woods. Below the 1-mile mark and just after a wide turnaround on the road, the Connie's Way Ski Trail departs on the right.

Connie's Way was created in memory of Connie Waste. A member of the AMC Pinkham Notch crew, Connie died of a heart attack in 1975 while playing touch football with her crew mates. She was 19. Her comrades created the 2.75-mile long Connie's Way as a living memorial to her in 1976. Her brother, Bill Waste, who still works for the AMC, reflects about Connie's Way, "The serenity, the beauty, and the peace you can get in the woods there is definitely in the spirit of who she was."

Connie's Way rolls up and down through unusual terrain. The trail passes by a series of huge glacial erratics. There are boulders and tall crags split by long crack systems. This is troll country—the small but dramatic features can be interesting diversions to stop and explore. Across the way to the east is the Wildcat Ski Area. The crowds over there make you appreciate your solitude here.

The trail finishes with a fun kick-and-glide through a conifer forest. After a gentle downhill on the final mile, turn left on the Blanchard Loop, then right onto the Go Back Trail. It is another 0.2 mile to the Pinkham Notch Visitor Center.

This tour is especially nice if you begin early in the day. Morning light filters through the trees, illuminating the birches that line the Old Jackson Road and accentuating the white snowcaps on the peaks above.

OTHER OPTIONS

The AMC Pinkham Notch Visitor Center has information on a variety of moderate ski tours in the notch. A free handout is available with a sketch map and description of eleven different Pinkham Notch tours.

Great Glen Trails (603-466-2333, www.mt-washington.com) has an excellent 40-km network of ski trails just north of Pinkham Notch, half of which is ungroomed backcountry terrain. They also rent backcountry ski equipment.

The Jackson Ski Touring Foundation in nearby Jackson (603-383-9355, www.jacksonxc.com) is nationally renowned for its 160-km network of trails, including a number of backcountry trails that link with the Pinkham Notch trail network.

Gulf of Slides

THE TOUR
The Gulf of Slides Ski Trail drops down from the base of the ravine from which the trail gets its name. There is excellent steep skiing in the Gulf of Slides itself and good downhill skiing on the trail.

DISTANCE
* 2.5 miles (Gulf of Slides Ski Trail)
* 0.5 mile (Main Gully, Gulf of Slides)

ELEVATION
* *Start* 2,032 feet (Pinkham Notch)
* *Highest point* 3,900 feet (top of Gulf of Slides Ski Trail and base of Main Gully); 5,000 feet (top of Gulf of Slides headwall)
* *Vertical gain* 3,000 feet from Pinkham Notch to top of slides

MAPS
AMC Map 1 (Presidential Range), AMC/Washburn *Mount Washington/Presidential Range,* USGS Mount Washington (1982)

DIFFICULTY
Most difficult/mountaineering

SNOWBOARDING
The Gulf of Slides is an excellent area for snowboarding. The Gulf of Slides Ski Trail is a sustained downhill ride. The gullies on the headwall of the Gulf of Slides offer challenging steep riding. This ski trail is lightly traveled, so snowshoes are needed for the climb.

HOW TO GET THERE
The Gulf of Slides Ski Trail leaves from the south end of the parking lot at the AMC Pinkham Notch Visitor Center.

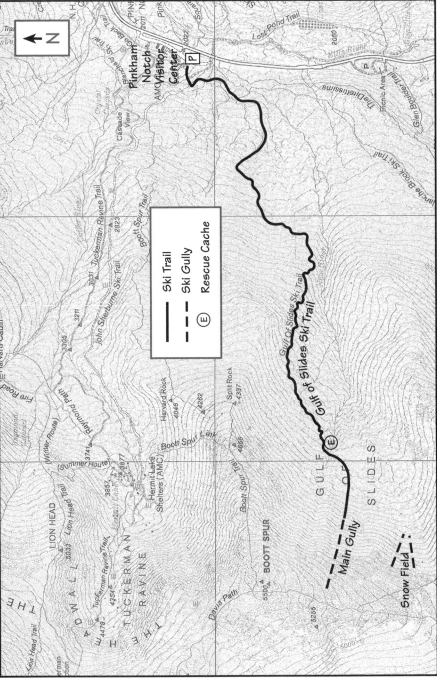

Mount Washington and the Presidential Range © Bradford Washburn

GULF OF SLIDES

The Gulf of Slides has long been overlooked by the majority of skiers. It is well away from the crowds that flock to the bowl in Tuckerman Ravine—indeed, it is unknown to many of the Tuck's regulars. That is precisely its appeal.

The Gulf of Slides is a wide ravine between ridges that run off of Boott Spur (5,500 feet) and Slide Peak (4,806 feet). The slides for which it is named form along the east-facing headwall and can be seen from NH 16 below. The Gulf of Slides holds some of the latest snow in the White Mountains outside of Tuckerman Ravine. It is a traditional spring skiing destination, with ski activity usually continuing from March through May.

Skiing in the Gulf of Slides has historically been reserved for the smaller number of skiers interested in exploring other slopes around Mount Washington. Although skiers began venturing into Tuckerman Ravine in the late 1920s, it wasn't until the early 1930s that those same skiers made their way into the Gulf of Slides. That they finally came was inevitable: The long snowfields of the Gulf are visible from a number of vantage points in the Mount Washington Valley and hold obvious promise for skiing.

The late Al Sise, one of the first of the Tuckerman skiers, recalls that the Gulf of Slides was simply "where someone would go to get away from the crowds. . . . It was not as awe-inspiring a place [as Tuckerman Ravine], but it was a nice place to get away from it all and ski."

The first skiers in the Gulf of Slides bushwhacked their way up the New River from the AMC Pinkham Notch Camp to reach the headwall. It was not a leisurely trip, according to the early accounts. Some skiers accessed it from the top by climbing up to the Davis Path, returning to Pinkham Notch by skiing the snow-filled bed of the New River—not an easy feat.

Interest and activity in the Gulf of Slides picked up enough in the early 1930s to warrant a bona fide trail. In 1935, master trail designer Charlie Proctor laid out the Gulf of Slides Ski Trail from Pinkham Notch, following the north bank of the New River into the Gulf. The trail was cut that same year by the Civilian Conservation Corps, and it has been maintained as a ski trail ever since. The trail was the site of a few races, but because of the lack of any shelters in the Gulf of Slides area, it was considered a less hospitable place for races than other, more developed trails in the valley. Unlike the Sherburne Trail, which has been widened and rerouted in places, the Gulf of Slides Ski Trail has not been significantly changed from its original state.

Lacking the crowds, the Gulf of Slides has not enjoyed the kind of ski lore of Tuckerman Ravine, where every ski run has a name and a reputation. The more popular runs on the Gulf of Slides headwall were given rather uninteresting names; few skiers today even know the runs have names. Brooks Dodge, son of the legendary AMC huts manager Joe Dodge and an early skier in the Gulf, says they were identified from north to south as the Boott Spur Gully, the Main Gullies, the Left Gully, and the Snowfield, which is the large prominent slope that lies on the flanks of Slide Peak. The names are less important than the fact that virtually all the gullies and snowfields on the headwall of the Gulf of Slides starting from Boott Spur have been skied and are skiable.

The Gulf of Slides Ski Trail starts at the south end of the parking lot at the AMC Pinkham Notch Camp and branches off quickly from the bottom of the Sherburne Trail. Beginning from the parking lot, the start of the trail is the same as that of the Avalanche Brook Trail; the trails diverge after 0.2 mile, where the Gulf of Slides Ski Trail heads right. The trail is about 20 feet wide and climbs steadily; the steepest grade is about 20 degrees. There are nice views to the east of the Carter-Moriah Ridge and the Wildcat Ridge as the trail climbs. There is a rescue cache with a litter just before the trail crosses the New River near the top of the trail. There are no views of the slides themselves until this point.

The Gulf of Slides Ski Trail is an enjoyable run in itself. Skied from the top, it is a sustained, 2.5-mile downhill run similar in character to the Sherburne Trail, although narrower and not as steep as the lower sections of the Sherburne. If there is avalanche danger on the slides (see note at the end of this section), just skiing the trail is a day well spent.

The upper end of the ski trail lies at the foot of the most prominent gully, which is just left of center on the headwall. This gully climbs about 1,000 feet in a half-mile. It runs all the way to the ridge at the top of the headwall. Looking up, there is another shorter and slightly narrower slide to the right of it. Both of these gullies get progressively steeper as they rise; the steepest sections are about 40 degrees. Skiers and snowboarders can climb up as high as they are comfortable and then descend.

From where the Gulf of Slides Ski Trail ends, one can also continue bushwhacking south through widely spaced spruce trees and enter the base of a very large snowfield that runs north from Slide Peak. This snowfield, which is not visible from the main gullies, has more moderate slopes than the gullies.

The gullies on the far right running down from Boott Spur are most easily accessed by climbing the steep Boott Spur Link Trail, which leaves south from the Tuckerman Ravine Trail just opposite the foot of the Lion Head Trail. From Pinkham Notch Camp it is 3.6 miles to the summit of Boott Spur via the Boott Spur Link Trail. The Main Gully at the center of the headwall can also be accessed in this way by dropping down from Boott Spur, although it is 0.8 mile longer than the approach on the Gulf of Slides Ski Trail. It is also possible to access the Gulf of Slides by hiking up Hillman's Highway or Left Gully and hiking south on the Davis Path until you can see the gullies and snowfields of the Gulf.

The preferred approach to the main gullies, however, is from the bottom, since it allows skiers to climb what they will ski and thereby assess conditions.

The Gulf of Slides is an extraordinary skiing area. A first reaction on seeing the slides and the snowfield is one of amazement that such terrain can be found in New England. Wide, open bowl skiing and steep alpine runs resemble the Colorado backcountry. Climbing high up on the slides, skiers get panoramic views up and down the valley. There is a wild, untamed feeling about the place.

A skier drops into the Gulf of Slides.

A trip into the Gulf of Slides is a good way to inspire skiers about the other possibilities for wilderness skiing in the White Mountains. The Gulf is one of a number of outlying ravines that are rarely visited by skiers. Oakes Gulf, Ammonoosuc Ravine, King Ravine, Jefferson Ravine, and the Mount Jefferson snowfields are just some of the many excellent skiing jewels that skiers with a lust for exploration have had to themselves. You need only pick up your map and head out. There is skiing everywhere, and the opportunities for exploring new terrain are limitless.

A word of caution: The Gulf of Slides is so named because it is highly prone to avalanches. Early in the winter, before the snowpack has consolidated, is the most unstable time. The gullies in the Gulf tend to avalanche more frequently than those in Tuckerman Ravine because the slopes in the Gulf are more uniform and the ground below the snow is smoother. On March 24, 1996, an avalanche tragically claimed the lives of two backcountry skiers who were standing at the bottom of the Main Gully. In their memory, their families provided funding for a new rescue cache that now lies at the top of the Gulf of Slides Ski Trail.

Check the signboard in the AMC Pinkham Notch Visitor Center, which lists avalanche conditions in Tuckerman and Huntington Ravines, for general guidance about snow stability in the surrounding area. However, the U.S. Forest Service does not monitor avalanche conditions in the Gulf of Slides, so the final assessment must be made by each skier.

At a minimum, carry a shovel, dig a snow pit where you plan to ski to check for the presence of shear layers, and observe the terrain for signs of recent slide activity. The Gulf of Slides should be avoided just after a snowfall, when its 30- to 40-degree slopes are most likely to slide. This is a remote area, and help will not be immediate in the event of an accident. Prevention—namely, not skiing slopes which you suspect are unstable—is essential.

John Sherburne Ski Trail

THE TOUR
A downhill ski trail from just above the Hermit Lake shelters to the AMC Pinkham Notch Visitor Center.

DISTANCE
4.8 miles round-trip from Pinkham Notch Visitor Center

ELEVATION
* ❋ *Start* 2,032 feet
* ❋ *Highest point* 3,950 feet
* ❋ *Vertical drop* 1,950 feet

MAPS
AMC Map 1 (Presidential Range), AMC/Washburn *Mount Washington/Presidential Range,* USGS Mount Washington (1982)

DIFFICULTY
More difficult

SNOWBOARDING
The Sherburne Trail is a great backcountry snowboarding descent. You don't even need snowshoes: the Tuckerman Ravine Trail is normally well packed, and the Sherburne Trail is downhill all the way.

HOW TO GET THERE
From Pinkham Notch Camp on NH 16, take the Tuckerman Ravine Trail 2.4 miles uphill to the Hermit Lake shelters. The Sherburne Trail starts across the wooden bridge that is next to the Hermit Lake caretaker's building (HoJo's).

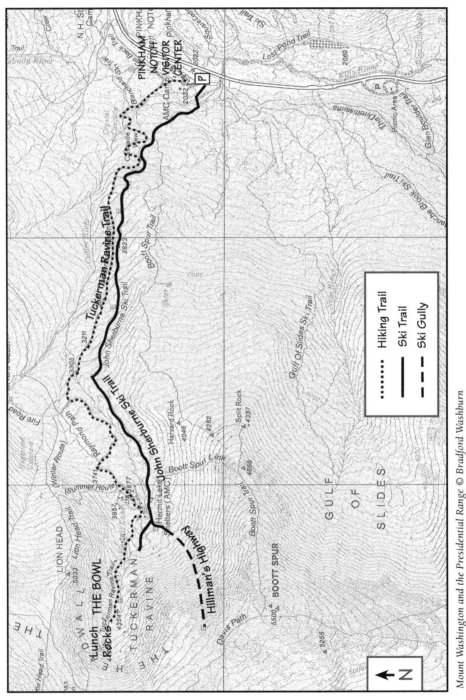

Mount Washington and the Presidential Range © Bradford Washburn

JOHN SHERBURNE SKI TRAIL

The John Sherburne Ski Trail is viewed by most skiers and snowboarders simply as the end-of-the-day run home after a day of skiing in Tuckerman Ravine. But the Sherburne deserves more attention than that. It is an excellent downhill run and a worthwhile destination in its own right.

The Sherburne Trail was designed and laid out by Charles Proctor and cut in 1934. It was named for John H. Sherburne Jr., a well-liked ski racer and member of the Ski Club Hochgebirge of Boston. Sherburne was instrumental in starting the famous "American Inferno" races in Tuckerman Ravine. He died unexpectedly of tetanus in 1934.

The need for a descending ski trail from Tuckerman Ravine was becoming more critical as the popularity of skiing in the Bowl increased. Before the Sherburne Trail was built, the Ravine was served only by the old Fire Trail, now known as the Tuckerman Ravine Trail. Skiing was always prohibited on the Fire Trail since it posed a serious threat to unsuspecting hikers ambling up the mountain. But Tuckerman Ravine regulars insisted that an alternative be found to walking downhill for more than 2 miles carrying skis. The solution then and now was the John Sherburne Ski Trail. The traffic rules that were established in the 1930s are still in effect today: Skiing downhill is strictly forbidden on the Tuckerman Ravine Trail, while the Sherburne is reserved solely for downhill skiing and snowboarding (that is, no snowshoeing or hiking, uphill or downhill, is permitted on the Sherburne).

The Sherburne is a wide trail that was cut with skiers in mind. There is ample room to choose your own line and ski it as you like. It is also the route that the rangers drive from Hermit Lake down to Pinkham Notch in their snow machines. This has a mixed effect. The snow machines pack the trail, so it holds snow longer, but the machines also create choppy tracks that can make skiing difficult. Fortunately, the Sherburne Trail catches many of the frequent storms on Mount Washington and is often replenished with a new layer of snow.

The route begins innocently enough 0.2 mile above HoJo's on flat terrain at the base of the Little Headwall. Early in the season it is possible to ski all the way from Tuckerman Ravine down to Pinkham Notch via the Little Headwall. Spring skiers may never know of the existence of the Little Headwall, since it has usually turned into a waterfall by late April. The Sherburne soon passes just south of HoJo's, separated from it by a wood bridge over the Cutler River. Most skiers who have come just to ski the Sherburne begin their descent at this bridge. The trail drops gently at the start. The views across the valley to the Wildcat Ridge and Carter Dome are worth stopping to admire. There are also impressive views back into both Tuckerman and Huntington Ravines to the west and northwest, respectively.

As with many trails of its era, the memorable moments on the Sherburne were all given names by the early skiers. The trail runs parallel to the south fork of the Cutler River but turns sharply southeast away from the drainage 0.6 mile below HoJo's. This turn is known as Windy Corner, and it was once the site of a cabin built by the Harvard Mountaineering Club. Windy Corner got its name

Skiing the Sherburne Trail, 1933. Photo by Winston Pote

because it was always blasted by wind from the ravines and was consequently icy and windblown. The U.S. Forest Service relocated the section of the trail at Windy Corner so it would be less exposed to the weather.

The Sherburne gets progressively steeper as it descends. At 1.6 miles, the S-Turn is reached. It is so named because the trail swings back and forth like the letter "S." From here down was considered one of the most difficult points of the Sherburne when races were held on it. Just below the S-Turn is the Schuss, a sharp left-hand turn with a steep, straight drop. The trail then passes through a sharp, narrow right-hand turn called the Bottleneck; then it goes into the Glade, an open, moderately steep slope. The final drop is Deadman's Curve, where the trail drops steeply and turns sharply to the right. This last section received its name in the 1930s when a skier hit a tree and was killed here. The tree was promptly removed. The steepest sections (up to 24 degrees) are encountered in the last third of the route. The trail is as much as 60 feet wide at this final section, so you are still left with many options as to how to negotiate the crux moves.

The Sherburne Trail can be deceptive. Over 2 miles of linking turns is no small feat at the end of a long day. This run can be a delight if you have the energy for it, and an endurance test if you've blown your strength having too much fun elsewhere during the day. It has certainly caught me off guard. I have skied this trail smiling one day and whining for my partners to wait up the next. Hence its well-earned nickname, the "sure burn."

The Sherburne Trail is an excellent introduction to down-mountain skiing for cross-country skiers who have learned to telemark at ski areas and want to try their skills in the mountains. Snowboarders will also enjoy this introduction to eastern trail riding. The trail is wide enough to take long turns, will certainly introduce you to some unpredictable snow conditions, and will call for some creative thinking in your approach to some of the natural obstacles.

Finally, the Sherburne Trail has the unusual distinction of being the gateway to one of the meccas of backcountry *glisse,* Tuckerman Ravine. If you are a newcomer to this sport, a side trip into the Bowl to see what you can aspire to ski or ride should give you new incentive to keep practicing your turns. The thrill of the steeps awaits you just around the corner.

Tuckerman Ravine

THE TOURS

A variety of very steep and extreme ski routes in and around Tuckerman Ravine on Mount Washington.

DISTANCE

From Pinkham Notch Visitor Center:

* ❄ 2.4 miles to Hermit Lake shelters
* ❄ 3.1 miles to floor of Tuckerman Ravine
* ❄ 4.2 miles to Mount Washington summit

ELEVATION

* ❄ *Start* 2,032 feet (Pinkham Notch)
* ❄ *Highest point* 4,400 feet (Tuckerman Ravine floor); 6,288 feet (Mount Washington summit)
* ❄ *Vertical drop* 4,256 feet from summit to Pinkham Notch

MAPS

AMC/Washburn *Tuckerman Ravine*, AMC/Washburn *Mount Washington/Presidential Range*, AMC Map 1 (Presidential Range), USGS Mount Washington (1982)

DIFFICULTY

Most difficult/mountaineering

SNOWBOARDING

Tuckerman Ravine is the most popular destination in the East for backcountry snowboarding. All routes described here can be snowboarded. The Tuckerman Ravine Trail is heavily boot-packed, so snowshoes are not needed to reach the Ravine (crampons may be useful on steep climbs that don't already have a boot track).

HOW TO GET THERE

Tuckerman Ravine is reached via the Tuckerman Ravine Trail, which leaves from the AMC Pinkham Notch Visitor Center on NH 16.

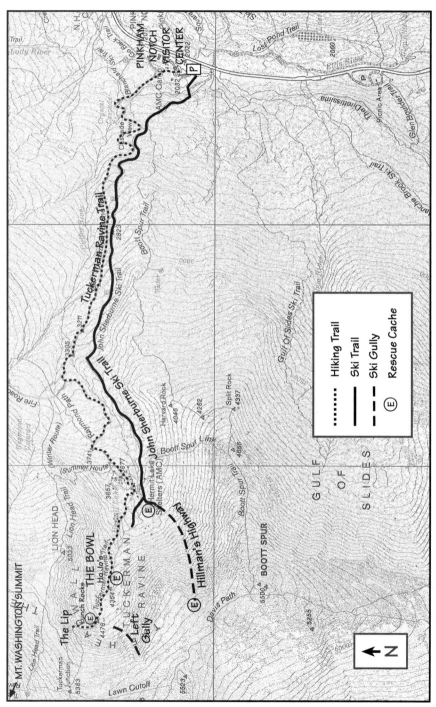

Mount Washington and the Presidential Range © Bradford Washburn

TUCKERMAN RAVINE

Tuckerman Ravine—referred to affectionately as "Tuck's," "Tuckerman's," or simply "the Bowl"—is where skiing legends have been made, broken, and made up. It is the home of some of the steepest established backcountry ski and snowboard runs in the country. The Bowl usually holds the last snows of the year, when every other place in New England has long since turned to rock and dirt. It is viewed by skiers alternately as a proving ground and a playground, depending on their abilities.

Tuckerman Ravine is actually a huge glacial cirque. It is shaped like a teacup, or bowl, that has been cut in half: the higher you go, the steeper the walls. The area is named for botanist Edward Tuckerman, who explored the White Mountains for two decades in the mid-1800s. Most of the snow that collects in the Bowl is deposited by wind, which generally comes out of the west-northwest and carries snow from the Bigelow Lawn and the Mount Washington summit cone. Snow on the floor of the Bowl may reach depths of 75 to 100 feet.

HISTORY OF SKIING IN TUCKERMAN RAVINE

No history of skiing in New England is complete without a look back at what has been going on in Tuckerman Ravine in the last century. Indeed, the skiing "firsts" in the Ravine serve as milestones in the story of how modern ski technique has evolved.

The first recorded skier on Mount Washington was a Dr. Wiskott of Germany, who wrote about his 1899 visit on skis to the mountain. Mount Washington was first skied from the summit in 1913 by Fred Harris, the founder of the Dartmouth Outing Club (DOC). He and a group of Dartmouth pals skied what is now the Auto Road. The following year, John Apperson, best known for being the first to ski Mount Marcy in the Adirondacks in 1911, reportedly skied up to Tuckerman Ravine. The era of ski exploration on the mountain began in earnest in the spring of 1926, when AMC hutmaster Joe Dodge and several of his friends ventured into Tuckerman Ravine on skis, skinning up and skiing the lower slopes of the Headwall. Among this first crew was the late Al Sise. Sise, a colorful figure who was still ski-racing until his death in 1992, once recounted to me the story of his first trips into the Bowl. "We were intimidated by the Ravine," he conceded. "It was a mighty impressive place—awe inspiring."

Former AMC Ski Committee chair William Fowler proclaimed on a radio show in 1934, "When we consider that this past summer people skied on the Headwall of Tuckerman's as late as July 4th, we realize that it is one of the seven wonders of New Hampshire, rivaling the Great Stone Face and the Flume."

Sise remembered the time when "there was nobody there—not a soul except us." This changed quickly and dramatically. The first skiers told their friends, who promptly told other skiers about the vast, challenging ski potential of the Ravine. Like any religious shrine, Tuck's required some sacrifice from its devotees: These first skiers had to bushwhack more than 3 miles up the Cutler River to reach the Bowl. As skier traffic increased, the AMC and the U.S. Forest Service were finally persuaded to construct the Fire Trail from Pinkham Notch to Hermit Lake in late 1932. This trail, now known as the Tuckerman Ravine Trail, is still the main thoroughfare for climbing up to the Bowl. The construction of the John Sherburne Ski Trail in 1934 made getting down from the Ravine even easier, enabling people to ski down from Hermit Lake to Pinkham Notch in less than 30 minutes when there was sufficient snow. Providing easy access in and out of the Bowl was a turning point in the history of skiing in Tuckerman Ravine.

By the early 1930s, the word had spread wildly among the budding ski community about Tuckerman Ravine. In 1930, the AMC ran its first ski trip to Tuck's. In April 1931, Dartmouth Outing Club skiers John Carleton (U.S. Olympic ski team, 1924) and Charlie Proctor (U.S. Olympic ski team, 1928) became the first to ski over the Lip of the Headwall down to the Ravine floor. By 1932, the snow trains from Boston to New Hampshire were ferrying more than 10,000 people per season to the North Country, and many of them were coming to ski in Tuckerman Ravine.

The first of three "American Inferno" races was held in the Ravine in 1933. It was reported in the June 1933 edition of the AMC journal *Appalachia:*

> The climax of the ski racing season this year was also another step in the conquest of Mount Washington under wintertime conditions. Up until this year the Headwall of Tuckerman Ravine, which is a drop of nearly a thousand feet, had been run by only a handful of people, . . . But this spring the snow was so unusually deep in the Bowl that the angle was perceptibly less and the Ski Club Hochgebirge of Boston [which included some of the best racers of the era] thought the time was ripe to conduct a race they had had in mind for some time—a summit-to-base run, including the Headwall. They christened it the "American Inferno," after a famous course at Murren, Switzerland.

Hollis Phillips of the AMC won the race with a time of 14 minutes, 41 seconds. Most of the other 10 skiers finished in about 20 minutes.

Skiing the Inferno was an amazing accomplishment even by today's skiing standards. The race course plunged more than 4,200 feet in about 4 miles. The first race started on the summit of Mount Washington, dropped into the Bowl via Right Gully, and continued to Pinkham Notch on the narrow Fire Trail.

As traffic increased into Tuckerman Ravine, skiing standards were pushed to new heights. The Inferno was the best gauge of this progress. In the second American Inferno, held in 1934, legendary Dartmouth racer Dick Durrance astounded the skiing community by winning in 12 minutes, 35 seconds. Yet no one could have predicted how dramatically this speed record would fall. It happened in the most famous race ever held in Tuckerman Ravine—the third American Inferno in 1939.

Toni Matt was an unknown in the American skiing world. A 19-year-old Austrian, he had just been brought to the United States to teach at the Cranmore Mountain Ski School in North Conway. He had never heard of Tuckerman Ravine, but when told about the race there, he was game to enter. The race was postponed twice due to bad weather. It was finally run on April 16, 1939. The summit conditions as the racers awaited their start were zero degrees Fahrenheit with a 60-mph wind. Matt caught his first glimpse of the Headwall as he climbed up it; he had never even seen the Sherburne Trail, which constituted the lower half of the race course. By contrast, his competitors, especially Durrance of the DOC, were veterans of numerous descents of the mountain.

What occurred next was to become one of the greatest moments in ski history. As an observer recounted in the December 1939 issue of *Appalachia*:

> An adequate description of Toni Matt's run cannot fail to take your breath away. From below in the Ravine, he was seen to come tearing down the cone in one long arc, and with one swoop that was hardly a check he dropped over the Lip of the Ravine, came straight down the headwall, across the floor, and on down the brook bed to the Sherburne Trail. On the trail he ran with an ease and abandon that left one gasping. He cut the corners close, never traveling an extra inch. His time of 6:29:2 practically halves any previous time, and he finished looking as fresh as when he left for the ascent four hours before.

Matt finished a full minute ahead of Durrance, who came in second. He simply took the Headwall straight, a feat few have dared to repeat. It is estimated that he hit 80 mph on his descent. Matt confessed later that he did not *plan* to *schuss* the Bowl:

> I figured I'm gonna make three or four turns over the Lip itself and on into Tuckerman Ravine. And before I knew it, I dropped over the Lip and there wasn't any *sense* in turning; it wouldn't slow me down anyway! I decided it's much safer to go straight than to go by turning on this kind of pitch and I was stupid enough and strong enough to be able to stand up. . .

A summit-to-base race such as the American Inferno has never been held again (bad weather has thwarted several other attempts). Toni Matt passed away in 1989 at the age of 69, one month after the golden anniversary of his epic descent. His record time lives on.

❄ ❄ ❄ ❄ ❄

The first era of ski exploration in the Bowl was in the early 1930s. Skiers from the Dartmouth College ski team would come every spring. The first descents of the classic lines—Right Gully, Left Gully, Chute, Hillman's Highway, and the Lip— occurred during this period, most likely by skiers from Dartmouth and Harvard.

Hillman's Highway was named for Harry Hillman, a Dartmouth skier who enjoyed exploring the less-traveled areas. The late Sel Hannah, a well-known local skier of the era and member of the Dartmouth team, told me, "Hillman was a colorful, wild guy and a damn good skier. Everybody would be over on the Headwall, but he used to go up there [to Hillman's Highway] all the time and promote it. So eventually a lot of other guys went over there too." Hannah, for his part, was responsible for the first descent down the Center Headwall in 1937–38.

The next major era of exploration in Tuckerman Ravine belonged to one remarkable man. Brooks Dodge was born in 1929 and grew up in the shadow of Mount Washington. He was the son of AMC huts manager Joe Dodge, and thus had the good fortune to live in Pinkham Notch. This upbringing was to serve him well. He first skied over the Lip at the tender age of 13. He went on to attend Dartmouth, was a member of that renowned ski team, and earned berths on two Olympic ski teams (1952 and 1956).

Dodge left his greatest mark on skiing in his own backyard. Between 1946 and 1952, Dodge had a singular passion: skiing the steepest, boldest, and most elegant lines on Mount Washington and the surrounding mountains. He made first descents of a dozen different routes, most of which were frighteningly steep. Dodge's Drop, which is left (as you look up) of Hillman's Highway, was named for him and is one of his best-known routes. Among others he was responsible for are Duchess (it had been skied once before him); Cathedral; Lion's Head Gullies 1, 2, and 3 (gullies between Right Gully and Lion's Head); Sluice; Boott Spur Gullies 1, 2, and 3 (gullies to the left of Dodge's Drop); and the Chute Variations (left and right, respectively, of Chute). His most difficult run was the Icefall, a route down through the cliffs just left of the Lip which forms only occasionally.

Dodge insists that he didn't have any agenda in his skiing conquests beyond satisfying his hunger for good skiing. "Each spring, I'd go up and do the ones where the snow was good," he told me. "I didn't have any specific goals to do them all. I just looked for the best skiing. I didn't like to ski where there was another track—I always liked smooth fresh snow."

"I never considered those runs worth a damn unless I could ski top to bottom without a stop," he said of his skiing ethic. He credited his ski achievements to the unusual technique that he developed. He insisted that the popular stem christie required too much space and did not provide the precise, controlled turns needed for skiing steep, narrow gullies. So he devised his "two-pole turn" for the steeps: a quick jump turn, "keeping your tips on the snow at all times and pivoting on the tips of your skis. You can turn very quickly in tight spaces," he explained. Dodge would also wait for what he considered to be safe snow conditions: one to one and a half inches of soft snow on a hard surface. He did all of his skiing on seven-foot-long, metal-edged hickory skis with cable bindings that were secured down by a heel latch.

Brooks Dodge raised the bar for skiing in Tuckerman Ravine to new heights. More than a half-century later, only a handful of modern skiers can match his turns (among them is his son, Brooks Dodge III, a noted ski photographer and prolific Mount Washington skier in his own right). His achievements confirm that what matters most in pioneering new mountain descents are creativity, tenacity, and boldness. High-tech equipment is no substitute for skill and passion. When Dodge began skiing in Tuckerman Ravine there were seven established routes; when he finished, there were nineteen. In the years since he made his mark, no major routes have been established in Tuckerman Ravine of the high standard and enduring quality of those skied by Brooks Dodge.

THE DHARMA OF TUCKERMAN RAVINE

The annual pilgrimage to Tuckerman Ravine is the world's grandest, oldest, biggest celebration of sliding on snow. Nowhere else on earth do people come together so faithfully and in such numbers to revel in the joys of snow. Tuck's is anathema to many of the values of modern society. It takes hard work to get there, there are no rules, dire consequences can follow from mistakes, and you have nothing to show for your courageous efforts save for a fleeting track in the snow. For this, people return again and again. In Tuck's, you are free.

Skiing in Tuckerman Ravine today is as exciting and heart-stopping as it ever was. The sensation of climbing the Headwall and standing at the top with your heart racing and palms sweating as you try to talk yourself into dropping into the fall line is repeated with each run and each step higher that you take. The first time you ski over the Lip into the Bowl will be a moment you remember for a lifetime. As Toni Matt recalled of his maiden voyage: "Going over the Lip is a terrifying experience, especially for the first time. It's like jumping into a 600-foot-deep hole from a speeding car."

A snowboarder starts down Left Gully.

Fear. It is an intoxicating part of the Tuck's experience. Fear is the mind's rational reaction to being in insane places. At best, fear has a useful moderating effect on behavior. At worst, it paralyzes you. The best skiers do not claim to conquer fear. They harness its energy, control it, learn when to heed it.

All the routes in Tuckerman Ravine are for expert skiers and snowboarders. Just because the skier before you skied something effortlessly doesn't mean that you can follow his or her tracks. The normal rules of gravity apply here: If you leap off a cliff and fall, or somersault down a rocky couloir, you are very likely to get hurt.

Warnings aside, every backcountry skier and snowboarder should make the pilgrimage to the Ravine at some point. The skiing, scenery, history, and terrain are unmatched. It is a place where ordinary folks shed their workaday persona and, for a moment, live large. Some return as heroes in their own minds, proud just to have survived the hike. Others return humbled, or inspired.

Being in Tuck's is not a wilderness experience in the traditional sense. On a nice spring weekend you are joined by thousands of fellow seekers. You will see people descending the Headwall on everything from downhill skis, telemark skis, and snowboards to inner tubes, rubber boats, plastic sleds, and rear ends. A circus? Perhaps. But this is the steep culture of Tuck's. Enjoy it. This is a celebration, after all, and it wouldn't be complete without the people.

TUCK'S NUTS & BOLTS: WHEN TO GO, WHAT TO BRING

THE SEASON

The prime skiing season in Tuckerman Ravine runs from late March to around Memorial Day. Skiing usually continues through June and often until the Fourth of July. As summer approaches, the terrain becomes more limited and the ski conditions get progressively more difficult. Warm spring days in Boston may be perfect spring skiing in the Ravine.

For tape-recorded weather and avalanche information for Tuckerman Ravine, call the AMC Pinkham Notch Visitor Center at 603-466-2727, or check the excellent Mount Washington Observatory website at www.mountwashington.org.

HOW TO GET THERE

From the AMC Pinkham Notch Visitor Center on NH 16, it is a three-mile hike up to the bottom of Tuckerman Ravine.

"ARE WE THERE YET?"

It typically takes the fittest hikers about two hours for the climb; slower-moving parties usually take about three hours or longer, depending on pace. The descent from the Bowl to Pinkham Notch takes about 45 minutes if you can ski all the way down the Sherburne Trail. If the Sherburne is closed and you have to hike, it will take about an hour.

"Is it open?"

Tuckerman Ravine is always open. The U.S. Forest Service has jurisdiction over Tuck's. In the past, rangers would close the Ravine when they deemed that snow conditions were hazardous. After years of criticism from skiers and climbers, the USFS abandoned this policy in 1982. In the mountaineering spirit, each person must now decide for him- or herself what, where, and when they can ski. Even during periods of extreme avalanche danger, you will likely be warned (via a ranger or a posted sign) that conditions are unsafe, but no one will stop you. This is as it should be—long live the freedom of the hills.

What to bring

This is a backcountry area. There is no food or shelter in Tuckerman Ravine. Bring plenty of water—consider bringing two liters on hot days. You can refill your water bottle in the Cutler River at Hojo's (no guarantees, but the water is generally safe here). Pack food, and bring storm gear. It is colder and wetter in the Bowl than at the trailhead. Be prepared for winter conditions, especially if you plan to hike above the Lip. If you will be hiking anywhere outside the Bowl (i.e., above treeline), you should carry a map and compass—whiteouts and fog are common around the Mount Washington summit.

Where to stay

If you plan to spend several days skiing in Tuck's, you may as well stay in the neighborhood. For people interested in camping out, there are eight shelters at Hermit Lake (next to Hojo's) with room for 84 people. Five of the shelters are enclosed, and the other three are open-air affairs. There are also three tenting sites in the woods near Hermit Lake. The lean-tos and camping sites are filled on a first-come, first-served basis. You can buy a ticket to stay overnight at Hermit Lake in the AMC Pinkham Notch Visitor Center, so you will know before you hike up whether there is room for you. On spring weekends, all sites are usually filled by Friday night. Camping is forbidden anywhere else in the area.

If cooking over a camping stove and crashing in a sleeping bag is not your style, you can stay in bunk-bed comfort at the AMC Joe Dodge Lodge, located right at the trailhead in Pinkham Notch. The epic all-you-can-eat meals are famous. Call ahead for reservations at 603-466-2727. Finally, there are numerous inns and hotels within a 15-minute drive of Pinkham Notch. You can obtain info and make reservations by contacting the Mount Washington Valley Chamber of Commerce and Visitor's Bureau at 800-367-3364, or on the web at www.4seasonresort.com.

How to ski

The most important thing to bring with you to Tuckerman Ravine is common sense. Use good judgment and be realistic about what you can do here. Rather than being hell-bent on "going over the Lip" at all costs, try another goal: skiing well. Work on making good, controlled turns on lower-angle slopes, gradually moving up to steeper terrain as you improve. Learn to read corn snow: Notice how it changes throughout the day, and adapt your technique to the different types of snow that you encounter. Figure out when the snow is best to ski. You will soon progress from just getting down the Headwall to actually being able to ski it—one of the greatest thrills in Tuckerman Ravine.

MOUNTAIN HAZARDS

Tuckerman Ravine is not Disneyland. There are real mountain hazards to contend with. As of 1998, 31 people have been killed skiing in Tuck's. Following are some mountain hazards to watch out for.

AVALANCHE

There is often significant danger of avalanche in the Ravine and on all surrounding gullies early in the winter or just after a snowstorm. Check the posted avalanche warnings in Pinkham Notch or at Hojo's. The final assessment of the avalanche hazard rests with each skier. Look for signs of avalanche activity around the Bowl; a recent slide is a warning sign of snow instability. Gullies that are crowned by a new cornice are probably wind-loaded and should be avoided. If you have reason to be concerned about the stability of the slope, ski a different line, or confine your skiing to the Sherburne Trail. A number of people have been killed or seriously injured by avalanches in the Ravine.

ICEFALL

On warm spring days, refrigerator-sized ice blocks come tumbling down the Headwall. The danger of falling rock and ice is especially high on warm days. Choose your picnic spot carefully: Look above you to see what you may be subjected to and avoid the most exposed places. Have an escape route (e.g., a large rock you can duck behind). Lunch Rocks is especially prone to icefall—heads up.

CREVASSES

As the spring progresses, the snow in the steep gullies and in the Bowl becomes undermined and crevassed. Give crevasses and holes a wide berth when skiing or climbing near them. Avoid routes that have crevasses. Crevasse falls are extremely serious, and extrication can be difficult or impossible.

SUN

The solar assault in the Bowl can be intense. You are simultaneously baked and broiled: sunshine gets you from above, and reflected sun can burn you from below. Wear sunglasses, sunscreen, and lip protection. Serious sunburn is a common problem, even in winter.

FALLING

If you fall when skiing or snowboarding, get your skis or snowboard downhill. Attempt to self-arrest by setting your steel edges hard into the slope, and/or driving the tip of your ski pole into the snow and putting your weight on it like an ice axe. Then breathe deep, say three Hail Mary's, and pray.

SKI AND SNOWBOARD ROUTES IN TUCKERMAN RAVINE

The skiable routes change from day to day and year to year in Tuckerman Ravine. A gully that you skied in perfect corn one day may be an icy luge run the next. Let the prevailing conditions—not your fond memories—dictate where you point your skis.

Several critical factors influence the difficulty and location of skiing in Tuckerman Ravine. Snow conditions, the hour of day, the depth of the corn snow, the firmness of the base, and the runout (in case of a fall) should all be taken into consideration when deciding where to ski in the Ravine. The steepness of each route varies from year to year depending on snow depth. Runouts also change: Rocks that menace you one year can be buried beneath the snow the next.

Tuck's can be cruel. You may make the long drive and even longer hike only to discover that the sun is not shining and the snow is hard. *The steepest routes in Tuck's should only be skied in good snow conditions.* Corn snow is best and safest, along with "Styrofoam" snow that can be edged; skiing on a bulletproof or icy snow surface can be suicidal on the steeps. Look for where the sun is shining, and anticipate whether your route will be in shadow after the hour it takes you to hike up to the top. This is part of the art of skiing here—predicting and responding to the ever-changing personality of the mountain. Treat the mountain with respect and you will be rewarded with a great skiing experience. Get cocky and ignore danger signs, and you could pay a stiff price.

ROUTES IN THE BOWL

(**Note:** Directional references are as you look up from the bottom of the Ravine).

A few orienting points in the Ravine: The Tuckerman Ravine Trail delivers you to the floor of **THE BOWL**. This refers to the Ravine proper, the bowl-shaped basin of snow which most of the gullies empty into. **LUNCH ROCKS** is the large area of boulders on the lower-right side of the Bowl. This is the gathering spot (or bleachers) for the vocal crowd of spectators who cheer on each skier and applaud the antics of people on the Headwall.

The most popular runs on the Headwall vary each year, depending on snow conditions in the Ravine. Following are the main routes around the Bowl. The first two routes, the Headwall and the Lip, are the most prominent and popular runs and are thus listed first.

THE HEADWALL

The most distinctive feature in the Ravine is the Headwall. The Headwall has a vertical drop of 800 feet from the Lip to the floor of the Ravine. The Headwall gets progressively steeper as you climb it. It starts out at 30 degrees at the bottom, then steepens to 40 degrees just below the rock band in the upper center of the Headwall. You can ski anywhere on the Headwall, provided there are not crevasses. Less experienced skiers can simply climb the lower slopes to the level they feel comfortable, then ski down.

Access: The most common routes climb to the left and right end of the rock band, stopping below the cliffs. Climbing up directly below the rock/ice cliffs in the spring is inadvisable due to the danger of icefall.

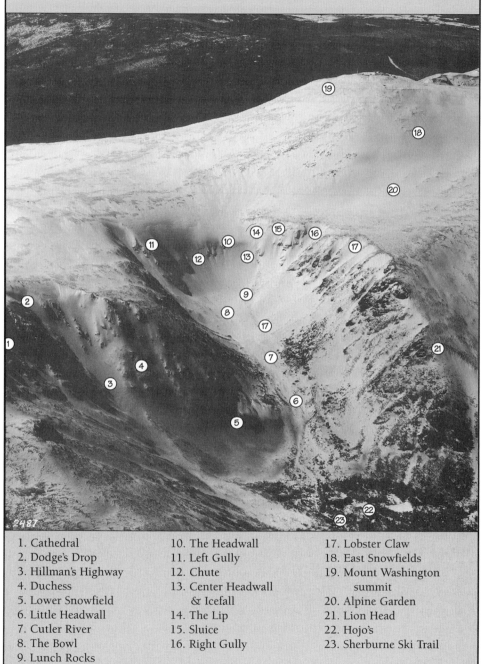

KEY TO ROUTES AROUND MOUNT WASHINGTON AND TUCKERMAN RAVINE

1. Cathedral
2. Dodge's Drop
3. Hillman's Highway
4. Duchess
5. Lower Snowfield
6. Little Headwall
7. Cutler River
8. The Bowl
9. Lunch Rocks
10. The Headwall
11. Left Gully
12. Chute
13. Center Headwall & Icefall
14. The Lip
15. Sluice
16. Right Gully
17. Lobster Claw
18. East Snowfields
19. Mount Washington summit
20. Alpine Garden
21. Lion Head
22. Hojo's
23. Sherburne Ski Trail

Tuckerman Ravine photo © Bradford Washburn, courtesy of Panopticon Gallery, Boston, MA

126

THE LIP

Skiing over the Lip and into the Bowl is the classic test piece of Tuck's. The Lip is on the upper-right side of the Bowl, the broad slot that forms above Lunch Rocks and to the right of the rock band. From the Alpine Garden above the Bowl, you glide gently across the flats, and then drop precipitously over the Lip. Earth falls away, sky rushes up to greet you, and your heart lodges in your throat. Late in the spring, the Lip melts and separates from the headwall and is no longer skiable.

Access: Climb up straight above Lunch Rocks toward the right side of the Lip. The slope gets progressively steeper until you exit the Bowl onto the Alpine Garden, a relatively flat area of alpine grass and sedge above the Ravine.

✳ *Length of run* 0.25 mile

✳ *Vertical drop* 700 feet

✳ *Pitch* 45–55 degrees, depending on snowpack

EAST SNOWFIELDS

Above the Lip are the gentle grades of the Alpine Garden. The long moderate slopes of the East Snowfields rise above the Alpine Garden on the Mount Washington summit cone. On clear days this is the sunniest, most relaxed ski terrain on Mount Washington. It is a good destination for skiers and snowboarders who are just getting their backcountry legs under them.

Access: The snowfields can be reached by climbing up the Headwall over the Lip, or more commonly, by ascending Right Gully.

✳ *Length of run* 200 yards

✳ *Vertical drop* 400 feet

✳ *Maximum pitch* 30 degrees

The following routes are listed in the order they are skied, from left to right.

LEFT GULLY

This is a beautiful long, classic, alpine gully that runs from the Bigelow Lawn to the floor of the Bowl. The main body of Left Gully is just out of view of Lunch Rocks, behind the large rock buttress left of Chute. With its northeastern exposure, this is one of the best and longest-lasting spring runs; I have skied Left Gully nearly from the top in early July. The headwall at the top right side of Left Gully occasionally forms a cornice that has been measured at 55 degrees, which would make it the steepest measured pitch of any run in the Ravine (without this cornice the Left Gully headwall is 45–50 degrees). In practical terms, this means you will be airborne between your first few turns. If you prefer terra firma, you can put on your skis just below this final steep pitch.

After the sheer entrance, the upper gully is a wide ballroom. The pitch relaxes and the gully narrows into a 20-foot-wide hourglass between towering rock walls in the center. This bottleneck is the most dramatic part of the run. The gully then reopens for its final turns all the way to the Ravine floor. Left Gully is avalanche-prone in mid-winter, since it gets corniced and wind-loaded.

Access: To reach Left Gully, you can climb up directly from the floor of the Bowl, or traverse across the Headwall below the Chute and then climb directly up the gully.

✳ *Length of run* 0.25 mile

✳ *Vertical drop* 800 feet

✳ *Maximum pitch* 55 degrees

THE CHUTE

The Chute is the big, bold, in-your-face line that forms the left edge of the Headwall. The huge top-to-bottom exposure of this gully makes it the most intimidating looking of all the runs. "Like skiing off the edge of a cue ball," is the apt way Brooks Dodge III describes it. Chute starts innocently on the Bigelow Lawn; you cannot see the route from the top. The route steepens gradually as you ski towards the edge of the Headwall, then it suddenly plunges straight down. Once you get started, you cannot turn back. A menacing rock buttress on skier's right bulges into the steep center section of the descent, forming an hourglass. Unlike the Lip, where skiers frequently take dramatic tumbles but only bruise their egos, a fall in Chute will likely have consequences. The lower-angle top section is usually wind-scoured, with snow quality improving as you descend into the Bowl. A star-struck audience on Lunch Rocks applauds the few skiers with the nerve—or ignorance—to perform on this run.

Chute also has several variations. Brooks Dodge's original Chute Left Variation descended from the snowfield between Left Gully and the main Chute and went all the way down to the main slope of the Ravine. This line rarely has enough snow to ski. The more common Chute Left Variation today angles from the snowfield on the upper left and enters the main Chute above the hourglass. Chute Right Variation drifts out towards the center-left side of the Headwall.

Access: The fastest approach is to climb up over the Lip and ski across the Bigelow Lawn to the top of Chute. Climbing directly up Chute is much more time-consuming, strenuous, and nerve-racking.

✳ *Length of run* 0.25 mile

✳ *Vertical drop* 750 feet

✳ *Maximum pitch* near 50 degrees

CENTER HEADWALL AND ICEFALL

These are the most technical ski routes in Tuckerman Ravine. An ice-covered cliff band separates the top of the Headwall from the more gradual slopes above the Ravine. The Center Headwall runs are actually left of center; dead center on the Headwall is a cliff. The two Center Headwall routes go right and left, respectively, around large rocks. This whole area in the center of the Headwall is very disorienting as you ski down into it. The key to skiing here is to *locate reference points as you climb up.* As you ski down, you must aim for these points, or risk getting lost and cliffbound.

The Icefall route forms sporadically through the rock band just left of the Lip. Brooks Dodge, who first skied this line, insists that this route no longer fills in enough to enable a descent "while remaining in contact with the snow at all times."

These are true extreme ski routes. The descents through Center Headwall and Icefall require intimate local knowledge of the terrain and perfect snow conditions. Skiing or riding through this area requires 5 to 25 feet of mandatory air. These routes are rarely skied by anyone other than a handful of Tuck's veterans. Great skiers and snowboarders have wisely backed off these routes. You probably should too.

Access: Climb via the Lip, and traverse left.

✳ *Length of run* 0.2 mile

✳ *Vertical drop* 900 feet

✳ *Maximum pitch* 55+ degrees

SLUICE

Sluice lies directly above Lunch Rocks, between the Lip and Right Gully. It is one of the steepest pitches in the Bowl. In its upper section the slope bulges out and becomes convex before easing back for its direct run at Lunch Rocks. The top of Sluice reaches high onto the Alpine Garden. If you are skiing down from the summit, Sluice is the most direct line (but not the easiest) from the East Snowfields into the Bowl. The top section is highly prone to avalanche or slough.

Access: The access to Sluice is to either climb straight up it or take an easier climb up neighboring Right Gully. From the top of Right Gully, walk to the Alpine Garden Trail, turn left, walk about five minutes, and Sluice leaves directly from the hiking trail. The top can be difficult to find; step out and make sure you are in the right place before heading down.

✳ *Length of run* 0.25 mile

✳ *Vertical drop* 800 feet

✳ *Maximum pitch* 50 degrees

RIGHT GULLY

An elegant straight chute that begins at Lunch Rocks and rises directly north, Right Gully was one of the first routes to be skied in the Ravine. It is wide at the top and remains fairly generous throughout its length. It bulges out steeply at the bottom where it joins up with Sluice. Be extra cautious when skiing in firmer snow conditions. The runout—right into Lunch Rocks—is unforgiving.

Right Gully is the easiest route to climb up out of the Ravine if you are headed to the summit. This route is prone to avalanche. It gets wind-loaded from the summit winds; avoid skiing here when there is a new cornice on top. Since it is facing south, it tends to have wet snow sloughs and loses its snow early in the spring.

Access: Ascend the gully from the bottom.

❈ *Length of run* 0.25 mile

❈ *Vertical drop* 800 feet

❈ *Maximum pitch* 40 degrees

LOBSTER CLAW (OR, RIGHT RIGHT GULLY)

This is the next prominent chute to the right of Right Gully. It derives its name from the way it breaks into two arching fingers at the top, resembling a lobster claw. The top of Lobster Claw is higher than the Lip, so it affords spectacular views over the Ravine. Lobster Claw is about 10 feet wide in its upper section, and the run maintains a comfortable consistent pitch of 35 degrees. Like Right Gully, this is a sunny south-facing run that builds good corn snow.

Access: Climb up the ski route from the bottom.

❈ *Length of run* 0.25 mile

❈ *Vertical drop* 800 feet

❈ *Maximum pitch* 35 degrees

ROUTES AROUND HILLMAN'S HIGHWAY

Rising directly from just beyond Hojo's on the left is the prominent long alpine gully known as Hillman's Highway. It is the main attraction in an area surrounded by a number of prominent descents. Following the Hillman's description, the routes are described from Boott Spur to Little Headwall (left to right).

HILLMAN'S HIGHWAY

Hillman's Highway is the longest of the routes around Tuckerman Ravine, with a vertical drop of 1,500 feet. It was first skied by Dartmouth skiers Harold Hillman and Ed Wells in the mid-1930s. Hillman's is less traveled since it is out of the Bowl proper and lacks the cheering section found at Lunch Rocks. That is part of its appeal: Hillman's is a place to get away from the "madding crowds" in the Bowl.

Hillman's has two entrances at the top. The left fork (when climbing up) is the steepest section of the run, around 43 degrees. The grade on the right fork starts more gradually, but then steepens to about 40 degrees and enters a rock-lined, 15-foot-wide narrows. The run then opens up to as much as 100 feet (depending on snow levels) for the lower two-thirds of the descent. There is plenty of room to make turns. But be careful when the sun is not shining on Hillman's. People have taken long unplanned rides on frozen snow here.

From the top of Hillman's there are nice views into Tuckerman Ravine of the Chute, the Lip, Right Gully, and Lion's Head. It is possible to hike up out of Hillman's to access Oakes Gulf, or to drop down into Tuck's (Left Gully is closest). The reverse is also possible: You can hike up out of Left Gully to go to Hillman's. If you are walking over from Tuck's on the Davis Path, look for a rescue cache in a cylindrical steel container that is just east of the trail. The top of Hillman's lies just below this. Hillman's Highway can be a nice final run. The gully ends at the Sherburne Trail, from where you can continue directly to Pinkham Notch.

Access: From Hojo's, cross the bridge over the Cutler River and turn right (west) on the Sherburne Trail. Follow the trail uphill, bearing left after a rescue cache. Hillman's Highway is the prominent snow gully that continues all the way up to the ridge.

❋ *Length of run* 0.6 mile

❋ *Vertical drop* 1,500 feet

❋ *Maximum pitch* 43 degrees

CATHEDRAL

This couloir is the narrow slot that plunges down directly from the summit of Boott Spur. It is located on the slope that forms the left (southern) boundary of Hillman's. There are two entrances from the top; the one on skier's right has the

Descending the top of Hillman's Highway (Wildcat Ski Area is in the background).

easier (lower angle) start. The gully connects with the bottom section of Hillman's Highway. Cathedral has several ice bulges in it and needs a lot of snow to be skiable. The climb up can be ornery, involving postholing through vegetation at the bottom before reaching the firmer snow. This north-facing line loses sun quickly, so it is best skied at mid-day when the snow is soft.

Access: The best access is to climb up from the bottom, starting on Hillman's Highway.

❋ *Length of run* 0.2 mile

❋ *Vertical drop* 700 feet

❋ *Maximum pitch* near 50 degrees

DODGE'S DROP

This ultra-steep gully was Brooks Dodge's signature run. It is the prominent line to the left of Hillman's Highway. When Dodge first skied it in the mid-1940s, his friends met him at the bottom and suggested that he give it an alliterated name, in the fashion of Hillman's Highway. "How about Dodge's Drop?" his friend proposed. Dodge liked it. "I'm not unhappy that a run is named after me," Dodge told me, "and I'm pretty happy with that run, too."

As well he should be. Dodge's Drop is a run that seasoned Tuck's die-hards aspire to ski. It is a frighteningly steep and committing descent. The top of the chute is almost always corniced. There are two entrances that merge into a narrow main gully. The top turns are about 50 degrees, and they are often rocky; a fall in the first 60 yards will likely result in a slide into rocks. After the two upper fingers merge, you enter a narrow chute that leads to an ice bulge between some rocks. This is the crux of the route; you must ensure that there is enough snow to ski over the ice flow. From here the gully opens and the pace relaxes. It goes over some bushes and merges onto Hillman's Highway.

Access: The easiest access to Dodge's Drop is to climb to the top of Hillman's Highway, then hike left to the top of Dodge's.

❋ *Length of run* 0.2 mile

❋ *Vertical drop* 700 feet

❋ *Maximum pitch* 50 degrees

DUCHESS

The broad rocky buttress that separates Hillman's Highway from the Bowl in Tuckerman Ravine is home to the Duchess. Looking up from Hojo's, Duchess lies just right of Hillman's. Its most dramatic feature is its funnel-like lower section that empties onto the Lower Snowfield. The route was first skied by Brooks Dodge in the mid-1940s. He named it after the Duchess Trail, a faint abandoned path that climbed from the Little Headwall to the top of Boott Spur and passed by the top of what is now the Duchess ski route.

Duchess greets her suitors by terrifying them: As you stand at the top, you look over your ski tips and peer straight down at Hermit Lake, 1,500 feet below.

There is no mistaking how high you are and how steep the route is. Making matters worse, you can't see the descent route beyond the first snowfield. The route is wide to start but narrows quickly. The skiable line drifts to skier's right, then back to the center. The route descends through a series of funnel-like chutes, some just wider than a ski length, before finally emptying out onto the Lower Snowfields. The maximum pitch is around 50 degrees.

Access: Climb Hillman's Highway. From the top, hike skier's left onto the prow of the buttress, where Duchess drops down.

✳ *Length of run* 0.3 mile

✳ *Vertical drop* 800 feet

✳ *Maximum pitch* 50 degrees

LOWER SNOWFIELD

The Lower Snowfield is the broad slope between Little Headwall and Hillman's Highway. This area can be skied on its own, or used to traverse between Hillman's and the Bowl.

Access: From Hojo's, ski up towards either Hillman's Highway or the Little Headwall, and you will run into the Lower Snowfield.

✳ *Length of run* 0.3 mile

✳ *Vertical drop* 700 feet

✳ *Maximum pitch* 35 degrees

LITTLE HEADWALL

This short pitch forms on the Cutler River on the way up to the Bowl. When the Little Headwall is in, it is possible to ski from the Bowl directly onto the Sherburne Trail. By springtime, it has usually turned into a waterfall, making it necessary to hike back down to Hojo's on the Tuckerman Ravine Trail.

Access: From the bottom of the bowl, bear right of the Tuckerman Ravine Trail, staying in the Cutler River drainage. The Little Headwall is a short steep drop halfway down the trail to Hojo's.

✳ *Length of run* 100 yards

✳ *Vertical drop* 150 feet

✳ *Maximum pitch* 35 degrees

Note on ski route data: Information on length of run, vertical drop, and maximum pitch is drawn from several sources: the U.S. Forest Service, measurements that I have personally taken, and slope pitch measurements taken over a period of years by several other veteran Tuckerman Ravine skiers. Data on maximum pitch can vary greatly from year to year. Where different sources conflict, I have chosen the source that I believed to be the best indicator of a route's difficulty relative to other runs.

Great Gulf

THE TOURS
Airplane Gully and Pipeline Gully are steep, elegant couloirs that descend one of most dramatic alpine ravines of the White Mountains.

DISTANCE
❄ 0.5 mile

ELEVATION
❄ *Start/highest point* 5,500 feet (Airplane); 5,533 feet (Pipeline)
❄ *Finish* 4,357 feet (Spaulding Lake)
❄ *Vertical drop* 1,100 feet

MAPS
AMC/Washburn *Mount Washington/Presidential Range*, AMC Map 1 (Presidential Range), USGS Mount Washington (1982)

DIFFICULTY
❄ Most difficult/mountaineering

SNOWBOARDING
These are superb steep mountaineering-oriented snowboard descents for expert riders.

HOW TO GET THERE
From Pinkham Notch: Climb to the summit of Mount Washington (4.2 miles, via either Tuckerman Ravine Trail or Lion Head Trail), from where it is another 1 mile north on the Gulfside Trail to the Westside Trail junction, which is near the top of Airplane Gully. From the west, you can take the Jewell Trail from the Cog Railway Marshfield Base Station (4 miles to Westside Trail junction).

The Marshfield Base Station can be reached via the plowed Mount Clinton Road (opposite the AMC Crawford Notch Hostel). The Mount Clinton Road is

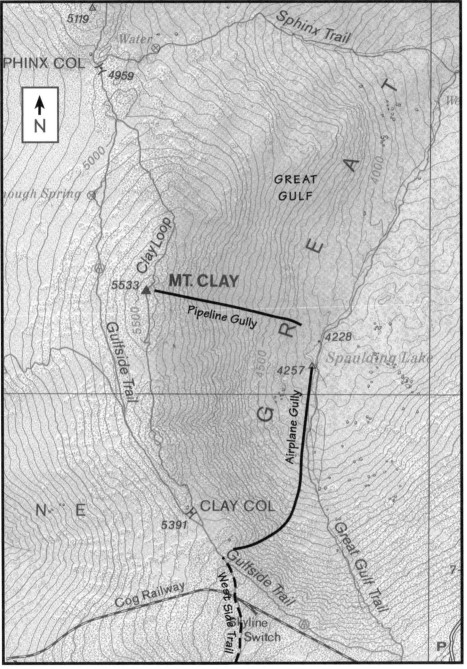

GREAT GULF

officially open only to Cog Railway employees in winter. The Cog Railway permits hikers and skiers to drive on this road, but you travel at your own risk; the road conditions will not be as manicured as NH 302. The Base Road from NH 302 is not plowed during the winter; it opens the last week of April.

The Mount Washington Auto Road (603-466-3988), which usually opens in mid-May, also offers access to the Great Gulf. Park at the 7.5-mile parking area and hike around the top of the Gulf on the Gulfside Trail.

The Great Gulf is the largest glacial cirque in the White Mountains. The walls of this massive ravine extend east 3.5 miles. The headwall is bounded on its south side by the Mount Washington summit cone, and on the west by the flanks of Mount Clay (5,533 feet). The Great Gulf drops over 1,600 feet from its rim to Spaulding Lake, which lies on the valley floor. This entire area lies within the 5,552-acre Great Gulf Wilderness, established in 1964.

The Great Gulf is one of the wildest places in the White Mountains. According to the *AMC White Mountain Guide,* Darby Field, who is credited with the first ascent of Mount Washington in 1642, made the first recorded observation of the Great Gulf. The name is credited to Ethan Allen Crawford, who, in 1823, got lost in cloudy weather on Mount Washington and reported coming to "the edge of a great gulf." Laura and Guy Waterman write in *Forest and Crag* that a Boston newspaper observed in 1909 that "until the present summer, the Gulf has remained almost as unknown as it was inaccessible."

For skiers, the remoteness of the Great Gulf in winter has been at once its attraction and its deterrent. There is simply no easy way to "get there from here." One indication of its out-of-the-way character is that the ski history of the Great Gulf has never been recorded. Photographer Winston Pote has stunning photos of skiing on the rim of the Great Gulf in 1938 and 1940, but there is no indication that Pote or his friends actually descended into the Gulf. The credit for first descents of all the major routes in Great Gulf may go to Brooks Dodge, the author of numerous firsts in Tuckerman Ravine, who skied six major gullies in the Great Gulf in the mid-1940s. Among them were what he called Clay Col Gully (now Airplane) and Clay Summit Gully (now known as Pipeline).

For those skiers who make the effort, the Great Gulf holds many rewards. Standing on the rim of the Great Gulf, you peer out over the wildest reaches of the White Mountains. The northern peaks of the Presidential Range—Mounts Clay, Jefferson, Adams, and Madison—stand like inaccessible beacons from here. To reach them requires traveling along the exposed spine of the Whites. They appear so close, yet are so far.

The terrain of the Great Gulf is remarkably alpine. A series of couloirs rake the rocky headwall. Many are hidden away, revealing themselves by surprise. You will be hiking or skiing along, when suddenly a spectacular corridor unfolds beneath you, offering passage through the vertical world of rock and ice. In summer, watery cascades tumble down the sides of the Great Gulf. In winter, these become skiable gullies. In any given winter, some gullies may form and others not. Such is the fickle character of these high mountain environs. I have skied couloirs in the Great Gulf that have appeared one year, only to vanish until several years later. Each trip into the Gulf is a surprise.

Airplane Gully is the most prominent and striking line of descent in the Great Gulf. The gully got its name from an incident on October 2, 1990, when an airplane crashed right at its top and tumbled down into the Great Gulf, killing three people. The wreckage was removed, but it is still possible to see the remnants of colored metal or glass lying on the ground at the top.

The top of Airplane Gully lies just north of the junction of the Gulfside and Westside Trails. A truck-sized boulder sits just northeast of the trail junction; below the boulder, a prominent 50-foot-wide gully plunges down the side of the Great Gulf. From the top of the gully, there is a vast sweep of land. There are views to the west of Mount Mansfield and Camel's Hump, of the Northern Peaks of the Presidential Range, and beyond to the more gentle contours of the Mahoosuc Mountains.

Dropping into the Great Gulf.

Airplane Gully begins with a bang. A cornice often forms on the top, forcing skiers to either ski through it or jump off. The top is about 50 feet wide, with a pitch of 44 degrees. The entrance can be intimidating, but there is plenty of room for turns . . . for now, that is. The gully gets narrower as you descend. Large boulders choke off the midsection to about 15 to 20 feet in width. Below this waist, the gully doglegs to the left, opens up, and continues plunging all the way to Spaulding Lake. The total vertical drop is 1,100 feet. However, most skiers stop well above Spaulding Lake in order to shorten the hike back up. The final few hundred yards to the lake are brushy.

Mount Clay lies north of Airplane Gully. Clay is a minor summit of Mount Washington, rising only 150 feet from the surrounding ridge. But Mount Clay has dramatic views and exceptional skiing. The rocky east face of Mount Clay is streaked with skiable gullies. The most prominent is Pipeline Gully. It departs directly from the Mount Clay summit and plunges straight down to Spaulding Lake. The entrance to Pipeline is about 20 feet wide with a gradual pitch, but it steepens and chokes off quickly to the width of a ski where a large rock juts in. The route remains narrow, drops over a waterfall, and empties onto snowfields above Spaulding Lake. Pipeline has a fairly consistent pitch of 40 degrees.

There are many other skiable gullies in Great Gulf as you walk south along the rim of the ravine. Two hundred yards south of Airplane is a steep headwall that drops into a wide snowfield, from where it is possible to join up with the lower part of Airplane. Continuing south, there are some shorter gullies that are not quite as steep. In good snow years it is also possible to ski on and around the Great Gulf Trail. Many of these gullies have several different names given them by locals; Airplane and Pipeline are the only ones that have stuck.

Skiers must take care to evaluate snow conditions in Great Gulf before jumping in. The gullies are prone to avalanche (I rode a small wet snow slide here in May 1997), and should be avoided after storms. Airplane Gully has a northeastern exposure and can take a while before the snow softens. Skiing steep rocky terrain when the snow is hard leaves you no margin for error. On the other hand, the Great Gulf is a pleasure to ski on sunny spring days.

A journey into the Great Gulf is a venture to the wilder side of the White Mountains. The first taste will spark your imagination about the vast skiing potential of the more remote high terrain of New England.

16

Oakes Gulf

THE TOURS

The sunny, south-facing gullies in Oakes Gulf offer wilderness skiing in a stunning remote glacial cirque. Double Barrel is a very steep gully located on the west side of the ravine.

DISTANCE

❋ Gullies range from 0.2 to 0.5 mile in length

ELEVATION

❋ *Start/highest point* 5,100 feet
❋ *Finish* 4,700 feet (main gully); 4,300 feet (Double Barrel)
❋ *Vertical drop* 400–800 feet

MAPS

AMC Map 1 (Presidential Range), AMC/Washburn *Mount Washington/Presidential Range*, USGS Mount Washington (1982)

DIFFICULTY

❋ Most difficult/mountaineering

SNOWBOARDING

Oakes Gulf offers fine steep riding. You will ride down a gully, then hike up and out the same way.

HOW TO GET THERE

From Pinkham Notch, it is 4.6 miles to the AMC Lakes of the Clouds Hut via the Tuckerman Ravine/Tuckerman Crossover Trails, and about the same distance via Hillman's Highway and the Davis Path. The shortest approach to Oakes Gulf is via the Ammonoosuc Ravine Trail, which ascends from the Mount Washington Cog Railway Marshfield Base Station. It is 2.4 miles from the Base Station to the AMC Lakes of the Clouds Hut, from where it is another 0.2 mile on the Dry

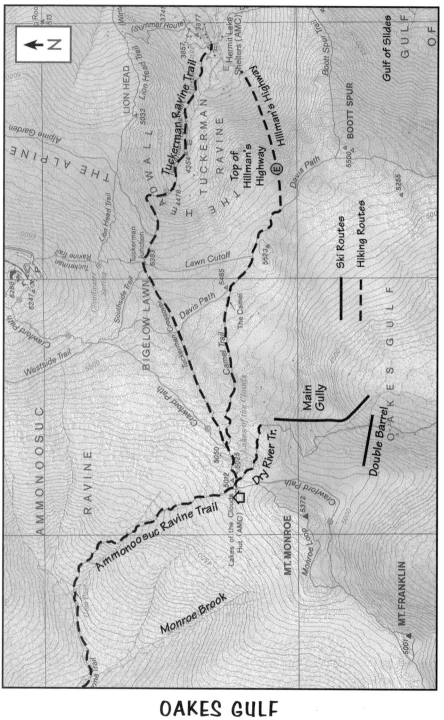

Mount Washington and the Presidential Range © Bradford Washburn

OAKES GULF

River Trail to the top of Oakes Gulf (see information about winter access to the Marshfield Base Station in the previous chapter).

Oakes Gulf is a large glacial cirque that bounds the south side of the Mount Washington summit cone. It resembles a vast horseshoe ringed by 5,000-foot peaks. Oakes Gulf has a special appeal among the remote ravines. This south-facing basin is a sunny getaway from the more traveled ski destinations such as Tuckerman Ravine. The ski gullies in Oakes Gulf are shorter and not quite as steep as found elsewhere, but the beauty and isolation of this place, combined with the soft spring snow, make for a memorable day of backcountry skiing and riding.

Oakes Gulf is defined by Boott Spur on the east and Mount Monroe on its western boundary. It cradles the Presidential Range–Dry River Wilderness, a 27,380-acre tract of land established by Congress in 1975. Oakes Gulf is named for William Oakes, a botanist who began studying the White Mountains in 1825. Brooks Dodge skied four or five gullies in Oakes Gulf during the mid-1940s. These may have been the first ski descents here; the ski history, like the place itself, is obscure.

The extra effort required to reach Oakes Gulf keeps traffic to a trickle. But on fine spring weekends I usually encounter a few other intrepid ski explorers here. As with the Great Gulf, the least arduous and most direct route to Oakes is from the west side of Mount Washington, via the Ammonoosuc Ravine Trail. The trail climbs steeply at the top; it is easiest to remove skis and walk up the steep pitches. Once at the Lakes of the Clouds Hut, continue on the Dry River Trail 0.2 mile to a height-of-land. As you begin to descend from here, you are sliding into Oakes Gulf.

The most popular ski route in Oakes Gulf is this main entrance gully. The Dry River Trail drifts right, while an obvious snow gully heads directly down to the valley floor. The gully begins gently and steepens briefly to about 38 degrees. This passageway is wide enough that less experienced skiers can feel comfortable swinging longer turns or traversing. The gully drops 350 vertical feet before reaching light vegetation. Most skiers stop at this line of scrub and hike back up this or another nearby gully. For more vertical, you can continue down a narrow, lower-angle gully of open snow through the scrub as far as you like. It is about 1,000 vertical feet of skiing from the top of the gully to the valley floor of Oakes Gulf.

For skiers who lust for the thrills found in Tuckerman Ravine but don't want the crowds, Oakes Gulf offers Double Barrel. This is a steep gully with two distinct channels that plunges down into the Gulf from a long ridge off Mount Monroe (5,372 feet). To reach Double Barrel, take a high traverse from the Main Gully around the west side of the bowl. You may have to scramble across some bushes, but you will eventually arrive at snowy chute that drops all the way to the ravine floor. This is the left "barrel" of Double Barrel. It is 45 degrees at the top, moder-

Dropping into Oakes Gulf from the Dry River Trail.

ating as you descend. This left side of the gully is about half the length of the right side, and a narrow rock ridge separates them.

The right side of Double Barrel begins at the rim of Oakes Gulf, at about 5,000 feet. The view down the gully is unnerving from here: The right chute pinches off to about 5 feet between large rocks midway down and you cannot see what lies beyond. This right "barrel" starts at about 38 degrees, quickly pitching up to 45 degrees. It then opens up and empties out onto the valley floor about 800 vertical feet below. As with any steep mountaineering gully, you should hike up from the bottom to assess snow conditions, as well as to take the full measure of your courage.

The hike up the west flank of Oakes Gulf is worthwhile just for the views. Nearby ski areas such as Wildcat and Attitash appear insignificant out here. Mount Washington appears as a large white rock pile to the north. Impressive large cliffs block the passage in the center of the Oakes Gulf headwall. The multiple summits of Boott Spur meld into the sprawling Bigelow Lawn. These flat grasslands tumble down into long gullies that rake the headwall of Oakes Gulf. These long white chutes all appear tantalizingly skiable. Oakes Gulf suddenly looks much bigger than it did from the valley floor. It is a place you could return many times to explore on skis or a snowboard and not come close to exhausting its potential.

The walk along the Mount Washington summit ridges over to Oakes Gulf on a calm, clear day is spectacular. But the remoteness of Oakes Gulf often deters skiers, and with good reason. The Mount Washington summit area is not the place to be in a storm or a whiteout. If weather is moving in, make an early exit and head back down a trail that gets you below treeline quickly. Note that the Lakes of the Clouds Hut is closed for the winter. Be sure to have a map and compass (and know how to use them), as whiteouts up on this ridge are common.

From the bottom of Oakes Gulf, you can climb out the Main Gully next to the Dry River Trail and return the way you skied here. From the top of Double Barrel, you can walk a short distance due east to intersect the Crawford Path. Turn right, and you will arrive back at Lakes of the Clouds Hut. From here, you can backtrack your route. If you have come up from the Marshfield Base Station, you can ski the Ammonoosuc Ravine Trail, or loop back by skiing down Monroe Brook, on the north side of Mount Monroe. After a 0.3-mile bushwhack at the bottom, Monroe Brook intersects the Ammonoosuc Ravine Trail 1 mile east of the Marshfield Base Station.

PEMIGEWASSET WILDERNESS REGION

The area in and around the Pemigewasset Wilderness is home to some of the most scenic and isolated backcountry skiing in New England. The official Pemigewasset Wilderness Area consists of 45,000 acres, designated as wilderness in 1984. It is one of the few places in New England in which multi-day ski trips can be undertaken without crossing roads. There are numerous possibilities for long ski tours in this area. Skiers can link day after day of high-quality touring and still not come close to exhausting the potential of this region.

The highlights of skiing in "the Pemi" include gaining access to high mountain ponds that are rarely visited in the winter; spectacular views of the Franconia Ridge to the east and the Presidential Range to the north; and a sense of isolation that is unusual in the heavily traveled mountains of the Northeast. All this is complemented by the fact that the skiing in the Pemi is exceptional—for the most unlikely reason.

Ironically, the trails in the Pemi owe their high quality to the fact that they were once the access routes for overzealous timber barons who ravaged the region at the turn of the century. Skiing along the Thoreau Falls Trail or the Shoal Pond Trail, observant skiers may notice that the trees on the parallel-sided paths would not grow as they do by accident. The first time I skied down the tunnel-like passageways, I could not help but imagine that I was skiing down railroad tracks, which I dismissed as poetic fancy. But my mind's eye was right: miles of railroad tracks built by logging tycoons indeed once crisscrossed the Pemigewasset Wilderness. The story of these early lumbermen and their wilderness railroad empires is told in fascinating detail by C. Francis Belcher in his book *Logging Railroads of the White Mountains* (AMC, 1980).

The Zealand Valley and the Pemigewasset River Valley caught the eye of J. E. Henry, the most famous and colorful logging boss in New Hampshire history. In 1884, Henry opened the Zealand Valley Railroad, which plied the route now covered by the Zealand Road (FR 16) from NH 302 all the way through Zealand Notch to Shoal Pond—a distance of more than 10 miles. Henry employed up to 250 people, housing them in small villages established deep in the woods of the Zealand Valley. Little trace now remains of these logging camps. Even the town of Zealand, once a bustling business center that had its own post office (it was located just west of the current Zealand Campground), has vanished into the brush.

Henry's legacy in the Zealand Valley was one of ecological devastation. Beginning in 1886, large quantities of slash caused the first of several catastrophic fires that swept through the valley all the way up the slopes of Whitewall and Zealand Mountains. The clearcutting and fires prompted one writer to dub the area "Death Valley" early in this century. Belcher quotes an 1892 newspaper editorial from the *Boston Transcript:*

> The beautiful Zealand Valley is one vast scene of waste and desolation; immense heaps of sawdust roll down the slopes to choke the stream and, by the destructive acids distilled from their decaying substance, to poison the fish; smoke rises night and day from fires which are maintained to destroy the still accumulating piles of slabs and other mill debris.

The ecological recovery of the Zealand Valley is nothing short of remarkable. Along the trail to the AMC Zealand Falls Hut today, the forest has regenerated with birches and other second-growth trees, and the area is now home to the largest lynx population in the state. Some evidence remains of the destruction that once reigned there, but it is no longer the blight it once was.

Henry's attention was next brought to the vast lumbering opportunities that lay just south of Zealand Notch in the Pemigewasset Valley. In the mid-1890s, Henry began focusing his efforts on logging this virgin wilderness. Once again, the railroad was the preferred means of transporting people and lumber. Henry oversaw the construction of rail lines from what is now the Kancamagus Highway (NH 112). The trains ran north alongside the East Branch of the Pemigewasset River to 13 Falls, and east over what is now the Wilderness Trail to beyond Stillwater Junction. Logging trains would normally make two round trips a day between Lincoln and the logging camps. In the summer, a fare of 75 cents was charged to bring tourists in to see the vast logging operations. Belcher quotes from a 1926 book:

> On gala days in the height of the summer season two or three flat cars used to be rigged up with extemporized railings and filled with chairs, and a hundred or more excursionists made the trip up into "Henry's Woods," to wonder at the new mountains and valleys, exclaim over the winding road, marvel at the various camps, and raid the cook's quarters for hot doughnuts.

Despite the criticism that may rightly be leveled at Henry for his plunder, skiers will appreciate that his rights-of-way endure as a well-constructed bed for the trails on which they now ski. As Belcher notes, "Even today the drainage ditches along these sections are doing a fine job of handling rainfall runoff. . . . Past, present, and future trampers [and skiers!] in these areas stride along easily where Henry's laborers sweated profusely for his avenue to a fortune."

The tours described here are by no means the only "classic" routes in the Pemi. They represent a sampling of the high quality of skiing and the unique aesthetics of the area, covering a full range of difficulty. Some of the routes are most easily done from a base camp either at the AMC Zealand Falls Hut or from a campsite, while others can be comfortably done in a day from a trailhead.

PARKING

A White Mountain National Forest parking permit is required at all trailheads in the Pemigewasset Wilderness (see page 43). Parking permits may be purchased at the USFS Visitor Information Center at the Lincoln Woods trailhead on the Kancamagus Highway.

MAPS

The best map of the Pemigewasset Wilderness region, including all the tours described in this section, is AMC Map 2 (Franconia-Pemigewasset). It is worthwhile to use the most current edition of this map since a number of trails have been rerouted or renamed in recent years. The DeLorme *Trail Map & Guide to the White Mountain National Forest* is also a good color map of the entire region.

USGS maps of the Pemi often do not include the most updated information, so I have omitted listing them on these tours.

SNOWBOARDING IN THE PEMI

Mount Hale is an excellent expert snowboard tour. It is the only tour in this section that is rated for snowboarding.

The other tours in the Pemigewasset Wilderness that are described here are not suitable for riding. The Pemi is characterized by gentle rolling terrain—great for cross-country ski touring, but not much vertical for snowboarding. However, some of the high peaks that border the Pemi, including the summits of the Franconia Ridge, offer good, steep riding, but in a very remote setting.

Zealand Falls Hut Tour

THE TOUR
The Zealand Road (from NH 302) and the Spruce Goose Trail lead to the Zealand Trail and the AMC Zealand Falls Hut.

DISTANCE
❋ 6.2 miles to the hut

ELEVATION
❋ *Start* 1,500 feet
❋ *Highest point* 2,600 feet (Zealand Falls Hut)
❋ *Vertical gain* 1,100 feet

MAPS
AMC Map 2 (Franconia-Pemigewasset); U.S. Forest Service sketch map *Zealand Valley Cross-Country Ski Trails,* usually posted at trailhead.

DIFFICULTY
❋ Moderate

HOW TO GET THERE
From the junction of NH 3 and 302 in the town of Twin Mountain, drive east 2.3 miles to a sign for the Zealand Campground on the right. Parking is in a plowed lot on the north side of the road, a quarter-mile east of the trailhead. The route begins on the unplowed Zealand Road (FR 16), which has a large gate across it.

A ski trip to the AMC Zealand Falls Hut is one of the best of the few hut tours in New England. The AMC Zealand Falls Hut is one of only two AMC mountain huts that are open in the winter (see "Carter Notch Hut Tour" chapter for

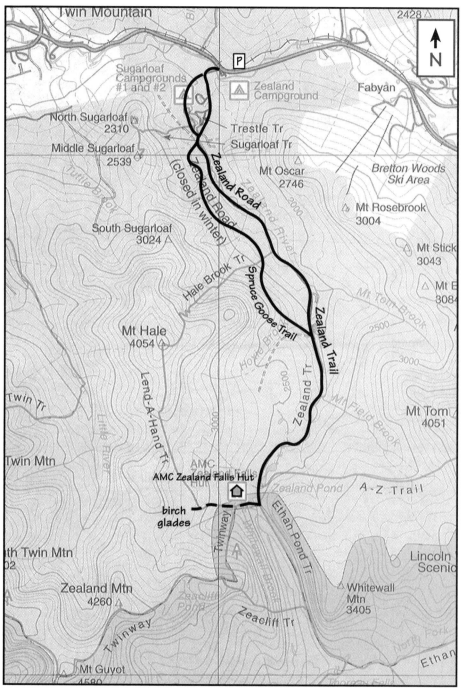

AMC Map 2 (Franconia–Pemigewasset)

ZEALAND FALLS HUT TOUR

the other one). From the Zealand Falls Hut, skiers have easy access to a number of excellent day trips that travel deep into the Pemigewasset Wilderness. The hut may be used as a base for a day trip, or as one stop on a multi-day ski trip through the Pemi.

The concept of hut-to-hut travel in the winter has unfortunately never been seriously developed in New England. Huts have long been the preferred means of mountain lodging in Europe. This tradition has only recently caught on in the United States, notably with the excellent Tenth Mountain Trail in Colorado.

The benefits to skiers of hut-hopping are many: being able to travel with light packs for several days while covering long distances, gaining access to remote wilderness, and meeting other winter travelers who can offer ideas and suggestions on interesting routes to seek out. The Zealand Falls Hut provides New England skiers with a taste of this experience.

The route to the hut begins on the gated and unplowed Zealand Road (FR 16) and finishes on the Zealand Trail. There are two ways to reach the Zealand Trail: ski on Zealand Road for 3.5 miles to the junction with the Zealand Trail, or take the Spruce Goose Trail 4.1 miles to reach the same trail junction. Most people opt for the shorter route. For variety, you can do both: ski the road on the way into the hut, and ski the trail out.

If you opt to ski the Spruce Goose Trail, you will start on the Zealand Road, cross the Ammonoosuc River on a bridge, pass a trailhead for the Flat Iron Ski Trail, and 50 feet later come to the blue-blazed Spruce Goose Ski Trail. This trail was constructed in 1977 by the Young Adult Conservation Corps so that skiers could be separated from snowmobilers on the Zealand Road (snowmobiles have since been rerouted onto their own trail, which lies east of the road). The Spruce Goose winds its way through the woods parallel to the road, about 600 feet away. The Spruce Goose Ski Trail is not the most scenic trail, crossing as it does through a number of recently logged areas. These clearings can be a good place to spot wildlife.

At 0.8 mile from the start, the trail passes through the Sugarloaf II campground. Bear around to the right side of the campground, and the Spruce Goose continues into the woods at the second Trestle Trail sign on the right. Shortly after the campground, the trail joins the Zealand Road for several hundred feet in order to cross the Zealand River on a bridge, reentering the woods on the right just beyond the bridge. The trail continues on easy, rolling woods terrain, before ending at the Zealand Campground and rejoining the Zealand Road on another bridge.

From the last bridge, you leave the road and continue on the Zealand Trail. From the bridge, it is 2.7 miles to the hut, following the old railroad grade for about a mile. The trail passes alternately through tunnels of birch and tall, sparsely wooded second-growth forest. Zealand Notch comes into view as the trail winds around beaver ponds and open meadows, evidence of the wildlife that has repopulated the area.

The AMC Zealand Falls Hut lies at the top of a small knoll just west of the trail. The hut was built in 1932 and was renovated in 1989. It was intended to link the western AMC huts with those in the Presidential Range to the northwest. It gets its name from the cascades on Whitewall Brook, which are just below the hut.

There are several nice glades to ski near the hut. The so-called Caretaker Glades—a favorite of Zealand Hut caretakers—are just west of the hut as you ski toward the Lend-a-Hand Trail. About 0.8 mile up the Zeacliff Trail is the top of a long birch glade that can be skied back down towards the hut.

OTHER OPTIONS

For another hut-based skiing option, there is a yurt-to-yurt ski trail system that opened in 1998 in the Phillips Brook Backcountry Recreation Area near Lancaster, NH. For information, contact 800-TRAILS8.

Zealand Notch Tours

THE TOURS
Ski from the AMC Zealand Falls Hut through Zealand Notch to Thoreau Falls and Shoal Pond, with an option to continue down to the East Branch of the Pemigewasset River.

DISTANCES
Round trip from AMC Zealand Falls Hut:
* 4.8 miles (Thoreau Falls)
* 7 miles (Thoreau Falls and Shoal Pond)
* 16.8 miles (East Branch of Pemigewasset River)

ELEVATION
* *Start/highest point* 2,637 feet (Zealand Falls Hut)
* *Lowest point* 1,800 feet (East Branch of Pemigewasset River)
* *Vertical drop* 837 feet

MAP
AMC Map 2 (Franconia–Pemigewasset)

DIFFICULTY
* Moderate

HOW TO GET THERE
This route can be accessed from AMC Zealand Falls Hut (see previous chapter, "Zealand Falls Hut Tour") or from the Wilderness Trail (see "Pemigewasset River Tours" chapter).

Zealand Notch is one of the most dramatic land formations in the White Mountains. It was once a typical V-shaped stream-eroded valley. But the ice sheets that covered New England gouged their way down to the ocean and left Zealand

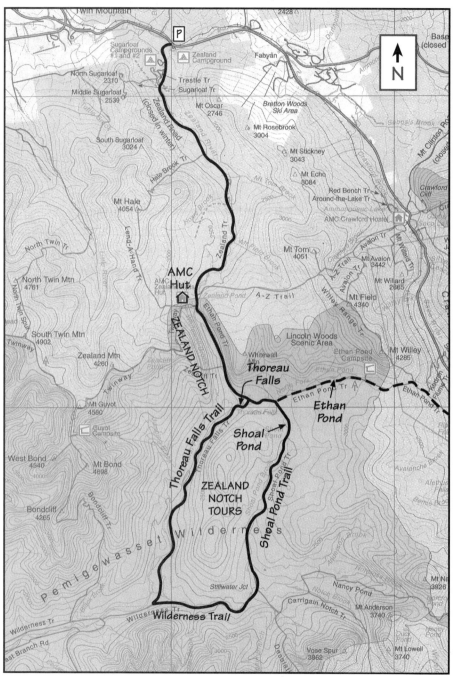

AMC Map 2 (Franconia–Pemigewasset)

ZEALAND NOTCH TOURS

Notch with the characteristic U-shape of glacial valleys. The notch becomes more impressive as you enter it. The steep rock walls of Whitewall Mountain jut overhead to the north, the blocky refuse of the glacier lies strewn about the valley floor, and the tree-covered slopes of Zealand Mountain rise to the south. A typical ski tour through the notch will usually involve stopping every few minutes just to marvel at the views.

One of the classic ski tours of the White Mountains is the trip through Zealand Notch to Thoreau Falls and Shoal Pond. You can extend this into a tour of the heart of the Pemigewasset Wilderness by continuing down the valley to the Pemigewasset River.

From the Zealand Falls Hut, the Ethan Pond Trail follows the old railroad bed of J. H. Henry's Zealand Valley Railroad into the notch. The trail contours at 2,500 feet along the sparsely vegetated sides of Whitewall Mountain, the name of which presumably derives from the chalky color of the cliffs on its flank. Old scars from the huge fires that swept through here at the turn of the century are still visible on the rocks. The trail offers clear views of Mount Hale and the Mount Hancock–Carrigain ridge and glimpses of the expanse of wilderness that lies just beyond the southern end of the notch.

Skiing across the steep slopes of Whitewall Mountain can be disconcerting if the snow is firm or icy. The trail narrows in width to about 3 feet in places and drops off rather steeply, keeping you on your edges on some exposed sections.

From the southern end of the notch, you have several choices. If you are going to Thoreau Falls, turn right on the Thoreau Falls Trail and reach the falls in 0.1 mile. Thoreau Falls is an icy, snow-covered cascade that drops off precipitously, providing a sweeping view of Mount Bond, Mount Guyot, and the Zealand Ridge (in heavy snow years, expert skiers have skied the falls). Consider adding a jaunt over to Shoal Pond to your tour before returning to the hut. Shoal Pond is about a mile from Thoreau Falls. It is 3.6 miles from the pond back through Zealand Notch to the hut.

If you are skiing the long loop to the Pemigewasset River, the best way is to descend on the Shoal Pond Trail to the Wilderness Trail and return via the Thoreau Falls Trail. The Shoal Pond Trail drops gradually over its 4-mile length, making it a pleasant cruise. The Thoreau Falls Trail is fairly flat, save for a short steep section just south of the falls. Trail signs clearly mark the way all along this route. This tour is long, but the terrain is gentle enough that strong skiers will enjoy the extended stretches of kick-and-glide skiing. If you are breaking trail just after a storm, it may be overly ambitious to try to cover all this ground in a day. In any case, you will need an early start in order to complete the tour in daylight.

Starting down the Shoal Pond Trail, you soon come to the isolated mountain pond that lies at 2,500 feet. High ponds are some of the most special places in the mountains. After skiing through the deep woods, the sensation of coming out onto a long, white, empty clearing with expansive views of Mounts Carrigain and Hancock is breathtaking.

The Shoal Pond Trail in the Pemigewasset Wilderness.

Traveling down the Shoal Pond Trail is one of the best ways to experience skiing the old railroad beds. The Zealand Valley Railroad came down through Zealand Notch all the way to Shoal Pond, with a spur to Ethan Pond. From the early 1900s until the 1920s, the East Branch & Lincoln Railroad was making two round trips a day between Lincoln and Camp 21, which was located on Shoal Pond Brook about a mile north of Stillwater Junction. The tracks continued a half-mile north of the camp to Labrador Brook. This area was once so devastated by logging that is was known grimly as the Desolation Region. As this tour demonstrates, nature has been remarkably resilient.

The ski tour continues through Stillwater Junction, once a major switching point and river crossing for the logging trains. Bearing east on the Wilderness Trail, it is 2.6 miles to the junction of the Thoreau Falls Trail. The Thoreau Falls Trail is flat for most of its length, traveling down some of the abandoned rail beds on the east side of the North Fork of the Pemigewasset River. Two major logging camps were once located on this route, although most of the tracks were on the opposite (west) side of the river from where the trail is now. The only trace of the activity that once thrived here can be seen in the scattered remains of bridge abutments along the river. The trail climbs up steeply just before Thoreau Falls.

The classic quality of this ski tour lies in the variety of terrain covered. Mountain ponds, abandoned railroads, babbling brooks, wide rivers, and waterfalls create an amazing array of scenery for one tour. Thanks to the logging tycoons, the skiing is excellent. And unlike other routes that start and end at a highway trailhead, skiing deep in the Pemi is a true wilderness experience. Long, uninterrupted views of mountain peaks that stretch for miles are not part of many New England ski tours. This trip to the heart of the Pemi is a chance to see the White Mountains at their wildest.

OTHER OPTIONS

The trip through Zealand Notch to Ethan Pond is another popular and pleasant tour day trip. It is 9.6 miles round-trip from the hut to Ethan Pond.

Skiers can opt to ski south from Zealand Hut and continue straight out the Wilderness Trail and Lincoln Woods Trail to the Kancamagus Highway. It is 15.7 miles from the hut to the highway.

19

Mount Hale

THE TOUR

A ski ascent of 4,054-foot Mount Hale on the historic Hale Brook Trail. The open summit has spectacular views over the Pemigewasset Wilderness and surrounding mountains.

DISTANCE

❋ 9.4 miles round-trip from NH 302 trailhead via the Hale Brook Trail

❋ 14.3 miles via AMC Zealand Falls Hut, the Lend-a-Hand Trail, and the Hale Brook Trail

ELEVATION

❋ *Start* 1,500 feet (NH 302)

❋ *Highest point* 4,054 feet (Mount Hale)

❋ *Vertical drop* 2,554 feet

MAP

AMC Map 2 (Franconia–Pemigewasset)

DIFFICULTY

❋ Most difficult

SNOWBOARDING

Mount Hale is an excellent expert snowboard descent. It demands nimble narrow-trail riding. Its one drawback is the hike in and out on the flat Zealand Road. Snowshoes are needed to climb Mount Hale. Consider staying at the AMC Zealand Notch Hut to make this an overnight tour. See "Zealand Falls Hut Tour" chapter for details.

HOW TO GET THERE

From the Zealand Road/NH 302 trailhead, ski south 2.5 miles on the Zealand Road or the parallel Spruce Goose Trail. Zealand Road crosses Hale Brook, and shortly thereafter the Hale Brook Trail (signed) climbs up fairly steeply to the right (west).

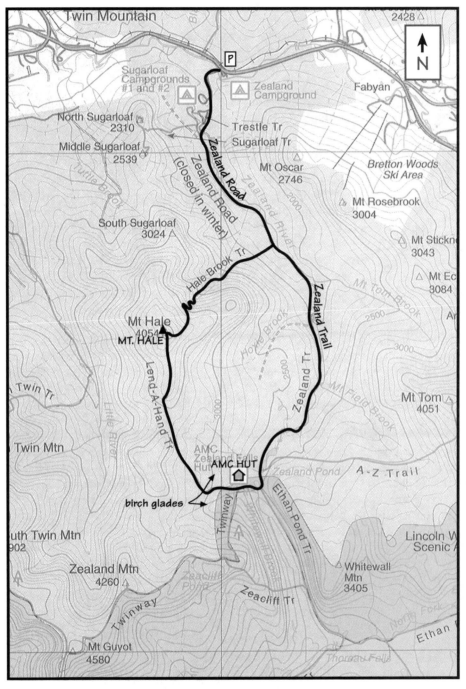

MOUNT HALE

From its bald, rocky summit, Mount Hale has spectacular views over the White Mountains. The scenery ranges from the peaks and valleys of the Pemigewasset Wilderness to the south, all the way to the Presidential Range in the north. Early fire wardens recognized that the mountain had a unique vantage point, and evidence of an old firetower can still be found on the summit. The mountain gets its name from the Rev. Edward Everett Hale, who authored the short story "Man without a Country" and was a frequent explorer of the White Mountains in the 1800s.

Mount Hale caught the eye of skiers from the earliest days of White Mountain ski exploration. Arthur Comey, who was the first to ski Katahdin, wrote in the AMC journal *Appalachia* in 1932: "The USFS Mount Hale Trail provides one of the finest runs in the White Mountains. The trail was built for a tractor, so that it has a good grade, just suitable for fast downhill running, with wide enough turns."

Mount Hale can be skied in two ways: as a day trip, or as a challenging alternative route out from the Zealand Falls Hut. Day skiers can start from NH 302 and climb and descend the Hale Brook Trail to the summit. From the AMC Zealand Falls Hut, the best access is the Lend-a-Hand Trail.

From the hut, climb around back on the Twinway for a short distance to where the Lend-a-Hand diverges right. It is 2.7 miles to the Mount Hale summit from this junction. Within a half-mile of steady but gradual climbing, the trail enters a large, open birch glade. Known as the Caretaker Glades, this is a favorite run of the hut staff and it begs to be skied. The trail climbs gradually until attaining the ridge that runs south off the Hale summit. The ridge has occasional open ledges and views, and a few very steep pitches that are most easily negotiated by climbing without skis if the snow is not too deep.

From the panoramic summit of Mount Hale, the Hale Brook Trail drops off steeply to the east. The trail is narrow at first, but it soon enters some open birch stands and begins some long switchbacks that traverse across steep slopes. The grade gradually lessens, but the trail never gets much wider than about 15 feet. The route demands an ability to link quick turns in a confined space or to be proficient at checking your speed without the option of wide, sweeping turns. The trail crosses the Spruce Goose Trail, which can be skied back to NH 302. The trail ends on the Zealand Road, from where it is 2.5 miles back to NH 302.

The descent of Mount Hale is a favorite among some avid White Mountain skiers. The route is very lightly traveled in winter by either snowshoers or skiers, partly because of its remoteness and difficulty. This tour is for strong skiers and snowboarders, and a party should have gear along to deal with the unexpected. The reward of journeying to where others don't go is that this is often a reliable powder run, even when other trails have only a light snow cover.

Pemigewasset River Tours

THE TOURS

This is an ideal tour for beginner skiers: skiing alongside the scenic Pemigewasset River on the Lincoln Woods Trail and Wilderness Trail, returning on the East Side Trail. A longer tour around Mount Hitchcock starts on the Kancamagus Highway (NH 112) on the Hancock Notch Trail, continues on the Cedar Brook Trail, and ends on the Lincoln Woods Trail.

DISTANCE

❋ 10.8 miles (Lincoln Woods Trail/Wilderness Trail–East Side Trail)
❋ 12.1 miles (Hancock Notch–Cedar Brook–East Side Trail)

ELEVATIONS

❋ *Start* 2,129 feet (Hancock Notch Trail); 1,157 feet (Lincoln Woods Trail)
❋ *Highest point* 3,100 feet
❋ *Vertical drop* 2,000 feet (Mount Hitchcock loop)

MAP

AMC Map 2 (Franconia–Pemigewasset)

DIFFICULTY

❋ Moderate

HOW TO GET THERE

The Lincoln Woods trailhead is located at a large parking lot 4.1 miles east of the White Mountain National Forest information center off the I-93 exit in Lincoln. The Lincoln Woods Visitor Information Center has maps, information, and hot drinks, and sells the necessary parking passes. The Hancock Notch trailhead is 5 miles east of this parking lot, just past the hairpin turn on NH 112.

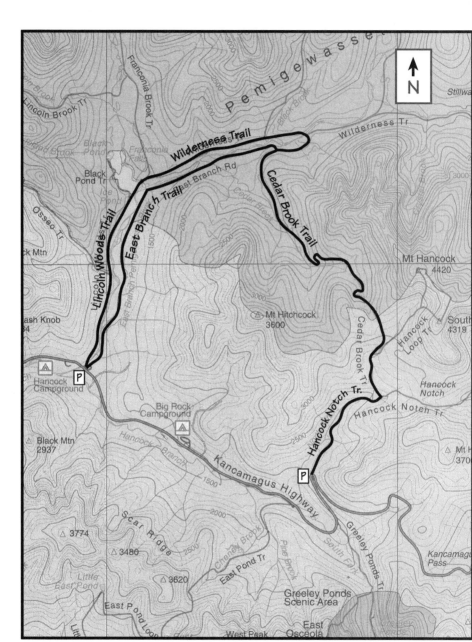

AMC Map 2 (Franconia–Pemigewasset)

PEMIGEWASSET RIVER TOURS

The Lincoln Woods Trail is probably the most popular ski tour for newcomers to the White Mountains. The trail was formerly named the Wilderness Trail. The U.S. Forest Service renamed the segment from the Kancamagus Highway to the Pemigewasset Wilderness boundary (at the Franconia Brook crossing, 3.2 miles from the road) the Lincoln Woods Trail; it is still called the Wilderness Trail to the east of Franconia Brook. This was done to demarcate where the official wilderness area started. The renaming was also intended to ensure that visitors did not expect the heavily used lower section of trail to be wilderness—at least not the solitary variety. As with most popular destinations in the mountains, the busy Lincoln Woods Trail attracts people for good reason.

The Lincoln Woods Trail is the gateway to the Pemigewasset Wilderness. On busy weekends, numerous cross-country skiers travel this scenic route. This trail was the main line of the logging railroads a century ago. The old railroad ties still constitute the foundation of this heavily trekked thoroughfare. The trails in the area of the East Branch of the Pemigewasset River and around Mount Hitchcock are generally wide and well graded, as they had to be to accommodate the many trains that plied the routes. The setting of the Lincoln Woods Trail makes for a classic cross-country ski tour as it travels alongside the wide river on nearly flat terrain. If your real joy in being on skis is just kicking and gliding for miles, this is the place to stretch out and cruise, while enjoying an exceptionally beautiful backdrop.

Two day trips showcase this area. The first is the tour up and down both banks of the East Branch of the Pemigewasset River. The tour starts and finishes at the Lincoln Woods Visitor Information Center located on the Kancamagus Highway. You can obtain maps and information here, as well as a hot drink. Head out on the Lincoln Woods Trail. The trail is groomed on weekends by the U.S. Forest Service up to the wilderness area boundary (3.2 miles in), so it should make for fast cross-country skiing. The Pemigewasset River meanders alongside the trail, offering glimpses of the peaks beyond. After crossing a bridge over the Franconia Brook, a sign informs you that you are entering the official Pemigewasset Wilderness Area, a 45,000-acre preserve created by Congress in 1984. The path now becomes the Wilderness Trail, and in another 1.5 miles, you cross Black Brook. The bridge on the right is the last of the old logging railroad bridges still left standing. At 5.4 miles, you cross the Pemigewasset River on a 180-foot suspension bridge and reach the junction with the Cedar Brook Trail.

As you cross the river and head west, the views get more dramatic. There are vistas of the Bondcliffs and the farther reaches of the Pemigewasset Wilderness. This view is the essence of the Pemi: It is one of the few regions in the Whites where you are surrounded by such a vast stretch of roadless outback.

You can return to the Lincoln Woods trailhead by skiing along the east bank of the Pemigewasset River. After 0.6 mile on the Cedar Brook Trail, you come to a junction with the East Side Trail. This is a much less traveled route alongside the river. From the wilderness area boundary (opposite where Franconia Brook joins the river), the trail widens into a grass road (FR 87—noted on maps as East Side Road). From here to the trailhead 3.2 miles away, the trail is presently groomed on weekends. The East Side Trail ends at the Lincoln Woods Visitor Information Center.

If you want solitude, you need only step a short way off the beaten path. A great day trip that avoids crowds and gets you pumping is to ski the 12-mile loop around 3,620-foot Mount Hitchcock. The route is best done east to west to maximize the amount of downhill skiing. You will drop 1,500 feet in 4.7 miles on the Cedar Brook Trail en route to the Pemigewasset River.

From the start on the Hancock Notch Trail, the route passes through mixed forest on rolling terrain, running slightly uphill and traveling on wide, old railroad beds and logging roads. The junction with the Cedar Brook Trail is reached after 1.8 miles. The route continues on the Cedar Brook Trail, which can be tricky to follow at the beginning. The trail crosses the North Fork of the Hancock Branch five times within the first 0.6 mile. The first few crossings can be avoided by staying on the east side of the brook and following a rough trail. The Hancock Loop Trail to the summit of 4,403-foot Mount Hancock heads off east about 150 yards after the last crossing. Watch for the blue blazes throughout this section. If you lose sight of them, you are off the route and should backtrack.

Passing the Hancock Loop Trail, the Cedar Brook Trail climbs about 400 feet in the next 0.7 mile to the height-of-land between Mounts Hancock and Hitchcock. This is a beautiful boggy plateau with lodgepole tree trunks jutting toward the sky. The trail meanders along flat ground through a high meadow for a short distance before beginning the long, gradual descent down to the Pemigewasset River and the Wilderness Trail. The descent follows old logging roads that slab along the east side of the Cedar Brook drainage. The trail has a number of drainage divots that must be approached cautiously if there is light snow cover. You soon pass a sign that marks the old site of Camp 24A, one of J. H. Henry's logging outposts. This whole drainage was the site of intense logging activity by Henry's company at the turn of the century. The Cedar Brook Trail was originally the access route to five different logging camps. Little evidence of this era now remains.

The Cedar Brook Trail continues its steady descent until it reaches the banks of the brook and makes a sharp right turn onto an old railroad bed at 4.1 miles. Soon after it passes through the clearing of the old Camp 24, the East Side Trail leaves to the left. This is the recommended route back to the Kancamagus Highway (NH 112). This trail is less traveled and shorter than skiing around to the Lincoln Woods Trail/Wilderness Trail.

The trip back on the East Side Trail is primarily flat—4.8 miles of double-poling and aerobic diagonal stride skiing. The trail hugs the East Branch of the Pemigewasset River, and the views are pleasant. Gliding effortlessly through the deep woods with a gurgling river alongside is what backcountry skiing is all about.

Nancy and Norcross Ponds

THE TOUR
A ski tour to the isolated and scenic Nancy and Norcross Ponds in the Pemige-wasset Wilderness.

DISTANCE
❊ 3.5 miles (NH 302 to Norcross Pond)
❊ 4.6 miles (Desolation Shelter to Nancy Pond)
❊ 13.2 miles (Nancy Pond Trail–Carrigain Notch Trail–NH 302 loop)

ELEVATION
❊ *Start* 950 feet (Nancy Brook trailhead); 2,167 feet (Desolation Shelter)
❊ *Highest point* 3,150 feet (Norcross Pond)
❊ *Vertical drop* 2,200 feet (to NH 302)

MAP
AMC Map 2 (Franconia–Pemigewasset)

DIFFICULTY
❊ Moderate (from the west)
❊ more difficult (from the east)

HOW TO GET THERE
The Nancy Pond Trail begins on the west side of NH 302, 2.8 miles north of the Sawyer Rock picnic area and 6.7 miles south of the Willey House Site in Crawford Notch State Park. Desolation Shelter can be accessed from the south via the Carrigain Notch Trail or the Wilderness Trail.

Perched high on a plateau on the edge of the Pemigewasset Wilderness is a small network of four mountain ponds: Nancy, Norcross, Little Norcross, and Duck Ponds. At 3,100 feet, they lie undisturbed and isolated, and offer sweeping views

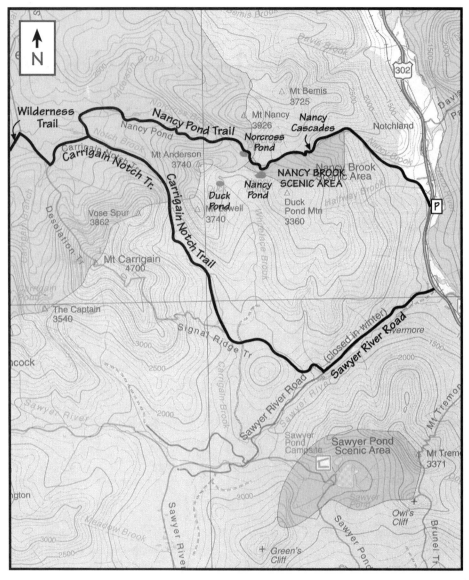

NANCY AND NORCROSS PONDS

AMC Map 2 (Franconia–Pemigewasset)

to the west of the entire Pemigewasset Wilderness. The actual boundary of the offi-
cial Pemigewasset Wilderness Area cuts between Norcross and Nancy Ponds. The
U.S. Forest Service designated 460 acres around Nancy Pond as the Nancy Brook
Scenic Area in 1964, to be maintained as much as possible in an undisturbed state.
This action was taken to preserve a stand of virgin spruce on the north slopes of
Duck Pond Mountain that overlooks Nancy Pond. This is one of the two largest
areas of virgin timber in the state.

The pond, brook, cascades, and mountain in this area that bear the name
Nancy trace their appellation to "the sad tale of Nancy." This romantic tragedy
took place in the 1820s; it was chronicled by White Mountain pioneer settler Lucy
Crawford in her *History of the White Mountains*. Nancy was an "honest girl" who
worked for a colonel in Jefferson. She fell in love with the colonel's servant, who
promised to take her to Portsmouth and marry her; she in turn entrusted all her
financial and domestic affairs to him. But Nancy's paramour was evidently a louse.
He surreptitiously left for Portsmouth with her money, but without her. She took
off the same day in hot pursuit, dismissing the warning of the locals that she not
brave the deep snow of Crawford Notch alone. "For such was her love, either for
the man upon whom she had placed her affections or the money she had placed
in his hands, that she was inflexible," wrote Crawford.

Traveling through the night, she covered 22 miles in an attempt to overtake
her fiancé. The sight of his tracks and the discovery of his still-smoldering camp-
fire urged her forward. But the effort proved too much. When a search party from
Jefferson set out to find her the next day, they found poor Nancy sitting by the side
of a stream, frozen to death. The stream where she had evidently fallen in and
soaked herself is now known as Nancy Brook.

When this tragic story was later related to Nancy's wayward lover, "his own
conscience was smitten and he became frantic and insane." He died several
months later. Thus was born the Nancy landscape that endures as a memorial to
"love's sweet victim, in her bloom."

The shortest approach to the ponds is via the Nancy Pond Trail from NH 302
in Crawford Notch. The trail follows old logging roads for the first 2 miles, then
crosses some landslides and a drainage. At 2.4 miles the trail reaches the Nancy
Cascades. These beautiful, ledgy falls are several hundred feet high. The trail skirts
the falls on the left via steep switchbacks through the woods. It is easiest to remove
skis and walk this section. The route then covers easy ground through a moss-cov-
ered virgin spruce forest, emerging at Nancy Pond in 3.5 miles. Norcross Pond, the
larger of the two ponds, is another 0.8 mile west.

It is possible to make a loop trip from Norcross Pond through Carrigain
Notch and back to NH 302. The Carrigain Notch Trail leaves the Nancy Pond Trail
2.8 miles west of Norcross Pond at a well-marked junction. The trail climbs moderately on an old logging road, reaching Carrigain Notch (elevation 2,639 feet) in
1.8 miles. The trail follows logging roads down from the notch, and several steep
downhill chutes must be negotiated. Easier ground is reached, and an area of
beaver activity is crossed. The Signal Ridge Trail junction is reached 2.3 miles after

the notch. Follow the Signal Ridge Trail over fairly flat ground for 1.7 miles until it ends at the Sawyer River Road. This road is unplowed all the way to NH 302. It is heavily used by snowmobiles, making it a fast 2-mile ski to NH 302. The Sawyer River Road meets NH 302 1.7 miles south of the Nancy Pond trailhead so you may want to spot a car. The total length of this loop is 13.2 miles, assuming you do a car shuttle.

The ponds are also a great destination for a party that is camping in the Pemi. Accessed from the west, the Nancy Pond Trail ascends an abandoned railroad bed that is a delightful, gentle, mile-long downhill run on the return. From Desolation Shelter, the Carrigain Notch Trail is followed for 1 mile until it intersects the Nancy Pond Trail, which continues straight ahead. The terrain is flat and straight, perfect for fast backcountry flat-tracking. The trail crosses a number of streams and brooks, some of which are bridged by single logs. Bold skiers can keep their skis on and test their balance on these; you can choose a less airy alternative by walking or skiing across a frozen drainage nearby. The route then parallels Norcross Brook as it climbs gently (skins are not needed) up the drainage that leads to Norcross Pond. The ski tour begins in dense fir and hemlock forests, which give way to open birch stands at higher elevations.

This ski tour offers access to a wild area. There is a wonderful sense of isolation at these ponds, wind-swept and eerie in their desolation. Few people ski to the ponds from the west because it is not a feasible day trip from the road. But the rewards make it worth the effort of planning an overnight trip. Norcross Pond is one of the more spectacular vantage points over the Pemigewasset Wilderness. It provides views of the Franconia Ridge, Mounts Bond and Guyot, and even a glimpse into Zealand Notch.

As you travel east, Nancy Pond lies another 0.8 mile down the trail. You can practice a little backcountry skating technique as you cross the snowy, wind-scoured ponds. Nancy Pond offers clear views of three slides on Mount Nancy. These slides would make good ski descents; logging roads can be followed on Mount Nancy to reach them.

Easy Day Trips in the White Mountains

A variety of easier backcountry ski trails have been developed throughout the White Mountains. They deserve special mention for novice skiers who are interested in skiing off the beaten path. They are listed here in an effort to introduce beginning cross-country skiers to the world of backcountry skiing and to entice them to continue their explorations.

The U.S. Forest Service (USFS) maintains a network of moderate backcountry ski trails. The **Nanamocomuck Trail** and the **Oliverian Brook Trail** off the Kancamagus Highway (NH 112), the **Smarts Brook Ski Trails** on NH 49 near Waterville Valley, and the **Hayes Copp Ski Trail** on NH 16 north of Pinkham Notch are some of the better trails. The aptly named **Moose Watch Trail** at the **Beaver Brook Ski Trails** on NH 3 near Twin Mountain is a good bet for wildlife viewing. Trails lead into the **Greeley Ponds Scenic Area** from both the Kancamagus Highway (9.3 miles east of I-93) and from the Waterville Valley Ski Area.

The USFS publishes pamphlets with sketch maps about these and other trails. These pamphlets are available at any White Mountain National Forest ranger station, or by contacting the Forest Supervisor, White Mountain National Forest, 719 No. Main St., Laconia, NH 03246 (603-528-8721).

Another beautiful backcountry tour over easy terrain is the **Wild River Trail** from the USFS Hastings Campground on ME 113 to Jackson, NH. The route is heavily used by snowmobiles on its northeastern end, which makes for fast, flat skiing. The trail begins 1.7 miles south on ME 113, where the road is gated. From where you park your car, you may either ski in alongside the Wild River or ski south on the unplowed section of ME 113 through **Evans Notch**. The scenic Wild River has been designated a Wild and Scenic River by the U.S. Congress, assuring that it will be preserved in its free-running state.

The Appalachian Mountain Club has developed an excellent network of backcountry ski trails near its **Pinkham Notch** headquarters on NH 16. The **Blanchard Loop**, the **Square Ledge Loop**, and the **Lost Pond Trail** are several of the popular easy tours. The AMC has a free map and pamphlet which describes and rates eleven trails. See the chapter on Pinkham Notch for more details.

MAINE

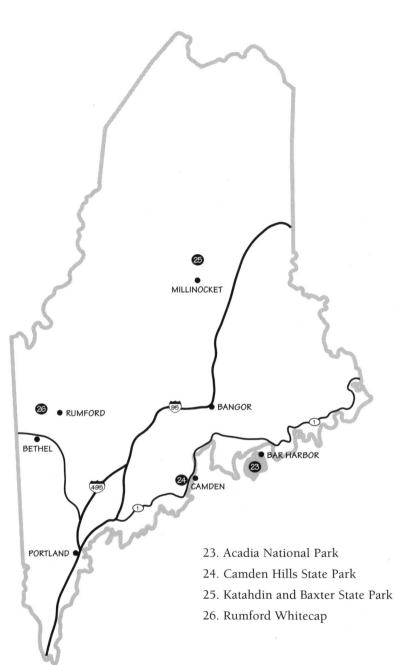

25
● MILLINOCKET

26 ● RUMFORD

95 ● BANGOR

1

BETHEL ●

495

24 ● BAR HARBOR

23

1 CAMDEN

PORTLAND ●

23. Acadia National Park

24. Camden Hills State Park

25. Katahdin and Baxter State Park

26. Rumford Whitecap

Acadia National Park

THE TOUR

A scenic ski tour on Acadia's carriage roads and trails to the summit of Sargent Mountain, where there is excellent skiing on large snowfields overlooking the Atlantic Ocean.

DISTANCE

❄ 5.6 miles round-trip to Sargent Mountain summit, via direct route

ELEVATION

❄ *Start* 400 feet
❄ *Highest point* 1,373 feet
❄ *Vertical drop* 973 feet

MAPS

AMC Acadia National Park (1993), DeLorme *Mount Desert Island,* USGS Acadia National Park and Vicinity (1971), Trails Illustrated *Acadia National Park* (1992). Maps are for sale at park headquarters.

DIFFICULTY

❄ Moderate

SNOWBOARDING

The unplowed auto road on Cadillac Mountain can be a fun, easy 3.5-mile snowboard descent, conditions permitting. You can also ride the steeper snowfields that drop to the west from the road. The carriage roads are not steep enough to ride.

HOW TO GET THERE

From the north, follow ME 198 to the Parkman Mountain parking area, a half-mile north of Upper Hadlock Pond. Park headquarters is just west of Eagle Lake on ME 233.

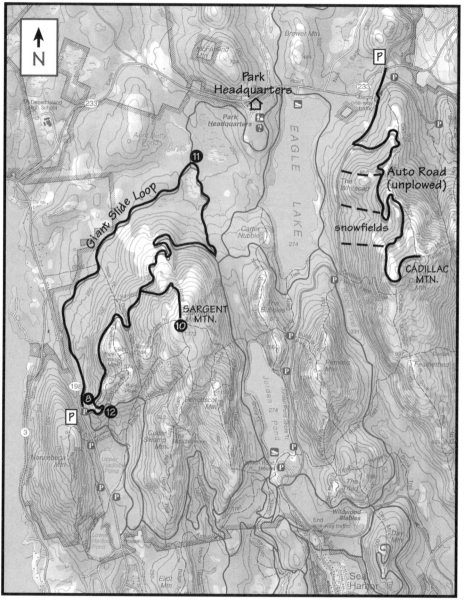

ACADIA NATIONAL PARK

Acadia National Park offers some of the most unusual backcountry skiing in New England, if not in the country. The reason is its setting: Mount Desert Island sits in the Atlantic Ocean just off the coast of Maine. From the island's rocky, bare mountain summits, skiers have a 360-degree view of miles of rugged Maine coastline and outlying islands. With the exception of the Olympic Mountains in Washington, no other mountain range in the continental United States comes to mind that offers skiers the opportunity to ski high snowfields with an ocean backdrop. Here is a breathtaking setting for an afternoon of easy cross-country skiing, with enjoyable downhill skiing options.

Acadia is also special for the glimpse of cultural history that it offers. It was once a summer haven for blue-blood families such as the Fords, Carnegies, and Morgans; ME 3 leading into neighboring Bar Harbor was once known as "Millionaire's Row." The most popular ski routes in the park travel over paths originally laid to accommodate the horse-and-buggy ramblings of the Rockefellers and their friends. John D. Rockefeller Jr. did not fancy having to hike the island's narrow foot trails. So in 1917 he hired the noted landscape architect Frederick Law Olmsted, designer of New York's Central Park and Boston's Emerald Necklace, to design and oversee construction of 51 miles of carriage roads. This elaborate network of roads took a quarter-century to build. Rockefeller later donated most of these carriage roads to the federal government when Acadia National Park was created. These paths are now a unique hallmark of Acadia. No motorized transport, including snowmobiles, is allowed on the carriage roads.

Skiers in Acadia will appreciate what went into the construction of these paths. They are lined with shark's tooth–shaped slabs of pink granite. Known as "Rockefeller's Teeth," these stones were locally quarried and cut by hand. Turns and curves on the 16-foot-wide paths were designed to direct the attention of horse-and-buggy passengers to scenic vistas. When bridges were needed, Rockefeller saw to it that they received no ordinary treatment. The sixteen bridges on the carriage roads, an attraction in themselves, were built with stones painstakingly cut by local masons. The carriage roads were extensively rehabilitated from 1992 to 1995.

A classic ski tour in Acadia would naturally include a taste of all of these unique features, along with good skiing. Sargent Mountain fits the bill perfectly. Sargent is a 1,373-foot peak lying directly across from Cadillac Mountain (1,530 feet), the highest point on the East Coast. A carriage road that forms a horseshoe around the north slopes of Sargent goes higher (780 feet) than any other carriage road in the park. What few winter travelers have discovered is the reward for leaving the carriage road to climb to the summit of Sargent. Skiers are in for a treat when they step off the beaten track here.

From the north side of the Parkman Mountain parking lot, turn right. Within 100 feet, you come to a junction with a carriage road. You may turn right here if you want the most direct route to Sargent Mountain (2.8 miles to the summit). Otherwise, a longer tour can be taken by turning left and skiing the Giant Slide Loop, which, when combined with a trip to the Sargent summit, is a 9.8-mile loop. Should you choose the latter route, you will ski for 3.2 miles on flat terrain before coming to carriage road junction 11, where you turn right. You climb for 200 feet, cross six small bridges that span a wandering stream, and then make a sharp right at junction 10 onto a carriage road that climbs gently along the north face of Sargent Mountain. After 1.7 miles, the Sargent Mountain Trail leaves on the left, leading to the summit in 0.8 mile.

While skiing the carriage roads, note the intricate stonework that forms the borders of each path. It is also worth looking over your shoulder where the path turns in order to see what the original landscape architects were directing your attention to at each point. The path affords nice views to the west of Somes Sound, the only natural fjord on the eastern seaboard.

The trail up Sargent can be negotiated easily without climbing skins. Snow conditions on the summit slopes can be icy and somewhat treacherous. It will probably be easiest to carry your skis the short distance from treeline to the summit when this is the case. From the summit, the Atlantic Ocean glistens off to the south, the horizon broken only by occasional coastal islands. The wind-swept summit ridge tells the story of the glacier that shaped the landscape. Estimated at 2 miles in thickness, the icecap slid over Acadia from the north, leaving deep north-south scratches in the rocks and grinding the island mountains into the characteristic domes that form the park's skyline. The lakes below were merely puddles that formed where the earth was scooped out by the icecap as it made its way into the ocean.

Walking north along the summit ridge, you soon come to a series of snowfields that drop down the northwest slope of the mountain. These snowfields are hidden until you are practically on top of them. Depending on how much snow has fallen that year, you may link together a series of runs of several hundred feet each. These open slopes provide perfect moderate terrain for telemarking. It is easy to spend all afternoon exploring the skiing possibilities on the north slopes. But you can spend as much time just taking in the incredible panorama here.

Late in the season, when the prevailing winds deposit snow on the southern slopes of the mountain, there is good open skiing on the ridge going south from Sargent Mountain over Penobscot Mountain and down into the Amphitheater.

To return to your car from the summit of Sargent, drop back down the Sargent Mountain Trail and go left on the carriage road. There is not much of a downhill grade on the carriage roads, since they were designed to contour gently around the mountain. Go right at junctions 12 and 13; the Parkman Mountain parking lot will appear shortly on your left.

Snow conditions in Acadia are difficult to predict. The coastal climate may cause it to snow in Acadia when there has been little precipitation elsewhere in Maine, or it may rain here when snow has dumped in the interior of the state. A call to park headquarters (207-288-3338) is helpful, but even the rangers tend to be overly pessimistic about the skiing possibilities. In mid-March, after rangers warned that I would be walking the whole route, I enjoyed a great day of skiing on Sargent. A better source of ski information is Cadillac Mountain Sports in Bar Harbor (207-288-4532), where you can also buy maps and rent skis.

Cruising along the summit of Sargent Mountain in Acadia National Park.

The best skiing in Acadia is generally from February through early March, although there is often snow by Christmas. Good skiing can continue on north-facing trails and slopes well into March, long after south-facing slopes have melted into rock and mud. Bar Harbor volunteers have, in recent years, been grooming and setting ski tracks on the entire carriage road network on weekends. The packed snow stays longer, which has helped extend the ski season.

The rule of thumb in Acadia is this: Don't wait—ski the snow when it falls. But lacking a recent storm, it is still worth defying the pessimists and heading to the summits. At best, you may be surprised to find great skiing; at worst, you will have to settle for hiking and savoring Acadia's world-class views.

OTHER OPTIONS

Cadillac Mountain offers good skiing off the auto road, which climbs 3.5 miles to the summit from a parking turnout on ME 233. The auto road is shared with snow-mobilers, so trail conditions may be icy or choppy. Ski up the auto road or the North Ridge Trail. When skiing down the auto road, look to the west for skiable snowfields. There is a particularly nice run off the snowfields on the Whitecap, a prominent knoll to the west.

The western side of Mount Desert Island seems to hold snow the most reliably. A nice ski tour departs from the south end of Long Pond. Ski the Great Pond Trail and climb up the Great Notch Trail. Return to your starting point on the Cold Brook Trail. Depending on snow, you can add longer loops to this basic tour.

The 51 miles of carriage roads are the most popular destinations for cross-country skiers in the park. The ski tour around Otter Point on the Park Loop Road (sometimes plowed in one lane) is exceptionally pretty where the road passes right alongside the ocean. The *Winter Activities Guide*, available from park headquarters, describes a number of other routes on the carriage and park roads.

Camden Hills State Park

THE TOURS
Coastal mountain skiing with panoramic views over the Penobscot Bay and the Maine coastline.

DISTANCE
* ❋ 7 miles (Ski Shelter Trail/Cameron Mountain Loop)
* ❋ 2.8 miles (Mount Battie Road, round-trip to summit)

ELEVATION
* ❋ *Start* 250 feet
* ❋ *Highest point* 1,101 feet (Bald Rock Mountain)
* ❋ *Vertical drop* 851 feet

MAPS
USGS Camden (1973) covers Mounts Megunticook and Battie; USGS Lincolnville (1973) covers Cameron Mountain and Bald Rock. The AMC Camden Hills map covers the whole park. *Camden Hills State Park Trails System* is a sketch map listing trails and descriptions that is available from the ranger. The USGS maps are available at the Village Shop or the Owl & Turtle Book Shop, both in Camden.

DIFFICULTY
* ❋ Moderate

SNOWBOARDING
The Mount Battie Auto Road may be reasonable to ride if there is hard snow. The other terrain in Camden Hills State Park is generally too gentle for snowboarding.

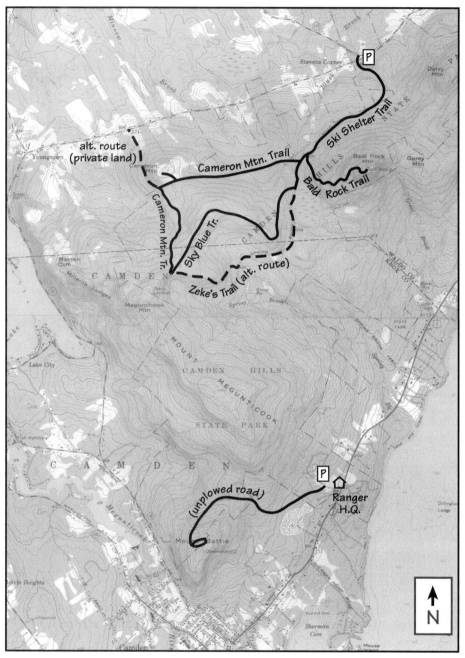

alt. route
(private land)

Ski Shelter Trail

Cameron Mtn. Trail

Bald Rock Trail

Cameron Mtn. Tr.

Sky Blue Tr.

Zeke's Trail (alt. route)

(unplowed road)

Ranger
H.Q.

N

USGS Camden and Lincolnville

CAMDEN HILLS STATE PARK

HOW TO GET THERE

To reach the Ski Shelter Trail trailhead, take US 1 north from Camden. Pass the ranger headquarters and the Mount Battie Auto Road entrance after 1.6 miles, and continue for another 4 miles to the junction of ME 173 north. Turn left on ME 173 and go 2.2 miles to Youngstown Road. This intersection is known as Stevens Corner. Turn left here, and the trailhead is immediately on the left.

The Camden Hills are a tightly grouped range of mountains clustered on the Atlantic coast just north of the town of Camden, ME. Mount Megunticook (1,385 feet) in Camden Hills State Park is the highest point on the mainland coast of the eastern seaboard (Cadillac Mountain in Acadia is the highest point on the East Coast, but it is on an island). For those who can never decide between going to the sea or to the mountains, the Camden Hills, like Acadia National Park, is one of the few places where people can do both. As one Capt. John Smith wrote, Camden lies "under the high mountains of the Penobscot, against whose feet the sea doth beat." The experience of skiing high on a mountain snowfield with the ocean unfolding below you is exhilarating.

Skiers may be surprised to learn that the ubiquitous Civilian Conservation Corps trail builders made their presence felt all the way to Mount Megunticook. The current Slope Trail on the north side of Mount Megunticook is the approximate location of an old hand-graded CCC ski trail that was rated intermediate to expert. In its heyday, it was 30 to 60 feet wide. This trail was relocated in 1977 because of serious erosion problems. Virtually all trails in the park were used and rated for skiing throughout the 1930s. What the CCC saw in the Camden Hills then is still true today: It is an area that tends to accumulate good quantities of snow and has excellent terrain for skiing.

The summits of the Camden Hills are steeped in the history of the early wars that touched this area. Zeke's Lookout, a prominent viewpoint off Zeke's Trail, was named for an old patriot who stood watch from this point. His job was to warn the townspeople of enemy movement in Camden Harbor and Penobscot Bay during the War of 1812. A local person was paid twenty-five dollars to clear a rough road up Mount Battie in 1814 and to haul three cannons to the summit for the purpose of defending Camden from a naval attack.

Some of the best and most scenic skiing can be found on the northern side of the park. Bald Rock (1,101 feet) and Cameron Mountain (811 feet) have exposed summits with views of Penobscot Bay. Both peaks are accessed via the Ski Shelter Trail.

The Ski Shelter Trail is an old fire road that led to a now defunct ski shelter. The trail is now used by both snowmobilers and skiers in the winter. Ski up a gradual rise for 1.3 miles until you reach a gazebo and a four-way trail junction. Heading off left, it is 0.8 mile up the Bald Rock Trail to the summit. Turning right, it is

Skiing on the summit of Bald Rock Mountain, overlooking the Penobscot Bay.

a mile to Cameron Mountain. The trail up Bald Rock climbs steadily but gradually through mixed forest. The trail is 10 to 12 feet wide, and with new snow it is an excellent moderate downhill run. From the cliffbound summit of Bald Rock, there is a panoramic view all the way to Cadillac Mountain in Acadia and a vista of the entire Camden Hills region. There is a small snowfield on the north side of the summit which can be skied.

The ski to Cameron Mountain is on flat terrain following an old town road and passing abandoned farmland. This is an old CCC trail that was used as part of a ski descent from Zeke's Lookout. Cameron Mountain itself is a treeless blueberry knoll rising 100 feet above the ski trail. It serves as a fun, gentle telemarking hill, with a nice view to the northeast of the Penobscot Bay. Cameron Mountain is on private land, so skiers should inquire at park headquarters about permission to ski on it. From Cameron Mountain, you may continue briefly north on the trail to a junction. Bearing right at the junction will bring you back to Youngstown Road, where there is no official parking and no trail sign (utility pole 91 is the only marker). Bearing left, the Cameron Mountain Trail continues, climbing uphill to its junction with the Sky Blue Trail. This trail wanders downhill through open blueberry clearings and passes some huge, old black spruce trees before meeting up again with the Ski Shelter Trail.

Another enjoyable ski tour in the park is up the unplowed road on Mount Battie (800 feet). From the parking lot behind the ranger's house, it is 1.4 miles uphill to the summit, and an enjoyable, sustained downhill ski back. The stone tower on the summit was erected in 1921 as a monument to local men and women who fought in World War I.

A plaque on the summit honors the poet Edna St. Vincent Millay, who drew inspiration for some of her most famous poems from her hikes in the Camden Hills. It is easy to understand why she was so struck by what she saw. From the summit, you are treated to a classic Maine vista of gentle, rounded hills, a patchwork of farm and pastureland in the valleys, and the sea stretching off endlessly in the distance.

OTHER OPTIONS

A popular local skiing destination for those looking for flatter terrain is the Tanglewood area, located just north of Duck Trap. The area has a number of easy cross-country ski trails.

In the event there is no snow on the coast and you still want to make turns, the nearby Camden Snow Bowl is a historic local attraction. Run by the town of Camden, this hill has old-style narrow-trail skiing and sells two-hour lift passes. The Snow Bowl is best known for its terrifying toboggan run, which drops 400 feet down an icy sluiceway. Bring a change of underwear.

Katahdin and Baxter State Park

THE TOURS
Ski mountaineering routes in the Chimney Pond area and ski touring around Russell Pond are some of the classic ski routes in the park. A north-south traverse of the park is a spectacular multi-day trip.

DISTANCES
* 10.2 miles from Golden Road–Mile 14 (parking) to Roaring Brook bunkhouse
* 3.3 miles from Roaring Brook to Chimney Pond; 7 miles from Roaring Brook to Russell Pond
* 40 miles, north-south traverse, from Matagamon Gate to Golden Road–Mile 14

ELEVATION
* *Start* 528 feet (Golden Road–Mile 14)
* *Highest point* 5,267 feet (Katahdin summit); 2,914 feet (Chimney Pond campground)
* *Vertical drop* 2,353 feet (Katahdin to Chimney Pond)

MAPS
AMC Mount Katahdin and Baxter State Park and the DeLorme *Map and Guide of Baxter State Park and Katahdin* cover the entire park. USGS Mount Katahdin (1988) covers Katahdin and its surrounding basins.

DIFFICULTY
* Most difficult/mountaineering (Katahdin)
* Moderate (Roaring Brook, Russell Pond, and other lowland routes)

SNOWBOARDING
The gullies around Katahdin can be snowboarded by expert riders. You will need snowshoes for the long approaches.

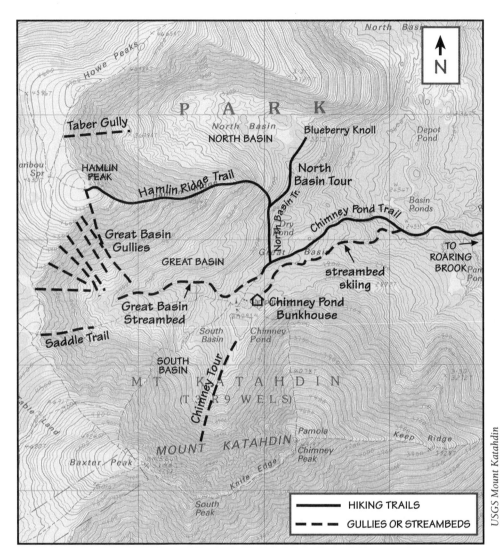

KATAHDIN

USGS Mount Katahdin

FEES & REGULATIONS

Baxter State Park charges fees for camping within the park. Call park headquarters (207-723-5140) for an information packet on visiting the park in winter. Applications for overnight stays in the park and payment must be received two weeks before your arrival.

HOW TO GET THERE

Follow I-95 north to the Medway exit (exit 56), then go west on ME 157 to Millinocket. Follow signs to the park. It is 14 miles from Millinocket to a large plowed parking area on the south side of the Golden Road (the plowed logging road just outside the park boundary).

Man is born to Die, His Works are Short-lived
Buildings Crumble, Monuments Decay, Wealth Vanishes
But Katahdin in All Its Glory
Forever Shall Remain the Mountain of the
People of Maine.
—Governor Percival P. Baxter

"It was vast, Titanic, and such as man never inhabits," wrote Henry David Thoreau of his 1846 ascent of Katahdin. Like Katahdin which crowns it, Baxter State Park has a way of reorienting one's sense of space and time. Covering 202,064 acres, the park is home to 46 mountain peaks and ridges, 18 of which are over 3,000 feet tall. While Baxter State Park is not the largest tract of wilderness in New England (that distinction lies with the 750,000-acre White Mountain National Forest), it *feels* bigger and wilder than any other place. That's partly due to its remoteness: The park is a full day's drive from urban centers such as Boston or Portland, and it is surrounded by thousands of miles of forest and rivers. The vastness of the place often stuns New Englanders, who are more accustomed to the tighter confines of the northern woods.

Baxter State Park is arguably home to the best wilderness skiing in the East. With its numerous mountains, valleys, and lakes, it is unmatched in the region as a destination for extended ski expeditioning.

Katahdin roars up out of the rolling terrain of northern Maine in a cacophony of ice, rock, and snow. At 5,267 feet, it is the highest point in Maine. It is stunning in its severity, a striking contrast to the undulating lake-pocked countryside around it. "What a place to live, what a place to die and be buried in! There certainly men would live forever, and laugh at death and the grave," Thoreau wrote of Katahdin in *The Maine Woods*.

Katahdin is strikingly incongruous for a New England peak. Its serrated ridgeline and the long, sweeping gullies that run off its summit are more reminiscent of the Alps than a Maine mountain. Its massive size is at the same time awe-inspiring and intimidating. The summit ridge is part of a 4-mile-long plateau that rises 4,500 feet above the surrounding lowlands. This so-called Table Land is bounded by a number of impressive glacial cirques, or basins.

Katahdin, an Indian word meaning "greatest mountain," is actually comprised of a series of summits that ring the horseshoe-shaped Great Basin. These include Baxter (the highest), South, Chimney, and Hamlin Peaks, and Pamola. The Penobscot Indians feared the mountain, believing that Pamola was a wrathful god with the power to destroy those who climb the peak. Today, the most dramatic— and feared—feature of the mountain for hikers and climbers is the Knife Edge. Rightly described as "the most spectacular mountain trail in the East" by the *AMC Maine Mountain Guide,* the Knife Edge is a mile-long section of the summit ridge between South Peak and Pamola. Lying at nearly 5,000 feet, it narrows to 24 inches in some sections, and plunges thousands of feet on either side.

Just as remarkable as the park itself is the fact that so large a place exists in Maine that isn't being relentlessly logged. The defenders of the park fought tirelessly for this honor, and it took no less than a former governor of Maine to make it happen.

Baxter State Park was conceived in an unprecedented act of love and stubbornness. Percival P. Baxter, governor of Maine from 1921 to 1925, had crusaded while in office to preserve the lands around Katahdin from rapacious loggers. The timber companies successfully fought him off, so Baxter decided to make an end run around them: he would simply buy the lands and give them to the state to preserve as a park. Between 1930, when he purchased Katahdin itself, and 1962, Baxter bought and donated more than 200,000 acres of land to the state of Maine. The land is protected by the former governor's covenant, which declared that the park would "forever be left in its natural wild state, forever be kept as a sanctuary for wild beasts and birds, and forever be used for public forest, public park, and public recreational purposes." Today, Baxter Park is the fourth largest state park in the nation.

BAXTER STATE PARK NUTS & BOLTS: THE DREADED RED TAPE

First-time winter visitors to Katahdin may be surprised to find themselves confronting one of its most difficult obstacles before leaving home: the Baxter State Park bureaucracy. Baxter is notorious for the rules and regulations that govern entry into the park in winter (defined as December 1 to April 1). This includes submitting an application and payment at least two weeks in advance of arriving for a special use permit (which can be denied) for camping or climbing; designating a "trip leader" and two alternate leaders for whom outdoor résumés must be submitted; requiring a minimum of four people per party for overnight stays; and providing a day-by-day itinerary of where visitors intend to stay. Once inside the park, there is more. If you are staying at Chimney Pond and hiking, you must: sign in and out daily with a ranger; get your equipment and party checked out by park rangers if you are climbing above treeline; and depart by 8 A.M. for any technical ascent. Only after all these conditions have been met may you head off into the solitude of the park.

Mountaineers have long considered the rules and regulations of Baxter an affront to the ethic of self-reliance. Guy and Laura Waterman, writing in the climbing journal *Off Belay* in 1977, charged that the rules "stifle the 'freedom of the hills' so successfully that many climbers simply avoid Katahdin rather than submit."

Park authorities explain in their literature that the purpose of the regulations is "to promote safety of all persons using the Park and to protect the Baxter State Park Authority and its staff from unnecessary search and rescue efforts." These rules actually represent a relaxation of past practices, when every party member had to submit a medical form signed by a doctor.

Buzz Caverly, park director, insists that the rules exist to protect the fragile natural resources. He notes that the park is closed during April and May (unfortunately, the best time for spring skiing) to "give the resources a rest." And, he told me bluntly, "We don't agree with the philosophy that you have the right to die in the mountains." In spite of these precautions, 21 people did die in Baxter State Park between 1963 and 1998.

The rules and regulations for Baxter change periodically. Suffice it to say that a trip to the park must be planned *at least* one month in advance, and that park authorities must have your application and payment in hand two weeks before your arrival. Applications for winter use are accepted starting November 1.

If you are even considering a trip to Baxter, contact the Baxter State Park Authority, 64 Balsam Drive, Millinocket, ME 04462 (207-723-5140), well in advance and request their literature and applications for winter use. If you plan to ski in any of the basins (that is, off-trail above treeline), this is considered "technical climbing" and you must apply for a special permit and provide additional information in your application. Note that park authorities are still debating whether or not to require helmets for skiing above treeline; inquire with them whether you should bring one.

The park freely concedes that its paperwork requirement can be onerous. But, as park naturalist Jean Hoekwater points out, "It's an exercise in expedition planning and accountability. We take it seriously."

The silver lining for those who successfully negotiate this gauntlet of bureaucratic hurdles is that you have the park to yourself and the other select few paperwork survivors. The crowds who have overrun places like Tuckerman Ravine are absent here. Enjoy the solitude.

HISTORY OF SKIING ON KATAHDIN

Katahdin was first climbed in 1804 by Charles Turner, who later became a U.S. congressman. Henry David Thoreau climbed it in 1846, and wrote about it in his classic *The Maine Woods*.

The ski history of Katahdin is more obscure. The first recorded winter ascent of Katahdin was made in 1892. In March 1926, Arthur Comey, a noted blazer of the Appalachian Trail and an influential city planner, made the historic first descent of Katahdin on skis. Comey skied up and down the Saddle Trail. He also reported skiing in North Basin and descending some of the Great Basin Gullies.

Comey wrote of dropping onto the steep Saddle Trail, "The greatest thrill of all comes when one dips the ski-points over its rim." He was both humble and humorous in his description of his technique: "If the runner is a bit tired and not

Skiing in the shadow of Katahdin in Baxter State Park.

particularly expert, he will probably use the 'Sitz-Telemark' turn, said to have been invented by Professor Sitz for just such occasions." Comey was an early pioneer of creative approaches to eastern skiing. Laura and Guy Waterman recount in *Forest and Crag* that Comey "skied through krummholz, over rocky ridges, and even up fire tower ladders."

Comey was a phenomenally prolific skier. By his own account he logged 1,115 miles on skis over three winters. But he was also a contentious figure among mountaineers. The Watermans recounted that he had a "skyrocketing temper" that resulted in his being banned from the Bemis Crew, a gung-ho group of top New England climbers from the 1920s. One of his partners observed, "The trouble with Arthur Comey is that I can never tell which way he will jump, except that it is generally the way I don't want him to."

After Comey's early ski exploits, there is virtually no recorded ski history of Katahdin for another half-century. In 1980, a group from the University of Maine at Orono that included Dave Getchell and Tad Feffer skied Taber Gully in North Basin, along with the next gully north. These elegant 30–40 degree couloirs may have been skied earlier, but there is no record of the descent. In 1984, some ski patrollers from nearby Squaw Mountain are reported to have skied Black Gully, a steep ice-climbing route that ascends Baxter Peak. This 50+-degree couloir would rate as an extreme ski descent. In 1986, Dick Hall, Winslow Ayer, Gary Faucher, Roger Zimmerman, and Dean Mendell freeheel-skied the Chimney Couloir, Katahdin's classic climbing gully that ascends South Peak.

SKI ROUTES IN BAXTER STATE PARK

Telemark guru Dick Hall compares a first visit to Katahdin to "going to Disneyland"—you just ski around checking out the views and size of the place but don't really plan to accomplish much. There is something to say for this approach. Winter visitors to the park need not set an ambitious itinerary. It is enough to come to take in the grandeur of the mountains. The bunkhouses, with their views of the summits, are a good base from which to take day trips.

Two areas of major interest to skiers are the Chimney Pond area and the Russell Pond area. The Chimney Pond region is the most popular destination for winter climbing in the park. It lies at the foot of Katahdin in the heart of the Great Basin. Skiers can make reservations to stay at the bunkhouse, to camp in a lean-to, or to pitch a tent, all next to Chimney Pond. The Chimney Pond bunkhouse can feel a bit dank and crowded when it is full, but with the wood stove roaring, it is a warm refuge. Some people prefer tents or lean-tos to the close quarters of the bunkhouse.

THE APPROACH

The long ski in from the Golden Road is the first test of your commitment and your packing job. Park authorities now require that parties take two days to ski to Chimney Pond, going only 10.2 miles to Roaring Brook the first night (they may exempt parties who have previously skied to Chimney Pond in a day, and allow them to continue the practice). You ski in on a relatively flat snow-packed road. Heavily laden parties often drag their gear in plastic kiddy sleds, which works reasonably well if you are only going as far as Chimney Pond (the flimsy sleds are unsuitable in deep snow elsewhere in the park). Bring wax for this tour; plodding along the flats with skins makes it unnecessarily slow going. And remember to bring blister gear—Second Skin or Compeed work best—for the inevitable hot spots on this long haul. Enjoy the scenery, strike up conversation, zone out. Use this long approach to put physical and spiritual distance between your distracted outside world and Katahdin. Be here now.

The ski from Roaring Brook to Chimney Pond is strenuous. The Chimney Pond Trail climbs 1,400 feet in 3.3 miles (by contrast, the approach to Roaring Brook rises about 1,000 feet in 10 miles). Most people are carrying in food and gear for a week, which increases the grunt factor. The two days to ski in and one to get out explains why winter trips to the park usually require at least a week.

The reward for the trip to Chimney Pond is the humbling view of South Basin. It is a north-facing glacial cirque that wraps like a horseshoe around Chimney Pond. Large snowfields drop from the upper cliffs of the Cathedral Buttress on the west side of the ravine, and on clear days you can see the summit of Baxter Peak.

CHIMNEY POND

An enjoyable moderate tour from Chimney Pond is to ski the streambed down to Basin Pond. Follow the Saddle Trail as it cuts east through the campground and you will quickly come upon a 15-foot-wide streambed. Turn right, and start skiing. It makes a meandering steady descent toward Basin Pond, picking up speed just before emptying out onto the pond.

For more dramatic scenery, ski south across Chimney Pond and up onto the steep slopes of South Basin. You can ski up to the base of the gullies that ascend Pamola and Baxter Peak, going as high as you feel comfortable and skiing down. One of the better routes of this nature ascends the drainage that flows out of Chimney Pond up toward the base of the Chimney, a prominent gully in the left corner of the ravine. Note that the South Basin slopes are steep and often avalanche-prone (see "Avalanches" in this chapter).

North Basin

Another moderate ski tour from Chimney Pond is the trip over to North Basin. This is a beautiful traverse that links Katahdin's two most dramatic ravines. North Basin is lightly traveled, especially in winter. It is a wild, remote place, with spectacular walls and gullies that rise 1,500 feet to the summit of the Howe Peaks. The northern wall, called the Taber Wall by climbers, is a huge cliff.

The route into North Basin follows the North Basin Trail. From the Chimney Pond campground, ski slowly down the Chimney Pond Trail toward Basin Pond, and at 0.3 mile you will see the trail junction on the left with the North Basin Trail. The trail climbs through a spruce forest and soon rounds the lower buttress of Hamlin Ridge, passing a junction with the Hamlin Ridge Trail. The trail is moderately graded but can be rocky in light snow cover. The trail then contours into North Basin and climbs up **Blueberry Knoll**. This is a spectacular vantage point from which there are views into both North Basin and South Basin. The North Basin Trail ends here, but it is possible to bushwhack another 0.2 mile to the floor of North Basin where there are two small ponds. You can ski around the floor of the ravine right up to the cliffs.

Several prominent gullies tumble down the headwall that forms the western edge of North Basin. **Taber Gully** is the dramatic swathe that splits the horseshoe down the center. It is a classic 1,000-foot couloir, a straight shot from the Table Lands to the valley floor. The best approach from Chimney Pond is to climb the Hamlin Ridge Trail. It is a 2-mile hike to the summit of Hamlin Peak (4,751 feet). The hike up Hamlin Ridge is breathtaking, with giant views into both North and South Basins. Taber Gully begins steeply, at about 40 degrees, then eases back to a consistent 30-to-35-degree pitch all the way down. The gully is spacious at the top and bottom, but narrows to about 15 feet in the center. This is a thrilling descent in a wild landscape.

Great Basin

The best skiing around Katahdin is found in the **Great Basin Gullies,** on the north wall of the Great Basin. The Great Basin is the yawning glacial cirque bounded by Hamlin Peak on the north and Katahdin on the south; South Basin is a branch of the Great Basin. Between Hamlin Peak and the Saddle Trail, a series of snow gullies stripes the flanks of the Great Basin.

Starting with the **Saddle Trail** (itself a fine ski, and the route taken by Arthur Comey in his 1926 ski descent of Katahdin), there are seven more gullies en route to Hamlin Peak. The gullies are all of a similar character: each drops 800–1,000 vertical feet and averages about 30–35 degrees, often pitching up to near 40 degrees at the top. The gullies are 20 to 30 feet wide. They face south and southeast, the perfect exposure for growing corn snow. Directly opposite you are striking views of the ice cliffs that pour 2,000 feet down the flanks of Pamola. Look periodically at Pamola to see how the ice flows glow different colors at different times of the day. Dropping into the Great Basin here, you have the sensation of flying over all of Katahdin.

The easiest access to the Great Basin Gullies is to climb the Hamlin Ridge Trail; the first gully drops down directly from the summit of Hamlin Peak. These gullies are clearly visible from Chimney Pond. From the bottom of the gullies, you can ski a prominent streambed on the floor of the basin and follow it right back to Chimney Pond campground.

Skiers who are not comfortable on the steeps can access the Great Basin Gullies from the bottom. The lower slopes are at a moderate angle, so skiers can climb and ski up to their comfort level. From the campground, head out either on the Saddle Trail or the streambed and ski up into the Great Basin. Break off to the right (north), ski across the floor of the Great Basin, and you are at the foot of the gullies.

The skiing here is world-class, but there are potential dangers such as avalanches (see sidebar on next page.)

RUSSELL POND

The Russell Pond area is a ski adventure with a different quality than the high and wild skiing on Katahdin. Russell Pond is a peaceful crossroads in the midst of a vast, upheaved landscape. The pond lies in a pockmarked valley dotted with numerous lakes, all of them linked by small brooks. A trip to this area is a first-class wilderness ski tour. The terrain is gentle throughout the area.

From Roaring Brook Campground, skiers take the Russell Pond Trail. It crosses the Wassataquoik Stream and its drainages a number of times in the first 4 miles from Roaring Brook. At 3.3 miles, the Wassataquoik Stream Trail (listed on some older maps as the Tracy Horse Trail) diverges to the right. The Wassataquoik Stream Trail travels over flatter terrain than does the Russell Pond Trail in this section. It follows an old tote road and passes two lean-tos 5.6 miles after Roaring Brook. Camping is permitted at the shelters. The trip to the Russell Pond Campground is 7 miles via the Russell Pond Trail and 7.6 miles via the Wassataquoik Stream Trail.

Russell Pond is the gateway to the northern peaks in the park. From the pond there are views south to Katahdin and north to Traveler Mountain and Pogy Mountain. It is an exceptionally pretty area. Wildlife is abundant here; sightings of moose, pine marten, and other animals are common. Russell Pond Campground has a recently renovated bunkhouse and lean-tos. Reservations are required for both. From the Russell Pond area, day trips can be made into the remote Northwest Basin, to the many lakes that lie to the west, and east to view the remains of century-old logging activity.

AVALANCHES

The steep ski routes around Chimney Pond, North Basin, and the Great Basin require a high degree of both skiing and mountaineering skill. Skiers and snowboarders are warned that *the most extreme avalanche hazard in the eastern United States exists on the slopes and in the gullies of Katahdin and the Great Basin.* I met one party that had just taken a 300-foot ride after triggering an avalanche on an ice-climbing route on Katahdin; they were lucky to be skiing out and were heading for the hospital. Snow instability is typically highest early in the season, from January through early March, and just after snow or rain storms.

The Chimney Pond ranger is not a trained avalanche forecaster and is not a reliable source of information about avalanche hazard. At least one member of your party should be experienced in avalanche hazard evaluation, and all skiers planning to venture onto steep terrain should carry avalanche rescue equipment, including shovels, probes, and avalanche transceivers. You should dig snow pits to assess snow stability on steep slopes that you plan to ski. Choose your routes conservatively, and back off if you are uncertain about the conditions. *Avalanches on Katahdin are common!*

SKIING SAFE

The most important technique for skiing steep terrain is to use your head. Skiing gullies that are icy or have "bulletproof" hard snow is suicidal. An innocuous slip on a steep icy gully can result in a terrifying slide for life with no chance of stopping. With a little sun or soft snow, the same gully can be an enjoyable, forgiving, and reasonably safe descent. Baxter Park is not like a ski area; there is no easy way out if you get injured. Scores of people are needed to mount a rescue operation out here, and evacuation will take a very long time.

Use conservative mountaineering judgment. Assess your skills and the conditions honestly before committing to a route. Even if you back off a cherished descent, there are countless consolations—incredible views, thrilling hikes, and camaraderie with friends—just for being in this magical place.

Despite the moderate skiing on a trip to Russell Pond, skiers must still consider a winter ski trip anywhere in the park to be a serious undertaking. Severe weather can set in for days, making travel to all areas impossible. Extra food should be brought in anticipation of such unpredictable events.

BAXTER TRAVERSE

Traversing Baxter State Park is among the grandest and most ambitious back-country ski expeditions in the East. You will travel through one of the wildest parts of the North Country. This trip combines the isolation and rugged beauty of far northern Maine with the jaw-drop drama of Katahdin.

Traversing the park from north to south makes Katahdin the incentive and goal of your journey. Allow at least five to six days for the trip. It is possible to stay in bunkhouses (cabins with wood stoves) each night—if you stay on schedule. Anticipate moving slower than expected: When I traversed the park, the northern trails were fiendishly difficult to follow, often appearing and vanishing right before our eyes. We planned to stay in the bunkhouses, but we ended up camping in lean-tos when we didn't cover the miles that we expected. Be prepared to camp and travel in severe weather. You should be competent with off-trail map and compass navigation, since you may spend much of your time bushwhacking until you reach Roaring Brook. However, the forest up here is fairly open, making the off-trail travel quite reasonable.

The best time for undertaking this north-south tour is February and March. Rivers will have frozen by then (the Wassataquoik Stream is a major crossing), and parts of the trail may even have been recently broken out. The tour can be started just south of Matagamon Gate, due west of Patten, ME. The perimeter road is plowed up to the Dudley Matagamon Wilderness Campground, which is just east of the bridge that crosses the East Branch of the Penobscot River. From there, the route goes 4.1 miles along the unplowed perimeter road to the relatively new bunkhouse at Trout Brook Farm. The route then continues 7 miles to the South Branch Pond bunkhouse, and another 9.7 miles to the Russell Pond bunkhouse.

Some of the highlights of this area include the views of the wild and craggy Traveler Mountains. It is 7 miles from Russell Pond to the bunkhouse at Roaring Brook, and a 3.3-mile ski to Chimney Pond. Your final day is a 13.5-mile trip out to the Golden Road and Millinocket.

It is possible to eliminate one day of skiing by arranging a 9-mile snowmobile ride from the Dudley Matagamon Wilderness Campground to Trout Crossing; from there, it is a 2-mile ski to the South Branch Pond bunkhouse. You will also need to have your car shuttled around to where you will exit the park on the Golden Road. Inquire with the park for the names of local people who provide these shuttle services.

Rumford Whitecap

THE TOUR
A fine half-day ski tour up onto the long, bald summit cone of Rumford Whitecap. There are great views and enjoyable skiing on the summit snowfields.

DISTANCE
5.2 miles round-trip to summit from East Andover Road; 4 miles round-trip from Coburn Brook Road.

ELEVATION
❈ *Start* 640 feet (East Andover Road), 840 feet (Coburn Brook Road)
❈ *Highest point* 2,197 feet
❈ *Vertical drop* 1,557 feet

MAPS
USGS East Andover (1968). Maps are available from Mahoosuc Mountain Sports in Bryant Pond and True North Adventureware in Bethel.

DIFFICULTY
More difficult

SNOWBOARDING
The rolling terrain on this tour is not suitable for snowboards.

HOW TO GET THERE
From Bethel, take ME 2 north. Turn left (north) on ME 5 just before Rumford Point. In about 3 miles, turn right on a bridge over the Ellis River at a sign for Andover Road. Take the next sharp left onto East Andover Road, go 0.2 mi., and see a clearing and a sand pit on the right. Park here; the trail leaves from this parking pullout.

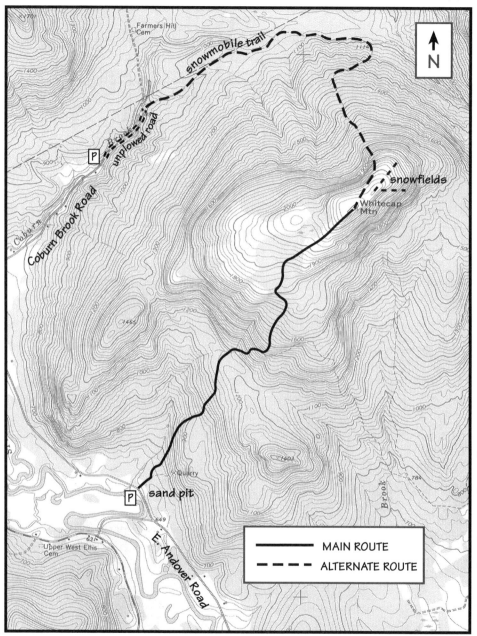

Farmers Hill Cem

snowmobile trail

unplowed road

P

Coburn Brook Road

Coburn

snowfields

Whitecap Mtn

1465

Quarry

P sand pit

Upper West Ellis Cem

E. Andover Road

Brook

| MAIN ROUTE |
| ALTERNATE ROUTE |

USGS East Andover (courtesy of Maptech)

RUMFORD WHITECAP

Skiers passing through Rumford notice two things. The first is the gigantic paper mill which seems to dwarf the town. But it isn't long before your eye is drawn to the prominent bald white summit, resembling an ice cream cone, that stands like a beacon watching over the landscape. Even the mill seems small in the shadow of this peak.

Whitecap Mountain—better known as Rumford Whitecap—has excellent ski terrain. The mountain is capped by a mile-long treeless summit ridge. Open slopes drop down in all directions. There is fun skiing with great views over a woolly part of Maine that sees few winter travelers aside from snowmobilers.

The town of Rumford is better known among Mainers for its paper mill than its skiing. Surprisingly, Rumford has developed a long and distinguished ski history—thanks to the mill.

When the Rumford paper mill opened in 1901, Scandinavian loggers were brought over to run the new operation. The Norwegians and Swedes, in turn, brought over their skis. It didn't take long before the surrounding hillsides were laced with ski trails. In 1923, the Chisolm Ski Club was formed in Rumford. The club was named for Hugh J. Chisolm, the owner of the mill. Rumford quickly rose to prominence as one of the leading Nordic ski centers in the Northeast. By the 1930s, there were a number of ski jumps around the town, and ski trains came here from Portland. In the ensuing years, Rumford has sent four cross-country skiers to the Olympics. The Chisolm Ski Club still operates a small alpine ski hill. The club also runs a renowned cross-country center, which continues to be a venue for top national and international cross-country ski races.

Rumford Whitecap is well known to locals, but not for skiing. It is home to abundant blueberry bushes along the open summit. Local residents hike the mountain throughout the summer to harvest the bountiful crop. The locals keep their skiing confined to the valleys.

There are several trails up Rumford Whitecap, but none of them is well marked. The easiest trail to find departs from the East Andover Road. From the sand pit, an old jeep trail leaves the left side of the parking lot and crosses a flat area. Continue straight; do not take a trail that leaves right to an old mica mine. The trail climbs steeply up several switchbacks, emerging onto a clearing where there are blueberry bushes. This is the southeast corner of the summit snowfields. Continue up to the summit ridge, where there is a delightful mile of skiing with great views. It is 2.6 miles to the summit via this route.

On the descent, be careful on the switchbacks. Below this steep section, you can weave through beautiful beech glades on skier's right. You can often make turns all the way back to your car.

Another route that is more obscure ascends the west side of the mountain and offers good skiing. From the sand pit, continue north on the East Andover Road for 1.8 miles, turning right on Coburn Brook Road. Drive to the end of the plowed road, park, then ski along the snowmobile road for 0.6 mile, passing several hunting camps along the way. Where the snowmobile road veers sharply left,

Cornice jumping on Rumford Whitecap.

continue straight ahead past a row of boulders onto an old jeep trail/snowmobile route. As you ski up this trail, you have views of the summit most of the way. The trail peters out, but it's a short bushwhack to reach a large, steeper open slope on the northwest end of the ridge. You will enjoy skiing this face on the descent.

From the summit of Rumford Whitecap, there are 360-degree views of the surrounding countryside. To the east are the towns of Rumford and Mexico, easily spotted by the permanent plume that rises from the paper mill smokestacks. To the south are the trails of the Mount Abraham Ski Area, and to the southwest are Locke, Barker, and Jordan Mountains—better known as the Sunday River Ski Area. Northeast of Whitecap is Black Mountain, with radio towers on the summit. The east face of Black Mountain is home to the Chisolm Ski Club's alpine and cross-country ski centers.

The most dramatic views from Rumford Whitecap are to the west. A large basin ringed by soft gray mountains unfolds here. In the distance there is a glimpse into Grafton Notch and the gnarled flanks of Old Speck. This is a wild, untamed part of Maine. Gone are the well-developed trail systems of New Hampshire; the hiking and skiing here has a rougher edge. This outback doesn't see many skiers, so you will have this wild place to yourself.

There is a good 300 vertical feet of turns down the east side of the summit. You are skiing over blueberry ledges here; take care to avoid any exposed vegetation. The north side of the summit also has nice snowfields.

After touring on the open summit for a while, the best skiing is right back down the way you came, whether from the south or the west. The open terrain around the summit has the feel of western mountains, and you can choose your ski line at will. You will finally return to your respective climbing trail and ski it back to your car.

Rumford Whitecap is a relatively easy mountain to travel on. The open views and the long treeless summits enable you to see where you are going most of the time, even if you lose the trail. Unlike other places in Maine, on this mountain you can "get there from here."

OTHER OPTIONS

Mount Blue State Park, located in Weld, lies north of Rumford. The park maintains 15 miles of groomed and tracked cross-country ski trails that travel through scenic rolling terrain. The trails on Mount Blue itself are narrow and not particularly hospitable to skiers. When I skied it with a friend, we affectionately dubbed it "Mount Black and Blue."

POSTSCRIPT
Protecting Our Wildlands

This book is about the past, present, and—most importantly—the future of skiing. Skiers and snowboarders are picking up where earlier generations left off and are returning to the backcountry. The possibilities of where we can go and what we can explore are almost limitless.

Our opportunity to travel freely in the backcountry cannot be taken for granted. The New England wilderness is shrinking, as large swathes of land are traded and sold to speculators and large timber companies. The Northern Forest, covering 26 million acres of land stretching from Maine to the Adirondacks, is under threat. It is an area that is home to a million people, and within a day's drive of 70 million more.

In 1987, a million acres of undeveloped Northern Forest land was sold by a timber company to a foreign investor. Since that time, several million more acres have changed hands. Clearcutting is on the rise—in 1992 alone, 60,000 acres of Maine forest were leveled. There is also a great risk of large undeveloped areas being chopped up and sold off as small real-estate parcels. The habitat of backcountry skiers—the high and wild places all around us—is at risk.

Backcountry users should be part of the solution. The Northern Forest Alliance, a project of the Appalachian Mountain Club, is working to create a sustainable future for the vast Northern Forest. The Alliance has proposed the creation of 10 wildlands across the Northeast. These areas range from a 1.3-million acre protected swathe around Baxter State Park to a 160,000-acre preserve in the western Adirondacks. The wildlands are intended to "maintain ecological balance, provide remote and wilderness recreation opportunities, provide solitude to rekindle the spirit, and support the region's forest-based economy."

You can help. Support the wildlands efforts near you. To find out who is working to protect the areas where you like to ski, contact the Northern Forest Alliance, 43 State St., Montpelier, VT 05602 (802-223-5256).

Value the backcountry enough to save it. Work with local environmental groups, land trusts, and the AMC to protect access to our wildlands. You just may discover your next favorite ski tour in land you help preserve.

APPENDIX A

Outdoor and Instructional Organizations

The following is a selective listing of organizations in New England that offer information or instructional programs related to backcountry skiing. This is by no means a complete list. Most downhill ski areas and ski-touring centers now offer telemark lessons in addition to other classes. Snowboard lessons are available at any downhill ski area.

Appalachian Mountain Club
5 Joy Street
Boston, MA 02108
617-523-0636 (Boston) or 603-466-2727 (Pinkham Notch, NH)
www.outdoors.org
   The AMC offers courses throughout the winter in telemark and backcountry skiing, avalanche assessment, ski touring, and mountain safety. The AMC offers an extensive selection of guidebooks and maps for all of New England.

Catamount Trail Association
P.O. Box 1235
Burlington, VT 05402
802-864-5794
www.catamounttrail.together.net
   The Catamount Trail is a 300-mile backcountry ski trail that runs the length of Vermont. It links 15 ski-touring centers along the way. The Catamount Trail Association offers maps and information about the trail.

Green Mountain Club
RR 1, Box 650
Waterbury Center, VT 05677
802-244-7037
www.greenmountainclub.org

The Green Mountain Club is the steward of Vermont's 270-mile Long Trail. It sponsors a variety of outdoor educational lectures and workshops. It is also a resource for maps and guidebooks about the Vermont backcountry.

Hurricane Island Outward Bound School
P.O. Box 429
Rockland, ME 04841
800-341-1744
www.outwardbound.org
The Hurricane Island Outward Bound School offers a wide range of winter courses in the White Mountains of New Hampshire and in the Mahoosuc Mountains of Maine. Winter mountaineering, backcountry skiing, and general winter wilderness courses are among its offerings. These courses provide a comprehensive introduction to winter skills.

North American Telemark Organization (NATO)
Box 44
Waitsfield, VT 05673
800-835-3404
http://planet.syr.edu/telemark/
Dick Hall is the grandmaster of telemark and backcountry ski instruction. Nobody teaches people the basics of cross-country downhill technique as well, and with as much fun, as he and his NATO instructors do. NATO offers courses all around New England for ski instructors, beginner skiers, and people interested in multi-day adventure tours.

Stonehearth Open Learning Opportunities (SOLO)
P.O. Box 3150
Conway, NH 03818
603-447-6711
www.stonehearth.com
SOLO offers backcountry first-aid programs, including wilderness emergency medical technician and wilderness first responder courses.

Wilderness Medical Associates
189 Dudley Road
Bryant Pond, ME 04219
888-945-3633
www.wildmed.com
Wilderness Medical Associates offers a full complement of backcountry medicine courses, from weekend first-aid classes to wilderness emergency medical technician courses.

APPENDIX B
Recommended Reading

AVALANCHE SAFETY

Daffern, Tony. *Avalanche Safety for Skiers and Climbers*. 2d ed. Calgary: Rocky Mountain Books, 1992.

LaChapelle, E. R. *The ABC of Avalanche Safety*. 2d ed. Seattle: The Mountaineers, 1985.

FIRST AID

Hubbell, Frank, and Buck Tilton. *Medicine for the Backcountry*. 2nd ed. Merrillville, IN: ICS Books, 1994.

Lentz, Martha, Steven Macdonald, and Jan Carline. *Mountaineering First Aid*. 4th ed. Seattle: The Mountaineers, 1996.

GUIDEBOOKS

Dawson, Louis W. *Wild Snow: A Historical Guide to North American Ski Mountaineering*. Golden, CO: American Alpine Club, 1997.

AMC Maine Mountain Guide. 7th ed. Boston: Appalachian Mountain Club Books, 1993.

AMC White Mountain Guide. 26th ed. Boston: Appalachian Mountain Club Books, 1998.

MOUNTAINEERING SKILLS

Gorman, Stephen. *AMC Guide to Winter Camping*. Boston: Appalachian Mountain Club Books, 1991.

Graydon, Don, and Kurt Hanson, eds. *Mountaineering: The Freedom of the Hills*. 6th ed. Seattle: The Mountaineers, 1997.

SKI HISTORY

Allen, E. John B. *From Skisport to Skiing: One Hundred Years of an American Sport, 1840–1940*. Amherst: U. of Massachusetts Press, 1995.

Allen, E. John B. *New England Skiing*. Dover, NH: Arcadia Publishing, 1997.

Federal Writers' Project. *Skiing in the East: The Best Trails and How to Get There*. 1939 ed. Irvine, CA: Reprint Services Corp., [n.d.].

Pote, Winston. *Mount Washington in Winter: Photographs and Recollections 1923–1940*. Camden, ME: Down East Books, 1985 (out of print).

Waterman, Laura and Guy. *Forest and Crag: A History of Hiking, Trail Blazing, and Adventure in the Northeast Mountains*. Boston: Appalachian Mountain Club Books, 1989.

SKI AND SNOWBOARD TECHNIQUE

Parker, Paul. *Free-Heel Skiing: Telemark and Parallel Techniques for All Conditions*. Seattle: The Mountaineers, 1995.

Van Tilburg, Christopher. *Backcountry Snowboarding*. Seattle: The Mountaineers, 1998.

MAPS

AMC topographic maps are the best general maps for skiing in New Hampshire and Maine. AMC topographic maps are available from AMC, 5 Joy St., Boston, MA 02108; 617-523-0636 or www.outdoors.org.

For navigating the back roads of New England the **DeLorme** *Atlas & Gazetteer* is indispensable. The editions for Maine (1998) and New Hampshire (1996) are available from DeLorme; 800-452-5931 or www.delorme.com.

USGS topographic maps are now available on CD-ROM. **Toposcout** offers all of New Hampshire on one CD-ROM, while Maine is covered by four CD-ROMs. Contact Maptech, 800-627-7236 or www.maptech.com.

USGS maps (on paper) are also available directly from the U.S. Geological Survey. USGS also publishes useful informational pamphlets on using its maps. Contact USGS at 800-USA-MAPS.

APPENDIX C

S System Ratings

Rating the difficulty of ski and snowboard routes runs the risk of being hopelessly subjective. A tour rated "most difficult" in one book may barely rate as a "moderate" run in another. At best, guidebook rating systems have been useful only for comparing routes within the same book. There is now an attempt to change this.

Skiers and snowboarders are trying to bring consistency into how tours are rated. Climbers have long benefited from having a standardized rating system; a 5.9 climb in New York is roughly comparable to a 5.9 climb in New Mexico. The advantage offered by a standardized rating system is that itinerant snow sliders can travel to a new mountain range and quickly glean information from a local guidebook about which tours match his or her abilities.

The "S System" originated in Europe as a way to grade the objective difficulty of ski routes. Versions of this system have recently been utilized by several American ski guidebook authors, notably Lou Dawson (*Colorado High Routes*) and Andrew Maclean (*Chuting Gallery*). The S System attempts to assign a rating based on the steepness and overall difficulty of a route. Good snow conditions are assumed, just as rock climbing ratings presume dry rock. This is a major assumption since, as noted earlier in this book, *conditions are everything:* breakable crust or other heinous and humorous incarnations of snow can quickly transform an easy tour into an epic ordeal.

In the interest of providing a way to compare the relative difficulty of northeastern skiing and snowboarding tours with tours found elsewhere in the country, I have provided S System ratings for the routes in this book. What follows is an adaptation of this system that takes into consideration the unique challenges present in eastern skiing and riding, especially narrow-trail skiing.

The S System in its unabridged form can be numbingly complex, requiring a translation key to interpret every rating (as in, "I just skied a great III S 2+ tour"). For the sake of simplicity and practicality, I confine my S ratings to whole numbers. I have eliminated prefixes (which rate the approach) and dispensed with intermediate grades (e.g., "S2+" or "S4-"). I also include my equivalent narrative rating (moderate, more difficult, most difficult, most difficult/mountaineering) that accompanies each tour description in this book. All these ratings presume basic competency in your chosen technique, be it freeheel skiing, alpine skiing, or snowboarding.

S ratings primarily rate the difficulty of the descent. The overall difficulty of a tour, which includes the steepness of the climb and the total distance covered, can significantly increase the challenge involved in any routes. For the best idea of what to expect on a tour, these S ratings should be used in combination with the detailed route descriptions and difficulty ratings given for each route in this book.

S0 (Moderate) Flat or slightly rolling terrain. Typically an easy Nordic ski trail.

Zealand Falls Hut Tour, Acadia National Park, Easy Day Trips in the White Mountains

S1 (Moderate) Easy low-angle terrain. Novice downhill technique—snowplow or sideslip—will suffice.

Pinkham Notch Tours, Zealand Notch Tours, Pemigewasset River Tours, Nancy and Norcross Ponds, Camden Hills State Park, Mount Garfield

S2 (More difficult) Slopes up to 25 degrees, equivalent to an intermediate run at a ski area. Trails typically have room enough for making turns at will, and have forgiving bailouts.

Dukes and Kimball Trails (Mount Cardigan), Mount Monadnock, Mount Moosilauke, Mount Chocorua, Carter Notch (from Jackson), Wildcat Valley Trail, Avalanche Brook Trail, Doublehead Ski Trail, Rumford Whitecap

S3 (Most difficult) Slopes up to 35 degrees, equivalent to an expert run at a ski area. Narrow trails will require sustained linked turns. Obstacles such as sharp blind turns or tight trees may be encountered. Solid downhill technique required.

Alexandria Trail (Mount Cardigan), Cannon Mountain, Sherburne Trail, Mount Hale, Carter Notch (from Pinkham Notch), East Snowfields (Mount Washington)

S4 (Most difficult/mountaineering) Slopes between 35 and 45 degrees. Falling may be dangerous. Avalanche hazard of route must be evaluated. Proficiency in skiing and riding steep terrain in difficult conditions is necessary.

Gulf of Slides, Oakes Gulf, Great Gulf, Katahdin, Tuckerman Ravine (Right Gully, Lobster Claw, Hillman's Highway, Lower Snowfield, Little Headwall)

S5   (Most difficult/mountaineering) Slopes between 45 and 55 degrees. Injury
      may result from falling. Multiple terrain obstacles present, including
      narrows, rocks, and trees.

      Tuckerman Ravine (Lip, Left Gully, Chute, Center Headwall, Sluice, Dodge's
Drop, Duchess)

      The S System currently tops out with the following two grades. Routes of this
severity exist in the Northeast, but are not included in this book. If you can ski or
ride at this level, you know where to go.

S6   Slopes continuously over 55 degrees. Extreme terrain. Rope work may be
      necessary. In all likelihood, "If you fall, you die."

S7   Slopes over 60 degrees. Looks dead vertical to most people, and most
      people would look dead if they tried it. You need a pilot's license to get
      down.

APPENDIX D

Emergency Contacts

NEW HAMPSHIRE

New Hampshire State Police
800-525-5555

Appalachian Mountain Club (Pinkham Notch)
603-466-2727

MAINE

Maine State Police
800-228-0857

Millinocket Police Department (for Baxter State Park)
207-723-9731

Note: These toll-free (800) telephone numbers can only be used when calling from within state.

About the Author

David Goodman is a writer, skier, and mountaineer who has written widely about the outdoors and other subjects. He is a contributing editor for *Ski, Powder,* and *Backcountry* magazines. His articles have appeared in *Outside, Travel & Leisure, Men's Journal,* and other national publications. He is a three-time winner of the Harold S. Hirsch Award for Excellence in Ski Writing, the highest award of the North American Ski Journalists Association— twice for his magazine writings and once for *Classic Backcountry Skiing: A Guide to the Best Ski Tours in New England.* He is also a recipient of the International Ski History Association's Ullr Award for his writings on ski history in *Classic Backcountry Skiing.*

Goodman has also written on subjects ranging from health care to international politics. He is the author of *Fault Lines: Journeys into the New South Africa* (University of California Press, 1999). His feature articles have appeared in the *Village Voice, Inc.,* the *Nation,* the *Boston Globe,* and other publications.

David Goodman is a graduate of Harvard University. He has worked as a mountaineering instructor for Outward Bound and is a wilderness emergency medical technician.

Goodman's travels have taken him to five continents. But he still insists that his favorite place to explore is in his backyard, the mountains of New England. He lives with his wife, Sue Minter, and daughter, Ariel, in Waterbury Center, Vermont.

About the Appalachian Mountain Club

BEGIN A NEW ADVENTURE!

Join the Appalachian Mountain Club, the oldest and largest outdoor recreation club in the United States. Since 1876, the Appalachian Mountain Club has helped people experience the majesty and solitude of the Northeast outdoors. Our mission is to promote the protection, enjoyment, and wise use of the mountains, rivers, and trails of the Northeast. We're committed to responsible outdoor recreation and we spearhead conservation and environmental efforts in the Northeast.

Members enjoy discounts on all AMC programs, facilities, and books:

OUTDOOR ADVENTURE PROGRAMS

We offer more than 100 workshops on hiking, canoeing, cross-country skiing, biking, and rock climbing and guided trips for hikers, canoers, and skiers.

MOUNTAIN HUTS AND VISITOR CENTERS

The AMC maintains backcountry huts in the White Mountains of New Hampshire and visitor centers throughout the Northeast, from Maine to New Jersey.

BOOKS & MAPS

We publish guidebooks and maps to the mountains, streams and forests of the Northeast—from Maine to North Carolina—and outdoors skill books written by backcountry experts on topics from winter camping to fly-fishing. Call 800-262-4455 to order AMC books or to receive a complete catalog.

To learn more about our workshops, facilities, books, conservation efforts, and membership benefits, contact us at:

The Appalachian Mountain Club
5 Joy Street
Boston, MA 02108
617-523-0636

Visit our website: www.outdoors.org

You'll never find this in bounds.

Black Diamond has been skiing the backcountry and making the best backcountry ski gear since 1984. For over a decade we have developed the most reliable and innovative products to make your backcountry ski experience the best it can be. For the most comprehensive line of backcountry ski equipment in the world, see your local Black Diamond dealer or contact us directly at ski@bdel.com.

Black Diamond
BACKCOUNTRY SKIING
ALPINISM ICE CLIMBING

2084 E 3900 S, SALT LAKE CITY, UT 84124, USA
(801) 278-5533, www.blackdiamondequipment.com

Share the Snow
Save your Soul

Billy & Jason practicing the buddy system.